About the Author

Iman Bibars acquired her PhD in Development Studies at the Institute of Development Studies, Sussex University. She is a co-founder and chairwoman of the Association for the Development and Enhancement of Women, an NGO providing credit and legal aid for poor women who head their households. As an Officer at UNICEF for six years, Dr Bibars managed the 'Urban Community Development' and 'Children in Difficult Circumstances' projects. An independent consultant since March 1998, she has worked with a number of international and multinational organizations such as the World Bank, UNDP Kuwait, UNDP Lebanon, UNIFEM, UNICEF Cairo, the Population Council MENA Office and the European Commission in Cairo.

I DEDICATE THIS WORK TO
AMR AND TAYMOUR, THE TWO MOST
IMPORTANT MEN IN MY LIFE
AND TO
U'M SABER, U'M NAGAH, SHADIA
AND MANY OTHER WOMEN WHO
HAVE CHANGED MY LIFE

Victims and Heroines: Women, Welfare and the Egyptian State

Iman Bibars

Zed Books
LONDON • NEW YORK

Victims and Heroines: Women, Welfare and the Egyptian State
was first published by Zed Books Ltd, 7 Cynthia Street, London
N1 9JF, UK and Room 400, 175 Fifth Avenue, New York, NY
10010, USA in 2001.

Copyright © Iman Bibars, 2001

Cover designed by Andrew Corbett
Set in Monotype Ehrhardt and Franklin Gothic by Ewan Smith

The right of Iman Bibars to be identified as the author of this work has been asserted by her in accordance with the Copyright, Designs and Patents Act, 1988.

A catalogue record for this book is available from the British Library

Library of Congress Cataloging-in-Publication Data: available

ISBN 978-1-85649-935-4 limp

Contents

Acknowledgements / vii
Abbreviations / x

1 Introduction: Gendering the State   1

The gendered nature of the state and its bureaucracies / 3
The state: a resource for women or a patriarch? / 8
Welfare bureaucracies as agents of a patriarchal state / 13
The Egyptian state and women / 14   Gendered citizenship
rights / 16   Women and the politics of needs interpretation / 20
Conclusion / 22

2 The Feminist Researcher among the Women   26

How the research was conducted / 27   Concerns regarding
feminist research / 29   The research sites / 33

3 Defining Female Headship   41

Definitions / 42   Typologies of women heads of households / 47
Factors affecting the status of women heads of households / 51
Prevalence / 54   Classification of women heads of households / 56
Findings of the fieldwork / 56   The perception and status of
women who head their households / 58   The experience of being
a female head / 61   Should women heads of households be a
priority target group? / 65

4 Women, Welfare and the State   72

Social security and the welfare state / 73   What is a welfare
state? / 73   The different types of welfare state / 75   Is Egypt
a welfare state? / 77   The Egyptian welfare system and women
heads of households / 81   Implicit patriarchal assumptions
behind needs interpretation / 85

5 The Politics of Exclusion   **88**

The mainstream contributory programme: social insurance programmes / 90   The social aid programmes: *Il Daman il Ijtimaii* and FHHs / 94   How women subvert the system: coping and opposing mechanisms / 100

6 Beyond the Veil: Religion and Welfare   **107**

Background and historical context / 108   The main features of the religious programmes / 112   Gender exclusions: assumptions shaping programme design and delivery / 114   How women subvert the system / 118   The politics of needs interpretation / 120

7 Women as Victims, Women as Survivors?   **124**

Who are these women and why did I choose their stories? / 124   Similarities and differences between the women / 125   Resourceful women: heroines? / 128   A man by day and a woman by night: mixed roles and responsibilities / 138   *Lamua'khdha malush lazma*: Excuse me he is useless / 140   Oppressed women: daughters of a lesser god / 146   What do these stories tell us? / 153

8 Conclusion: Do Women Resist?   **159**

Opposition versus resistance: a definition / 164   Feminism, post-modernism and cultural relativism / 167   Women, society and the state: a relationship of opposition or resistance / 171   The veil: a political act or an act of surrender? / 173

Bibliography   **179**

Index   **200**

Acknowledgements

During the course of this study I learned that without the support, warmth and love of my family, friends and colleagues I would not have survived the interesting but stressful journey of finishing this book.

This study would not have materialised without the professional support of my supervisor, Anne Marie Goetz. Her supervisory style gave me space to think for myself and at the same time her subtle guidance enriched me theoretically and academically. Her dedication to her students and quiet support for their work is remarkable. She welcomed me at her office and her home whenever I was in the UK, which made me feel among family in England and especially at IDS.

I would also like to thank Amr Mourad, my dear husband. His belief in me and encouraging words lifted my spirits the thousands of times that I fell into despair. His patience and tolerance of my moods and his continuous and loyal support helped me get through tense times.

The presence of our newcomer, Taymour, my son, who materialised in the middle of this study, was the sunshine that warmed my cold sleepless nights. I would also like to thank my mother, who baby-sat for me many nights and days, giving me the space to concentrate on finishing this work. There is also Maria, Taymour's dedicated nanny, who is a jewel and who has become a cherished member of our little family.

Among friends there were many who helped me and gave me the strengths I needed. There was Heba el-Kholy, my life-long friend, who never stopped believing in me and who urged me to continue when I had doubts. There were others who took time to find necessary material for me from different libraries such as Akram Habib, or those who read some of my early drafts such as Hoda el-Sada, Nadia Wassef and Hania Moussa. Special thanks to Mr Hany Hanna, for the layout of this study. There is also Nejla Tchirgi, who was among the first people who encouraged me to carry out the study.

In England I was surrounded by so much warmth from dear friends such as Katja Jobes, Meena Shivdas, Sue Ong, Ulrich Bartch, Gamza and many others, who were there when I needed them, offering advice, friendship and moral support. To Nadia Taher, my Egyptian friend in the UK, special thanks for the time she gave me in spite of her busy schedule. A lot of thanks to Buzz Harrison from AFRAS and Sarah Cook and Martin Greeley from IDS. They took time to read parts of my study, and their comments and advice helped me organise and clarify many of my ideas. Martin Greeley's comments gave me confidence and lifted my morale at a time when I was very low. To all these people, who cared enough to read and comment on my work, I am very grateful.

In addition, I cannot forget what Nabil Samuel from the Coptic Evangelical Organisation for Social Services (CEOSS) did and how he and his staff helped me in the early days of the research. Nabil, a colleague and a friend since the early 1980s, gave me the unique opportunity of working in one of the poorest urban areas in Cairo through CEOSS's local branches. CEOSS also funded part of the survey conducted for this research. Special thanks also to Ibrahim Makram and Nady. The station staff, including Maged Hosni, Amal Wahib, Hanan, Essam, Iskandar, Sanaa and others, made me feel at home when I encroached on their working space and stayed with them for five months. They introduced me to the community, helped me conduct several meetings and worked with me as volunteers during their holidays.

The British government and the British Council, here in Egypt, provided the critical financial support needed to begin my studies through the initial grant that covered my first year of the PhD. I am very grateful, for without such financial assistance, I would not have been able to join IDS.

I would also like to thank the Ford Foundation's office in Cairo and especially Humphrey Davies, the former representative, who believed in this study when it was still a draft proposal and who agreed to fund the second and third years. Without the generous grant of the Ford this work would not have seen the light. I would also like to thank Mr Steve Lawry, the current representative of the Ford foundation in Cairo, who continued Mr Davies's support for my work. The fieldwork in Cairo and Alexandria was covered by the Middle East Research Competition (MERC), and I take this opportunity to thank Salim Nasr, former programme officer, and Linda Herrari, former MERC coordinator, for their support and guidance. To Ghada Barsoum, Amany and Marina from Ford, I am grateful for their continuous assistance in sorting out all the complicated financial matters of the grant. And to Hana Ayoub, my dear close friend at Ford, thank you for always being there when needed.

Acknowledgements

Finally I would like to thank all those women whom I met and interviewed in the different areas. Their trust in me made it possible for me to write this study. These women have taught me a lot about how poor women live in urban Egypt, but more importantly they have taught me things about myself. My encounter with them and my exposure to new and more dramatic types of poverty made me revise and reflect on many aspects of my life, the personal and the professional. My response to their desperate situation is clearly stated in the conclusion as well as throughout this study. I am deeply grateful for their generosity in allowing me to enter their homes and their lives.

Abbreviations

ADEW	Association for the Development and Enhancement of Women
CDA	Community Development Association
CEOSS	Coptic Evangelical Organisation for Social Services
FHHs	female heads of households
IDS	Institute of Development Studies
LE	Egyptian pound
MOSA	Ministry of Social Affairs
MOISA	Ministry of Insurance and Social Affairs
MHHs	men-headed households
NGO	non-governmental organisation
UNICEF	United Nations Children's Fund

1
Introduction: Gendering the State

When I decided to study the social policies that affect the poor in Egypt – focusing on women who head their households (FHHs)[1] – I did not realise that these issues were and still are at the forefront of socio-economic debates, not only in Egypt but throughout the world. The economic life of the poor is becoming increasingly vulnerable, and governments worldwide are rethinking their social policies as a result of the globally changing economic and political environment. As Fraser (1989) states with regards to the USA, the first activity that takes place during periods of budget crisis is the 'war on welfare'. Economic stabilisation policies in many Third World countries, and especially in Egypt, entail not only reductions in social services expenditures and transfer payments, but also reductions of subsidies on basic foodstuffs and public transport. These reductions, combined with rising unemployment and falling real wages, cause increased poverty (Nassar 1998: 1–2). In addition, the Egyptian government's withdrawal from the provision of basic health and education services has increased the suffering of the poor, in general, and of poor women who head their households (FHHs) in particular. Women-headed households constitute a significant proportion of Egypt's rural and urban households. Although national estimates range between a minimum of 16% (Handoussa 1994: 1) and a maximum of 18% all over Egypt (Fergany 1993: 1),[2] more empirical work in urban areas put the figure at 30% (Farah 1997).[3] When examining the governmental social policies targeting FHHs, Handoussa criticised the economic implications of social aid programmes and called upon the state to provide a more comprehensive system (1994).

This study is an assessment of the impact of the Egyptian state's social policies and programmes on women who head their households (FHHs). Its main contention is that the state's social policies discriminate against FHHs because of gender biases: biases regarding the 'proper' composition of a household, and biases against the supposedly free and uncontrolled sexuality of some of the women heading their own households. However, the study found that women have discovered ways of contesting the current structures to get what they need from the state. The major findings of this study can be summarised by the following stories:

> MOSA[4] employee: You are cows and have no brains. I told you that I cannot enrol you in the aid programme. This is the law. You have a man to take care of you and you are his responsibility, not the state's.
> Nadia: But he divorced me last month and I have five children and cannot work. Mrs S. told me that I can come here and that the government will give me a monthly allowance.
> MOSA employee: The law says that you have to be divorced for one year to be eligible. And what did you do to make him leave you? Probably, you were not a good wife. Go now and come back in a year, and do not lose your morals now that you have no man to control you, or you'd better find yourself another husband'.[5]

This exchange is one example of how certain types of FHHs are perceived and stereotyped based on traditional cultural norms and values that aim to control the bodies and sexuality of women.[6]

> My son ran away from home and left me. He blames me for remarrying at my age. But tell me, what should I have done? I tried for two years to survive on my own after my husband died. I tried to work but could not find a part-time job, and I have no skills but to clean other people's houses. I went to MOSA and they gave me 34 pounds a month. But I need more than 200 pounds to barely survive and to pay for the children's school. I was unable to work. I really tried. (Sitohom, 32, widow who remarried, 'The Squatters')[7]

This quotation shows how the state's social policies reinforce women's secondary status and subordination within the family. By providing women with below survival-level incomes, the state does not offer them an institutional alternative to the male provider and it does not recognise them as actual heads of their families.

Nevertheless, women find ways to subvert the system. Several of the women I met were able to cultivate relationships with key people who facilitated their access to basic services. Aziza, in 'The Ezba',[8] was related through marriage to a civil servant at the central offices of the Ministry of Social Affairs. She urged him to introduce her to the employees at the social unit in her district and used this contact to provide services for her friends.

> A'm[9] Gomaa is my husband's great-uncle and he works in the headquarters of MOSA. He is a senior person there and is well connected. The people at the social unit are nice to me and help me because they expect to be helped by him in return. It is important to develop these networks with different

Introduction

government employees in order to get your work done. (Aziza, 36, wife of an *u'rzu'i*, 'The Ezba')[10]

Aziza's story shows that despite widespread stigmatisation, and societal and bureaucratic pressures, some women who head their households oppose these pressures and have developed culturally specific coping mechanisms.[11]

The three main propositions that are investigated in this study are:

1. That the state's social policies towards women who head their households reinforce their subordination through the provision of below survival-level incomes. These incomes do not provide an institutional alternative to the male provider.
2. That the state's welfare system is two-tiered, favouring men over women in its benefits and treatment of clients.
3. That despite stigmatisation, and societal and bureaucratic pressures, women who head their households oppose these pressures using culturally specific coping mechanisms.

The Gendered Nature of the State and its Bureaucracies

Western feminist research on welfare states and its bureaucracies suggests that they are structured in gendered ways and are imbued with masculine norms and values. Public social policies have been found to reinforce traditional gendered divisions of labour that further women's subordination (Fraser 1989; Nelson 1990; Ferguson 1984). '"Gender" refers to socially constructed and institutionalised roles based on biological and sexual differences. [For public bureaucracies] to be gendered is to reinforce these socially constructed roles which (in patriarchal societies) further oppress and victimise women' (Goetz 1992: 6).[12] For example, the assumption that women are or should be primarily housewives and mothers and secondarily workers permeates most policies of the state (Orloff 1993: 310–22). It affects women's material situation, for example, in justifying a discriminatory wage structure, a double burden of work, and unequal access to all types of basic services and credit. Specific areas of state policy such as fertility control, marriage and divorce legislation, and education are particularly relevant to women and their status (Afshar 1987). There is therefore a need to understand the state's role in gender relations, and the way its institutions manage, legitimate and construct power relations between men and women.

There is also a need to understand and address the complex nature of the state. One of the debates in literature about the state, in feminist and mainstream political science, is whether the state is 'a monolithic' entity that caters to its own self-preservation or a process of multiple and conflicting interests. In the writings of some conventional pre-feminist state theorists, socialist writers such as Frankel argue that the state is no longer seen as an object or an 'apparatus' but is a kind of 'social process' (1983). However, the writings of Bahro and de Jasay depict the state as a social actor in its own right and not just as a vehicle for other social interests (Bahro 1978; de Jasay 1985). Other analyses of the state, such as the work of Ursel (1986), address the state as unitary and rational in pursuing its interests or the interests of the 'class' or group it represents.[13]

This study acknowledges that the state is complex, as there are different and perhaps conflicting systematic divisions of interests that are embodied within it. I am not arguing in this study that the Egyptian state is monolithic but, as will be shown in the following chapters, that it is composed of different parts that treat gender and specifically women differently. There is a contradiction, for example, between progressive provisions for women in employment laws – issued by the Labour Ministry – and the conservative conditions placed on women's citizenship and rights in family matters as per the legal system. In this study I focus on only one part of the state, the social welfare system, and investigate the impact of its policies on gender relations and women's status. However, although my findings and conclusion refer only to the social welfare component of the state, many of the assumptions and practices regarding gender that characterise this part of the state could also apply to the other parts of the state.

The characteristics that Staudt (1990), Fraser (1989), Goetz (1992) and Pearce (1990) identify with welfare and aid bureaucracies – as being gendered structures and promoting gendering processes – apply to many Third World as well as First World countries. In this study, these characteristics are examined in relation to discussions about the adequacy and efficiency of the welfare system in reaching and serving poor FHHs in Egypt. I argue that the policies and welfare systems established are not haphazard. Indeed, they reflect a predominant ideology that maintains and reinforces the subordination of women. The aim of this study, then, is to analyse the state's social policies and to assess the impact of such gendered programmes and policies on the status and autonomy of poor women who head their households.

The empirical fieldwork was carried out in seven low-income urban areas where different types of FHHs were studied. Women's own opinions about the available social services were analysed. I examined the following welfare programmes of the state: the Social Aid Programme, which is administered by MOSA, and the Pension Programme for the destitute, which is administered by the Organisation for Social Insurance. Furthermore, because this study was carried out in Egypt, the role of the state

Introduction

could not be divorced from the influence of religious groups on the state's policies and actions towards women. In that context, three Islamic-affiliated and controlled welfare programmes were examined, as were two Coptic Christian programmes.

This study focuses not only on how women heads of households are perceived by the state and its bureaucracies, but also on how these women perceive their situation. I review the survival and coping mechanisms of this marginalised group and examine the impact of the available alternative social packages on women's position and autonomy.

My work is based on my belief that women are a particularly disadvantaged segment of society. They continue to play multiple roles – as managers of households, family income-earners and health agents – without much support for or recognition of their contributions. Traditional social theory argues that within the household there is a clear sexual division of labour whereby the man of the family is both the breadwinner and in control of the public realm, while the woman is isolated in the private realm. According to such a division of labour, women are mainly concerned with the reproductive and domestic activities of the household while men are in control of production and public representation (Moser 1989: 1799–800). This ideology is projected onto the public sphere in countries where a patriarchal culture permeates the different bureaucracies. It also becomes ideologically reinforced through such means as the legal and welfare systems, without the recognition that it reinforces woman's position as subordinate to that of the man (ibid.: 1800). It is these assumptions that I seek to investigate in this study.

The difference between this and previous studies on FHHs is that this study claims that the feminisation of poverty is not merely due to the deteriorating economic conditions of these women but is also related to the gendered ideology of the welfare state and its bureaucracy. Little if any of the literature on the state, welfare bureaucracies and public administration directly addresses the issue of FHHs. The few studies on FHHs and the state have taken place in developed countries and focus more on the welfare programmes of these states (Fraser 1989; Pearce 1985, 1990, 1993; Gordon 1990; Nelson 1990). Other studies describe the rising phenomenon of female headship and discuss the conditions and obstacles facing FHHs (Chant 1997; Folbre 1991), especially with regard to development programmes (Buvinic 1990, 1993; Youssef and Hetler 1983). When discussing the relationship between women and the development bureaucracies, other writers have either focused on rural areas (Goetz 1995a, Himmelstrand 1990), or have been more concerned with the status of and discrimination against women within the bureaucracies themselves and in WID programmes (Goetz 1992; Staudt 1990; Ferguson 1984).

Even fewer studies are available on the relationship between women heads of households, the state and its welfare bureaucracy in Egypt. A large number of the earlier studies on women-headed households focus on the impact of male migration on the structure of the family and the work patterns of women (Khafagy 1986; Zaalouk 1985; Khattab and Greiss 1976). In addition, the few studies dealing with social policies and the welfare state are either general and do not have a gender-specific focus, or operate from an economic perspective and thus do not offer a profound analysis of the impact of the existing programmes on women (Azer 1995; Nagi 1995; Nassar 1995, 1998; El Boraei 1997; Abdel Baset Abdel Mohsen 1997; Hakam 1995). Other studies are concerned with describing the characteristics of this new phenomenon and its demographic distribution (Fergany 1993, 1994a; Nawar 1994).

Handoussa examines social policies supporting the poor in Egypt. Her work highlights the deteriorating economic conditions of vulnerable groups – with a special focus on female-headed households – resulting from the Structural Adjustment and economic liberalisation programmes. The number of women reached and the economic implications of social aid programmes to the poor are briefly explained by the author, but there is no comprehensive analysis or description of the government's social programmes for this group (1994: 1–4). Another study by Nawar (1994) addresses women's need for more sympathetic social policies, but it does not investigate the comprehensive social policy programmes and systems provided by the government or by the informal and private sectors.[14]

In contrast, my study focuses on the social packages offered to women heads of households and the ways in which these packages either reinforce or challenge the discriminatory features of the social system under which they live. Furthermore, I have chosen to focus on the women themselves rather than on the concept of the household, as previous studies have done. It is also important to note that most of the previous studies, in Egypt, defined FHHs statistically as widows or divorcees; the broader and more subtle definitions adopted in this research were not previously used.

Hence this study is different for several reasons. First, it describes and analyses the Egyptian welfare system within a feminist[15] theoretical framework, clarifying the relationship between the state and women on one hand, and the ideology of the state in addressing women's needs on the other. Second, it also focuses on the growing phenomenon of the urban poor and their relationship with the state and the communities around them. Finally, this study represents and conveys the voice and opinion of low-income FHHs regarding governmental social policy and welfare programmes.

In this chapter I discuss some theoretical issues pertaining to women's

Introduction

reduced citizenship and the state's attempts to control women's will and sexuality.[16] The complexity of the relationship between women and the state in Egypt, especially with regard to 'needs interpretation' and the politics behind it, is also discussed in this chapter. Chapter 2 describes the tools and methods of research used and provides a brief background of the selected research sites and the reasons for choosing those areas in particular.

In Chapter 3 I discuss the debates in the literature on female headship with regard to definitions and perceptions. The personal experiences of different women heads of households and their ways of coping with their single status are explained and analysed. I show how these women are perceived by society and the state, and how they perceive themselves. I also explain why I believe these women should be a priority target group among the poor, and what type of assistance they need.

The Egyptian welfare state is analysed and contextualised within the different definitions of a welfare state in Chapter 4. The social assistance programme to the poor in general and female heads of households in particular is examined. This chapter analyses the continuation of sexism in the Egyptian social welfare system. This analysis shows how social welfare programmes hide sexist interpretations of women's needs. The chapter highlights the ideologies at the basis of the state's social policies and how the state succeeds in imposing its interpretations of women's and especially female heads of households' needs. I finally argue that the state indeed treats women as secondary to men and that the welfare system is two-tiered, favouring men and discriminating against women who head their households.

In Chapter 5, I adapt Martin Greeley's 1996 framework for analysing why and how development programmes fail to reach their intended beneficiaries. I apply this framework to the 'mainstream contributory' and 'social aid non-contributory' programmes of MOSA in order to analyse the main factors that exclude different types of women heads of households from accessing these services. Using Greeley's framework, I describe how exclusion can sometimes be built into the procedures and implementation practices of these programmes (what Greeley calls programme-driven exclusion). However, sometimes beneficiaries exclude themselves for various reasons, including an effort to avoid stigmatisation (what Greeley calls self-driven exclusion). Finally, I describe the ways by which these women circumvent the bureaucratic procedures of the social welfare system.

Chapter 6 is a description and analysis of the impact of religious – Islamic and Coptic – welfare programmes on women heads of households. Information on these kinds of programmes is notoriously hard to get, not just because of the familiar problems of accessing data from the NGO sector, with its sometimes informal approach to record-keeping, but because of the secrecy and defensiveness that surrounds the activities of some religious groups. This chapter presents new data on the functioning of these programmes, for the first time, and it analyses the way in which these religious welfare programmes perceive and treat low-income women heads of households. It also analyses the underlying assumptions at the base of their attitudes towards FHHs. The findings show the pernicious impact of gendered religious ideologies on women.

Chapter 7 consists of the voices and opinions of different types of women who head their households, drawing on interviews with women in Cairo and Alexandria. It is a glimpse of what female headship is like at the grassroots level and it reveals how different these women and their situations are. This chapter gives considerable space to extended citations from the interviews.

Chapter 8 concludes this study with a serious rethinking of notions of women's opposition and resistance. I argue that although poor illiterate women who head their households might oppose, object to and subvert their conditions, they nevertheless continue to act within the rules of the dominant group. They are 'coping within constraints' and not 'challenging the status quo with the aim for change'. In other words, their opposition – which takes shape in various forms of manipulation of oppressive traditions and oppressive state regulations – never becomes resistance, or an attempt to change the system as a way of seeking their liberation.

Various theoretical debates are relevant to this study, and are discussed in detail as they arise in the following chapters: debates pertaining to the definition of female headship are raised in Chapter 3. Debates regarding the nature and complexity of the state and its welfare bureaucracy are deliberated upon in Chapter 4, and notions of resistance are discussed in Chapter 8. However, in this chapter it is imperative to describe and analyse the theoretical debates pertaining to women and the state.

The State: A Resource for Women or a Patriarch?

States and their bureaucracies are central to development in many Third World countries. They determine economic policies and programmes and thus their impact on women is pronounced, for it is such policies that determine the distribution of resources between men and women (Goetz 1992: 9). Many recent analyses have recognised that states regulate gender relations through development programmes, in the labour market, and in the 'social' welfare sectors.[17] Consequently, studying and theorising about the state and its impact on gender relations is important for understanding how it affects and positions women.

Introduction

In their reviews of the history of theories of the state, Held (1985) and Knuttila (1987) show how slight is the attention of mainstream theorists to sexual politics and to the social position of women (Franzway et al. 1989: 3). Much of the mainstream literature on the state addresses issues of state autonomy and sovereignty without linking this to women, their roles and status. In addition, the state's role in defining the changing boundaries between the public and private spheres and how this is relevant to gender is not a subject addressed in the conventional theoretical debates about the state (Charlton et al. 1989: 2–3). The exclusion of gender analysis from mainstream theories of the state has contributed to the abstract nature of these theories and their focus on the relationship between the state and abstract de-gendered individuals.

In contrast, feminist theory has been preoccupied with gender relations, but only recently has it attended to the state in ways that would help explain the differences and inequalities between men and women. The feminist analysis of these conventional non-gendered theories of the state points out, first, that women do not have the same quality of men's citizenship, and, second, that the state seems to support capital by undervaluing women's labour and by supporting men in subordinating women. Nevertheless, when feminists began theorising about the state they were influenced by mainstream political and social thought.

The liberal pluralist approach has equated the state with the decision-making apparatus that is the arbitrator between competing social and economic interests. Although it recognises that different interest groups have different lobbying strengths and weight, those who use this approach continue to assume that politics is a matter of allocation in response to citizens' demands. Liberals thus argue that the state is neutral. Liberal feminists, on the other hand, admit that the state is not neutral and that it favours men. However, they believe that this situation can be changed either through including more women in the state bureaucracy or through pressures on the state from women's organisations (Ziller 1980; Friedan 1981). They see the sexism and patriarchy of social institutions as a case of imperfect citizenship, requiring change, and they see the state as the route to achieving such changes (Watson 1990: 6–7).

Liberal feminism reaches its conceptual limits when the demand for equal citizenship is not taken to its logical conclusion and women are not allowed to enrol in the army and bear arms. It is true that women have improved the quality of their citizenship to a certain degree by gaining the vote and the right to education and to an income, yet the state persists in creating gendered social structures. In other words, the state is more actively involved in shaping and affecting gender relations than liberal feminists admit (Franzway et al. 1989: 14–17).

The liberal feminist argument contains three problems that hinder its universal application. First, liberal feminists focus their theorising only on the liberal Western states of North America and Europe, making their theorising ethnocentric (Charlton et al. 1989: 10). Second, there is an implicit assumption that women's empowerment is applicable only to a democratic pluralist state, since most of the feminists' lobbying is carried out at the state level, through the state's various democratic apparatuses. For that reason they associate modern feminism with the liberal capitalist states only (Franzway et al. 1989: ix). They claim that countries such as China and Saudi Arabia do not have a feminist movement because they do not have the right political environment for liberal democracy (Charlton et al. 1989). One can therefore assume that the liberal feminist approach is not applicable to Egypt as well. For although the Egyptian government has been paying lip-service to democracy, independent political parties and interest groups do not have real opportunities for lobbying the government and its bureaucracies as in the Western democracies (Hatem 1992: 237).

Yet women's and feminist resistance in Egypt took different forms from those known in the Western liberal democracies. In other words, the liberal feminists' model for women's negotiation with the state is not the only route to women's participation.[18] The third problem with the liberal feminist argument is its belief that by increasing the number of women in the state's bureaucracies the gendered outcome will be altered: women do not necessarily form one homogeneous group with common interests (Molyneux 1985: 321), for not all women are necessarily feminists fighting for better policies for women. In addition, not all women belong to the same class, and because class intersects gender, class interests could supersede gender interests.

In contrast, the analyses of Marxist socialist feminists describe the capitalist state as acting mainly in the interest of preserving the dominant class relations, and creating the conditions for the accumulation of wealth. Marxist and socialist feminists focus on the social subordination of women and how that might be seen as useful for capital, securing the reproduction of the workforce, subsidising the wage via unpaid housework, and thus providing cheap labour (Barrett 1980; Eisenstein 1979; Burton 1985). In a number of debates, the state was seen as serving the capitalist interest by under-educating women, and organising the welfare system in such a way so as to support the patriarchal family form (McIntosh 1978; Ursel 1986). A major problem with the socialist feminist discourse is that it perceives the state's actions as shaped by a pre-given social structure, i.e. the capitalist class. There is no consideration of the idea that the state constitutes different categories of social, political and economic structures, and that certain social roles (masculinity and femininity) are products of the state's policies when translated by these structures. It is the state that creates the bureaucracies that produce gendered policies; it is the state that reinforces and not only reacts to a pre-given class or institution (Franzway et al. 1989: 20–6). Another problem with socialist feminism is that gender issues are subordinated to the need to liberate a given class from the domination of the capitalist class. The role of religion and its impact on state policies, on women and on the family is ignored in both liberal and Marxist analyses (Dahlerup 1987; Charlton et al. 1989).

Although feminists have a significant case against the state, its social policies and their impact on gender relations and women's marginalisation (Goetz 1991a: 43), Mackinnon (1989) is nevertheless correct in stating that feminists had not developed a specific theory for describing and analysing the state. This failure to provide a specific feminist theory of the state was a gap in feminist scholarship. The solution offered by some feminists was the formulation of what came to be known as the concept of the 'patriarchal state' and, more specifically for some, the patriarchal welfare state. This offered clear theoretical progress regarding the previous meaning of the state in feminist theory (Allen 1989: 22).

Feminist discourses about the welfare state and its systems have passed through several stages and schools. First, there was work on the discriminating character of the welfare programmes and their functions in reinforcing traditional sexist values and norms in the public and private sectors (e.g. McIntosh 1978; Law 1983; and Cummings 1980). This was followed by a structural critique of welfare itself, where its discriminating character was highlighted to demonstrate its role in reinforcing women's subordination. The argument was that such a system, through its double standards, reinforces the division between the public and private spheres and relegates women to an inferior position (Nelson 1990; Pearce 1985, 1990).

This was followed by the new left critiques of the welfare system, which adopted the 'social control model'. This group was anti-statist and included feminists such as Barbara Ehrenreich, Deirdre English and Alicia Frohman. Advocates of social control theory argue that the welfare system and the dependence of women on the state is a reflection of the shift from private to public patriarchy (Pateman and Gross 1986; Donzelot 1979). Carol Brown argues that public patriarchy is only an umbrella for men collectively to control the public sphere as opposed to their individual control of the private sphere. Most importantly, she argues that women have gained nothing from this shift and transfer of power (Gordon 1990: 22–3). Such feminists argue that women's lives in the welfare state are more dependent and more determined by state policies than men's lives. They are dependent on the state as clients (especially single mothers), as employees in the public sector, and as citizens – albeit weak citizens because they have no political power. They add that this dependency – as employees, consumers and clients – strengthens male power at a more structured level (Hernes 1987; Borchorst and Siim 1987). They argue that the state does play an indirect role in enforcing the subordination of women through supporting the specific model of a household based on the male as the main breadwinner (McIntosh 1978; Dahlerup 1987: 118; Nelson 1990; Abramovitz 1988; Gordon 1990: 23).

However, not all the feminist theorists are so antipathetic to the state and its welfare bureaucracy. Piven is critical of radical feminists who have hostile attitudes towards the state. She is uncomfortable with feminists who characterise women's relationships with the state as being dependent. She claims that radical feminists see an element of social control in every social relation, and argues that the benefits and gains won by women from state programmes should not be overshadowed by the fear that the state wants only to control and dominate (Piven 1990: 250–61). Dahlerup agrees with Piven and argues that women today have become independent of their husbands thanks to the state and its welfare programmes, for the state's support gives women the option of remaining single and avoiding dependence on men. Dahlerup challenges the notion that the state upholds and reinforces the subordination of women, arguing that the state is not the main force behind changes in women's lives or in their oppression. She criticises the feminist tendency to universalise women's oppression and adds that women in different places suffer differently (Dahlerup 1987: 105–19). Dahlerup's main point is that women's oppression stems from the whole structural setting of society and overcoming it requires simultaneous changes in the different social arenas.

In short, one of the main debates in the literature on women and the state is concerned with what was and is the impact of state policies on women. Whether the state provides stronger support for equality of the sexes and for more women's self-determination or whether its policies reinforce women's subordination and create new forms of male dominance are the main issues. An additional dimension of the latter question is whether the state reinforces women's oppression intentionally or not. Different conclusions have been reached and feminists have divided into two camps. The first camp argues that the state is gendered and serves male interests, and in the process oppresses women further. It is argued that it is in the interest of the state to promote class divisions and to exploit women for its own survival. It is cheap and easy to perpetuate traditional male and female roles. Women's reproductive roles maintain the household and produce the labourers and the soldiers who maintain and protect the state. The state stands to lose if this role is recognised in monetary terms and if women are given a choice about playing it (McIntosh 1978; Hernes 1987; Sassoon 1987; Goetz 1992, 1995a; Fraser 1989; Pearce 1985, 1990). The second camp argues that the state is neutral and that women must bear the brunt of the responsibility to lobby for their interests and gain more power (Piven 1990; Dahlerup 1987). It is these issues that I will address in the following chapters.

Welfare Bureaucracies as Agents of a Patriarchal State

Another dimension in the relationship between women and the state is the impact of state bureaucracy, especially the welfare bureaucracy, on the lives of women. Bureaucracies have become responsible for many tasks associated with development in health, industrialisation, capital accumulation, education and labour market policy, and therefore play a role that affects the lives of all people. In other words, they are a focal point and a central component for the empowerment or oppression of any social group, men, women or minorities (Staudt 1990: 5).

Traditional mainstream research on bureaucracy operates on the assumption that bureaucracies are gender, class and race neutral (Goetz 1992: 9). According to Weber, modern bureaucracy has the following traits: a complex rational division of labour, stability, a hierarchy, and a neutral and transparent and therefore public character (Ferguson 1984: 7). Thus to Weber the public world is rational and efficient and is separated from the private world, which is emotional and personal (Goetz 1992: 9). It is these elements of rationality, neutrality and objectivity that are challenged by feminists because they believe that these are defensive mechanisms that hide the politicisation and biases of bureaucracy (Ferguson 1984: 38). Feminists also argue that bureaucracies reinforce gendered relations through what they provide and regulate; they manage to relegate women to second-class status and reinforce their subordination to men in order to sustain the status quo (Goetz 1992).

Mainstream organisational theories have also tended to ignore these gendered aspects of bureaucracies as organisations. The relative powerlessness of women to influence agendas in the public administration and their inability to rise up to positions of control has been attributed to their under-representation. This is an over-simplification of reality. Inserting the bodies of women into public space will not solve the problem of under-representation of women's interests if they encounter male-dominated structures and masculine rules. The public organisational space is controlled by men and geared to respond to their needs. Working hours and schedules are both intolerant of and inconsiderate to the demands of childcare. In addition, 'maternity leave' affects women's performance, evaluation and promotions. The rules of the game are masculine, and these are what have to be changed to achieve real equality in treatment. Adding more women will certainly not solve the problem. There is a connection between masculinity and organisational power that has to be removed before women can be equally represented and be more effective in bureaucracies (Goetz 1992: 9).

In this context too, feminist theorists and activists are divided regarding their attitudes and approaches towards bureaucracy. Liberal feminism has appealed to the bureaucratic apparatus of the state to include women in the public sphere, seeking equal opportunity and affirmative action. Radical feminists reject the focus on integration because they see the existing system as flawed (Ferguson 1984: 4–5). Despite differences of levels of hostility towards bureaucracies, in the end some feminists agree that the state and its bureaucratic apparatus will only support the values that will lead to its preservation (McIntosh 1978; Mackinnon 1989). This study aims at determining the degree to which state policies and welfare bureaucracies in Egypt are gendered and the extent to which FHHs can promote their interests in their encounters with the state.

The Egyptian State and Women

Since the beginning of the twentieth century Middle Eastern women and female activists have been organising for emancipation and demanding social reform. They have made several gains during the last few decades. There is greater access to education and employment, and in many countries women have gained the right to vote. In addition, economic changes and migration throughout the region have obliged women to assume increased responsibilities for their households, though not necessarily with increased autonomy or power. While women themselves have often taken the initiative in demanding their rights, the state has also played a critical role, introducing changes and co-opting women's own initiatives (Peteet and Harlow 1991: 4–8).

Knowledge about the political history of Egypt is crucial to understanding feminist discourse and practice. The relationship between the state and women in Egypt has been fluctuating between periodical honeymoons where the state supported women's demands and longer periods of repression and tension.

Since the time of Mohammed Ali, in the modern state-building phase in the nineteenth century, the liberal phase in the 1920s and 1930s, the socialist phase under Nasser (1952–70), and the *Infitah* and capitalist periods under Anwar Sadat (1970–81) and Hosni Mubarak (1991–present), there have been shifts in rhetoric and emphasis (Badran 1991: 201–23).[19] For example, in 1956, the same year that the state gave women suffrage, the government banned feminist organisations, and in 1959 the state also suppressed feminist public expression, by incorporating feminist NGOs and groups within the state-controlled one-party system. However, the 1962 Charter regarded men and women as equals and called for the shedding of all obstacles that impeded the free movement and advancement of women.[20] Professional, educational and employment opportunities were opened for women (Badran 1991: 217–18). In other words the Egyptian state, during different political phases, sent out contradictory messages with regard to women. It imposed its own agendas at different times and thus defined the 'woman question' to suit its own purposes (Badran 1991: 228).

The periods of more progressive policies resulted not from egalitarian beliefs on the part of the state, but from political interests and pragmatic considerations during cycles of national development. Post-colonial states such as Egypt have incorporated women as citizens not for women's benefit but rather as part of political strategies and survival mechanisms. Thus it is important to distinguish between the state's genuine support and concern for women's status and liberation, on the one hand, and its willingness, on the other, to use women as symbols in the construction of national identities (Kandiyoti 1991e).

There is an explanation for Egypt's contradictory behaviour with regard to women's rights. Egypt's international survival after the mid-1970s depended on US support and Gulf money – from remittances but also from direct financial aid – while its internal legitimacy largely depended on appeasing its conservative masses. Under Sadat and even more so under Mubarak, the Egyptian state has been undergoing an internal conflict between its two identities, as an Islamic state and a modern democratic secular state. Kandiyoti traces this phenomenon to the emigration of many Egyptians looking for employment to the Islamic Gulf countries in the 1970s. As Egypt exported men and imported cash, it also imported the cultural and political influence of the Gulf. The increasing political influence of the rich oil countries strengthened the cultural and political prominence of local Islamist tendencies. Internal Islamic groups were either left alone or encouraged, or were able to corner the state into declaring its commitment to religious orthodoxy as means of upstaging more radical Islamist platforms in civil society (Kandiyoti, 1991b: 11–13). As religious and ethnic identities become increasingly politicised, the state has tended to sacrifice women's hard-won civil rights on the altar of a politics of identity that prioritises control of women.

In its conflict with Islamic groups the Egyptian state is losing ground, especially with the increasing dissatisfaction of the people with state performance, the widening gap between the rich and the poor and, finally, the increasing inefficiency and corruption of the political system. In an attempt to shore up its legitimacy, the state has chosen tactically to relinquish some of its responsibilities to protect women's rights in favour of reasserting traditional and religious controls over women.[21] Women's unequal citizenship in Egypt is one example of how state policies sacrificed the women's agenda and relegated women to a second-class category for the survival and preservation of the institution of the state itself.

Gendered Citizenship Rights

This study is concerned with the social rights of women and in particular FHHs. Social rights include social provisions offered to workers during unemployment and old-age pensions to strengthen their leverage with capital owners. They also include health insurance and equal access to other social services of the state (Fraser 1989; Orloff 1993). However, unless women are equal citizens, they will continue to be unequal in their access to all their rights, including social rights. According to the Egyptian constitution, all Egyptians are citizens with equal rights regardless of gender, age, race or religion. As an Egyptian I believed in our constitution and in my right to full citizenship. This assumption was shattered one Saturday morning as I applied to renew my passport. My previous passport had been issued in February 1991. In the interim, I was married but did not change my marital status in official documents such as in the ID card[22] or passport. To the state I was still a single woman. When I applied for a new passport as a married woman, i.e. as a wife, the state viewed me as a dependant. The government employee refused to issue my new passport or even process my papers until my husband came in person and consented in writing to the issuance of my passport, thus giving me explicit permission to travel and leave the country. An adult married Egyptian woman cannot travel or leave the country without the written consent of her husband. He has the right to stop her from travelling by adding her name to the list of criminals and suspects whom the state prevents from travelling abroad. The husband, on the other hand, does not need the written or verbal consent of his wife to travel. It was only then that I fully comprehended that women, including myself, are not equal citizens.

Women in Egypt depend on other more powerful individuals, usually men, to represent them in public and political structures (Baden et al. 1991). Usually they have their fathers or their husbands to represent them. The names of poor illiterate women in Egypt are put on their fathers' then their husbands' identity cards. They are not issued their own ID cards.[23] In addition, women cannot share their Egyptian nationality with their children as men can. Thus women's citizenship, representation and

Introduction

existence are conveyed through their male kin. Since women's citizenship and their legal existence is defined through their husbands or their male kin, a woman's citizenship is not considered by the state as equal to that of a man.

To be a full citizen one has to have full and socially approved social, economic and political rights. One must also have full control over one's own body and sexuality and over fertility and reproduction. A state is 'woman-friendly' to the extent that it provides women, regardless of age or marital status, with equal citizenship rights. According to Habermas, the citizen is a central participant in political debate and public opinion formation. Citizenship to him depends on the capacities for consent and speech and the ability to participate with others in a public dialogue. These capabilities are connected with masculinity in the male-dominated classical state: they are capacities that are denied to women, thus diminishing their citizenship. Consent in particular is a problematic notion for women, since many social institutions such as marriage assume women's consent for sexual intercourse. Cases of marital rape are an example of how women's consent is taken for granted and thus until very recently, in Western countries, a man could not be charged with raping his wife.[24] Carole Pateman states: 'women find their speech ... persistently and systematically invalidated in the crucial matter of consent ... if women's words about consent are consistently reinterpreted, how can they participate in the debate among citizens?' (cited in Fraser 1989: 126).

Finally, another reason for what is called the reduced citizenship of women is the soldiering aspect of citizenship. According to Fraser, the masculine citizen-soldier protector role links the public sphere (state) to the family. This is based on the assumption that men have the capacity to protect women and that women need this protection. This division between women and men as the protected and the protector introduces further friction to women's relationship to citizenship. It confirms the gender subtext of a citizen's role (Fraser 1989: 126–7). According to Charlton et al., the concept of citizenship as it emerged in the West in the twelfth century was associated with military acts of loyalty and commitment to the ruler. Women were excluded from these new institutions developed by monarchs to protect external sovereignty, with grave ramifications for women's status (1989: 23). This historical non-participation of women in the military contributed to their second-class status and delayed the extension of full citizenship rights to women (Charlton et al. 1989: 33). The historical association of political virtue and manhood with the military reinforces the public/private split and reduces women's legitimate claims in the public sphere (Brown 1992: 18).

Following the same logic, compulsory conscription in Egypt means that families ensure that their male offspring have an identity card (ID) rather than their daughters. The state penalises men above 16 years old if they do not have an official ID, but not women. The IDs are the state's monitoring tool to ensure that all eligible men are drafted into the army. This has major implications for women's legal position and citizenship. In Egypt, legal existence is tied to this piece of paper issued by the state, which verifies the name, age, gender, address and religion of its holder. Without an ID one cannot obtain a passport or driving licence or work in a formal public or private sector job, nor can one access state services. According to the state and its bureaucracies, an individual without an ID does not legally exist. Because women in Egypt cannot get drafted into the army, the state does not think it essential to monitor them through issued IDs. In most cases a woman's name is added as a dependant on her father's ID and later her husband's. As I will show in this study, women's lack of access to personal ID cards is one of the most serious constraints on their capacity to gain access to the state's social resources. In effect, it means that they lack an essential 'ticket' or marker for citizenship.

The fieldwork of a local NGO, the Association for the Development and Enhancement of Women (ADEW),[25] in one slum area since the late 1980s, demonstrated that a large number of poor FHHs have no identity cards. The NGO's members also found that this was perceived – by the women themselves – as the greatest obstacle in accessing the government's services, among other things. Heba el-Kholy, one of the founding members, states:

> Without the ID a poor woman cannot get access to subsidised goods, cannot get access to social security, cannot get access to pension, cannot raise a complaint to the police, and cannot even get her children into school. In short she is considered by society non-existent. A nobody. (el-Kholy 1994: 2)

In addition, the procedures for issuing an ID are extremely complex and intimidating for women – especially low-income women. El-Kholy notes that:

> The bureaucratic procedures and requirements to issue an ID for a forty-year-old illiterate woman are complex and lengthy. To issue an ID the applicant needs a birth certificate, access to two government employees who know the applicant in person and are willing to vouch for her and then stamp her application form, and to have the courage to finalise all that at the police station. A large number of the women living in squatter and slum areas were not born in Cairo and do not have a birth certificate and the process of issuing an alternative birth certificate is nearly impossible especially if one

does not have the time or money to go back to the village of origin and deal with the officials there. In addition the officials at the various bureaucracies are usually unsympathetic to these women and intimidating. (el-Kholy 1994: 5)

At another level, although many areas of Egyptian law remain discriminatory towards women, the personal status law, which is governed by one gendered interpretation of *Shari'a* (Islamic law) principles, is the most infamous as it affects women's lives and status in their immediate family and environment (Baden and Byrne 1996: 8; Kandiyoti 1991b: 10). Women do not have the same right to unilateral divorce as men. They have to go to court and prove that they have been harmed in order to be granted a divorce. At the beginning of the twentieth century, the wife could be divorced at her husband's whim. She was unable to divorce him (and still is unless the marriage contract stipulates otherwise). Several attempts were carried out by both men and women throughout the last century to modify and change these stipulations. However, very few changes took place, and the most progressive propositions have met with a great deal of resistance (Bibars 1988: 31).

Ideally, according to Penal Code statutes, a crime is, by definition, non-discriminatory. The penalty applies to the criminal regardless of class, race or gender. However, women are discriminated against in Egypt either due to the provisions of some laws in themselves or because of the ways in which some laws are executed. A powerful example is the crime of adultery, where women are treated unequally. A man is not considered guilty of adultery unless he is caught with another woman in his marital bed. On the other hand, a woman is an adulteress if she sleeps with a man anywhere. According to Egyptian law, the murder of an adulteress by her husband is a crime of passion and the sentence is thus reduced. However, a woman will be sentenced to a life of hard labour if she kills her husband under the same circumstances (Bahie el-Din 1994b). With regard to crimes of immoral acts such as female prostitution, women are the only party to be convicted. The man in most cases turns into a state witness and testifies against the female prostitute. He thus leaves the court as a free citizen.[26]

In addition, and according to the Egyptian Penal Code, an abductor (a man abducting a woman) is sentenced to life imprisonment and a rapist to death. However, if a rapist offers to marry the victim and she accepts, then he is set free.[27] It is rare in Egypt that a raped girl would refuse such an offer of marriage, since her parents would prefer this marriage than to be left responsible for a dishonoured daughter who is unlikely to have any other marriage prospects. In many cases she might face a death sentence by her parents or be treated as a source of shame to her family and be ostracised if she refuses.[28] Thus she is punished by society, her family and the legal system and is forced into being raped every night for the rest of her married life (Bahie el-Din 1994b). It is clear that discrimination against women exists in the Penal Code. Such discrimination has no religious basis in Islam or Christianity, but is based on traditional and cultural norms that influence legislation and the judges' use of their discretionary powers.

If, theoretically, all citizens are equal in the eyes of the law, for women to be discriminated against due to their sex means not only that the laws are gendered but that women are not considered by the state to be equal citizens. The Egyptian state's role in reinforcing women's reduced citizenship is evident in the personal status law, some aspects of the Penal Code and the nationality law.[29] These are tools used by the state to control women's lives and bodies in the interest of supporting male domination and women's socially and economically marginalised position. In spite of the rhetoric of equality in the constitution, law provisions and judges' interpretations of other provisions are extremely discriminatory against women. Although it is assumed that these laws are in accord with Islamic jurisprudence as in the cases of marriage, divorce and adultery, in reality Islamic law is less biased. For instance, according to Islam, and in very clear directives, it is nearly impossible to prove adultery and thus to punish those who commit it.[30] If in a rare case the adulterers confess, then both the man and the woman are stoned to death. The man does not turn into a witness and is not set free.

Finally, I have argued in this section that the state's actions and its motives are complex. Although at certain periods the state has acted generously towards women, according them certain social rights, it is these same rights that are the first to be sacrificed during any economic or cultural crisis. The contradictory nature of the state becomes clearer when comparing the state's labour laws, which recognise women's child-rearing roles, and the personal status laws of marriage and divorce, which treat women as dependants who are unable to make their own decisions.

Women and the Politics of Needs Interpretation

One important aspect of the relationship between the Egyptian state and women is their continued struggle over interpreting women's needs. My analysis of the Egyptian welfare system and its impact on FHHs shows the sexist interpretations of women's needs that are based on patriarchal definitions of households and family headship. Although such sexist interpretations are powerful and are sanctioned socially, they are contested. There is a conflict over needs interpretation and especially women's needs in Egypt. This struggle over needs talk is a natural result when groups

Introduction

with unequal resources – such as the state and women's groups – compete to make their interpretations of social needs the dominant discourse. Interpretations implanted in the practices of the state and its social welfare bureaucracy are only one type of discourses about needs. They compete with interpretations of oppositional Islamic groups, neo-liberal conservatives and women themselves. Therefore the state welfare bureaucrats are not the only agents engaged in interpreting women's needs (See Fraser 1989: 152–6).

Take the issue of childcare. Feminists argue that the state should provide subsidised, accessible and adequate daycare centres in order to allow women and especially FHHs to join the formal labour market. Social conservatives and especially representatives of religious groups advocate the women's return to the home in order to take care of their children. Poor man-less women with children want to work at well-paying jobs that also take account of their other caring jobs; jobs that provide them with an adequate income that constitute an institutional alternative to a male provider.

Consider also the issue of needs interpretation with regard to the recognition of female headship. Until 15 years ago, this term was never used in Egypt. When spoken of publicly at all, the phenomenon was defined to include widows, divorcees or deserted women only, and they were portrayed as helpless man-less women who were taken care of by any available male kin. Their needs were contained within the familial and domestic spheres. Then a number of feminists in a women's group (ADEW) began to identify this phenomenon and to broaden the definition and characteristics of female headship. Thus a new kind of public discourse emerged requesting the recognition of different types of female headship and demanding new rights. This new public discourse challenged traditional definitions of headship and questioned avenues open for women's participation in the paid formal sector. The discourse also questioned women's legal status and their dependence for legal and economic existence on men. In response to this oppositional needs interpretation, new conservative and especially Islamic groups contested the politicisation of FHHs' needs. They renamed female-headed households 'male-absent households' and argued that this is a familial problem whereby the males' absence created a dysfunctional family. The official needs interpretation by the state defined FHHs as aid recipients who needed to conform to certain rules in order to qualify for such assistance. Each of these competing groups is driven by its own ideology and is serving its own interests in interpreting women's needs. Only the powerful and dominant group will succeed in imposing its interpretation over others. This process of reinterpreting the needs of other groups for ideological purposes is what Fraser has called 'the politics of needs interpretation' (1989).

Fraser argues that it is necessary to focus on the 'politics of needs interpretation' and on the 'discourse of the interpretation of these needs' in order to bring to the forefront the contested character of needs claims. The real issue, in other words, is to reveal that needs interpretation is problematic and is contested by different groups within and outside the state (1989: 163). The aim of borrowing this framework from Fraser in this study is to prove that state and religious interpretations of women's needs are ideologically based and should be contested. Fraser argues that any theory for understanding needs claims should take into consideration the following:

1. The interpretation of people's needs is not to be taken for granted as unproblematic.
2. It is important to know who interprets these needs to serve which interests. Indeed, Fraser argues that defining people's needs is, in itself, a political act.
3. The socially accepted and available forms of public discourses for interpreting needs are not necessarily adequate or fair. Such public discourse is infused with patriarchal and masculine norms and values that work to the disadvantage of subordinate groups (1989: 155–6).

The process of interpreting people's needs is very important, especially in positioning women as secondary and subordinated. Equally important is to find out who interprets these needs and why. By determining certain meanings and reinterpreting their needs, bureaucracies and religious groups reinforce traditionally agreed upon discourses that see women as dependants.

Conclusion

The literature reviewed on the state, feminist theory, the welfare state, and debates on female headship opened up several new questions for my research. Many of the theoretical debates require more empirical work to illuminate them. Some of the questions raised, which I tried to respond to through this study, include whether the state is a resource for women, as liberal feminists claim, or whether it is a constraining factor that furthers their marginalisation and oppression, as radical feminists claim. How far can the state be made to work for women's interests simply by changing its personnel – adding more women, for example? Is the state a monolithic entity that serves the interests of one or more groups, i.e. are its policies a result of a male conspiracy or are its policies the 'unintended' result of conflicting interests? I dealt with questions related to what female headship is, how it is determined, and how this affects the status of women. Questions related to these new family structures and how they are perceived by society and the state are addressed in this empirical work. Questions regarding whether the state's social policies towards women and FHHs are but a reflection of society's perception of and attitude towards the same group of women are also examined. Finally, questions related to women's oppression and the empowerment project of feminism are raised. To what extent do these women actually resist the different systems of oppression and to what extent are such moments of subversion only mild deceptive and manipulative techniques that reinforce their secondary and marginalised position?

This study attempts to answer some of the above questions and at times raises related issues. Although there are no direct and clear-cut answers, I try to use examples from the field and the voices and stories of the women themselves to respond to these inquiries.

In this study two parallel, interacting and complementing themes are being investigated. The first theme is state social welfare policies and programmes and their impact on women's status and autonomy. The second theme is women's and especially FHHs' status within their societies, how they are perceived and positioned by members of their communities and their coping mechanisms. These two themes are connected by the contention in this study that state social policies towards women and especially FHHs are a reflection of and are influenced by how society perceives, positions and interprets women's needs. It is not feasible to understand the underlying assumptions at the basis of state policies without understanding how they originate from the patriarchal norms embedded in the community and its collective culture.

In the next chapter the methodology and research communities are described. Since I chose to study complex issues such as bureaucracy and the status and coping mechanisms of FHHs, it is imperative to explain in detail which research methodologies and techniques I used.

Notes

1. I refer to these women as female heads of households (FHHs). This refers to both the *de facto* and *de jure* women who are heads of their families, i.e. those who are the main or sole economic contributors to the family income. They are also those women who take on not only the economic responsibility of the household but its social and legal responsibilities as well. Chapter 3 provides a more detailed explanation of what I mean by FHHs.

2. More detailed statistics about the percentage and characteristics of FHHs will be given in Chapter 3.

3. It is also important to note that the national definition ignores many 'non-traditional' FHHs such as co-wives, wives of *Urzu'i* men and wives who are the main source

of income although their spouses work. Chapter 3 has more detail on these issues. In that sense these estimates are very conservative.

4. The Ministry of Insurance and Social Affairs will be referred to as MOSA. This is the ministry that manages and administers the state's social assistance programme to the poor.

5. I personally witnessed this dialogue in the social unit of 'The Tombs'.

6. As will be seen in Chapter 3, divorced women are more likely to be discriminated against than other types of FHHs. Divorcees are usually blamed for the failure of their marriage. It is necessary to point out that the aim of these citations is to show trends of bias against certain types of female headship. Although not all officials were that harsh and insulting to divorcees, the general trend was condescending.

7. For citations and quotations from field interviews I will state the person's name, her age, marital status and, finally, from which of the seven research sites she comes. Women's names used here are fictitious.

8. In Chapter 2, I will describe the research sites in detail. The names I gave to these areas are also fictitious.

9. A'm means uncle. Elderly men are called by their names preceded by A'm as a sign of respect.

10. An *u'rzu'i* is a man who has no regular job and in many cases is an unskilled labourer.

11. In Chapter 5, I will explain in detail three coping mechanisms that I identified during my fieldwork.

12. The accepted roles of women, in patriarchal societies, are socially imposed and limit them to the private sphere, consequently reinforcing males' superiority over females. (Both the square and round brackets are the author's.)

13. For feminist positions on this question, see the work of McIntosh 1978 and Mackinnon 1989. Feminist approaches to the state will be discussed fully below.

14. In addition, none of these studies on the social policy took women's opinions into consideration; they were desk reviews of decrees and policies.

15. Feminist theoretical framework, to me, is an approach that assumes that women are oppressed and that there is a need to change this oppression. See Chapter 2 for more detail.

16. As will be shown throughout this study, these controls are not explicit but implicit. There is no conscious male conspiracy out there. These policies are shaped by social biases and do not constitute a deliberate hatred of women.

17. On how the state and its policies affect gender relations, especially in the West, see Wilson 1977; Piven 1985; Sassoon 1987 and Gordon 1988.

18. For more information about the feminist movement in Egypt see Badran 1991.

19. Sadat's open-door policy to the West and the Western capitalist model for the economy was called the *Infitah* period, i.e. the opening period.

20. The charter is a political legal code that was established during Gamal Abdel Nasser's regime (1956–70) and superseded the constitution.

21. In 1971 the state's new constitution re-established the patriarchal forms of life and emphasised the distinction between the public and private spheres when it stated that men and women have the same rights as long as they are not against *Sharia'a* and not in conflict with women's duties at the household. Sadat encouraged and tolerated the emergence of the Islamic right. Women's citizenship rights have been compromised as the state acquiesced to Islamic and conservative demands.

22. Identity cards are the only official verification of name, age, address and profession of a particular person.

23. Women have the right to apply for ID cards. In fact few poor and illiterate women do, because they do not have the required documentation, such as birth certificates, and because it is easier to be tagged onto a man's card.

24. In Egypt to date marital rape is not acknowledged.

25. I am a founding member and the chairperson of this NGO. This is the first feminist NGO to work with FHHs in Egypt and to identify the problem of identity cards.

26. See the Gender Task Force Research Summary Paper 'Equality before the law' presented to the ICPD, 1994.

27. This has been changed by a ministerial decree in 1999.

28. There have been cases in the press of families killing a daughter who has been raped and who refused to marry the rapist. Women are still being blamed for 'bringing' rape on themselves.

29. While the right to Egyptian nationality is granted to a child born to an Egyptian father, to a child born to a foreign mother married to an Egyptian, to an illegitimate child born to an Egyptian mother and to a child born to an Egyptian mother and an unknown father or a father holding no nationality, this same right is refused to a child born to an Egyptian mother married to a foreigner (NGO Forum 1994).

30. As is clearly stated in the Qur'an (Surat el EFK), four witnesses have to witness the act of intercourse and a thread has to be passed in between the bodies of the two adulterers. If the thread does not pass between the two bodies (i.e. if their two bodies are not linked together through the intercourse), no one can prove they have been committing adultery unless they confess.

2

The Feminist Researcher among the Women

In this chapter, I not only describe the research methods used but also examine the deep dilemmas that I faced with regard to the assumption – in feminist research – that the research process itself will be a liberating experience for the subjects of the research. Finally, I describe the seven low-income urban sites of the research to provide a physical context for my findings.

The methods I adopted and the way I conducted my research were very important in themselves, inasmuch as they were essential to arrive at answers or raise additional questions regarding my research problematics. My work is based upon my understanding and interpretation of a feminist approach to research. This approach maximises the ability to explore women's experiences and to find out how they organise their lives differently from men. It is an approach that attempts to reach an un-exploitative relationship with the subjects who are being studied. Ultimately, feminist research strives to make a difference and to produce a kind of knowledge that could transform the patriarchal status quo. Feminist research emphasises the importance of understanding women's lives and ensuring that their voices, history and experience are not marginalised in any enquiry or research. When dealing with oppressed women, it is important to know about their lives and their perception of their situations, their relationships with their community, and, for this study, their perception of and relationship with the state through its welfare policies and programmes. For that reason using oral history and recounting women's stories was the most appropriate method. Oral history makes these women's voices audible.

Post-modern theory cast doubts on the extent to which we can rely on people's voices to deliver any kind of knowledge except for the most local, subjective and specific forms of knowledge. This study puts a great deal of stress on amplifying the voices of previously silent people because, I believe, they have something important to say about social systems of domination. I believe that what these women say is of broader significance and tell us interesting things about state power in Egypt more generally.

Nevertheless, post-modern feminists have rejected this method on the grounds that there is no one true account of women's oppression and that there is no universal women's experience. They also argue that it is important to examine how these experiences are interpreted by the women themselves and by the researchers (Grant 1987). I am aware of the effect of my subjective interpretation of their stories and equally aware that what I present is a middle-class interpretation. I nevertheless juxtapose the two different arguments and kinds of knowledge – that of the researched women and that of the state – as I understand them. The final aim is to contrast them and expose the contradiction.

The extended period of fieldwork – 20 months – that this research required, as well as the availability of funding, made it possible to experiment with different methodologies, both qualitative and quantitative. I intentionally began my work in the research sites by using qualitative methods such as semi-structured interviews, informal observation techniques and checklists. I wanted to learn about my communities first hand before trying out any other tool. I experimented with a quantitative research method only in one research site, 'The Shelters'. After five months of intensive ethnographic work in 'The Shelters', a survey was conducted with the help of a field supervisor and seven data-collectors. The survey was mainly used to assess the relevance of a quantitative method for studying women and for investigating feminist concerns.

How the Research was Conducted

I started the research by reviewing the state's laws and regulations governing welfare programmes. Access to data and official statistics were among the main problems. I tried to overcome this difficulty by using unofficial and personal contacts and resources. The scarce government sources that exist and to which I could gain access (many were inaccessible) were available in the form of annual reports, laws and decrees, and were not always consistent. Therefore, many of the figures – on the size of state welfare programmes' benefits – used in this study were taken from personal communication with officials and women rather than from official documents. However, all these documents were used as important background information on the procedures and criteria of the different governmental welfare programmes. Reports on the programmes of Islamic NGOs were even harder to get, but through personal contacts I gained access to many of their confidential reports, especially those on expenditures. I also reviewed the available literature on the Egyptian welfare system.

In addition, I carried out a number of semi-structured interviews with officials and policy-makers. In Cairo, I interviewed two high-ranking public officials from MOSA. In addition, I interviewed 25 different male and female government officials, Islamic administrators, church officials and NGO staff.

I followed a checklist in my interviews with all the officials. I had met most of the high-ranking officials before[1] and so our meetings were relaxed and sometimes informal. I had difficulties interviewing two low-level MOSA bureaucrats[2] in two areas and the employees of the two insurance offices.[3] My meetings and interactions with the female employees of the Islamic welfare programmes studied were friendly and cooperative. On the other hand, only two of the 18 male administrators of the Islamic NGO – which is running a very large orphan sponsorship welfare programme – agreed to meet me.[4]

Qualitative in-depth interviews were conducted with 444 women. More focused case-studies of 15 women from low-income, urban working-class backgrounds were then carried out. Of those 15 women, I chose to present eight cases only in this study. I did not present the remaining seven because in some way they repeat many of the issues raised in the eight case studies. The purpose of recounting their stories is to examine the aspects of their life histories that contributed to their status within their families and communities and their relationship to and perception of the state's welfare programmes.[5]

I interviewed all the women more than once. The value of re-interviewing was demonstrated repeatedly. It helped me discover discrepancies in information and, very often, problems of interpretation of the answers as well.

My findings are also based on my participation in various social situations, such as public meetings, social gatherings, weddings and circumcision ceremonies. In addition to the in-depth semi-structured interviews with selected women, other types of conversations also constitute the data of my study: a chance encounter in an NGO's office with a woman or a man; a long discussion with community leaders in one of their public meetings; a short conversation during a wedding. These constituted tips and data on the different areas that helped me understand the cultural and social context within which the women I studied lived.

In each area, I selected a range of informants to avoid partial accounts of the social situation. I used as many key informants as possible, making sure that they represented different geographical, religious, educational and income backgrounds and levels. Burgess describes a type of non-probability sampling whereby the researcher uses a small group of informants and, after working with them, is able to work with their friends and other groups through a 'snowball effect'. This sampling process follows the patterns of social relations in a particular setting and it was the technique that I used.

In all the research sites local NGOs were my entry point.[6] Their staff introduced me to many of the women and helped me identify the initial informants. Through the informants I focused on selecting *de jure* FHHs; at my request, they introduced me to widows, divorcees, deserted women and wives of imprisoned husbands. However, in my daily work with the NGOs I entered women's homes and got to know many more women who are not traditionally considered FHHs (wives of *u'rzu'i*[7] men, wives of unemployed men and co-wives). However, when my entry point was through the Islamic sponsorship welfare programme, most of the women interviewed were widows because the programme mainly targets orphaned children who have lost their fathers.[8] Finally, although the sample is not statistically representative, the fact that I found similar patterns in the seven research sites indicates that there is some validity to these findings.

On the other hand, one of the conditions of working through the NGO in 'The Shelters' was that I should conduct a sample survey of the population of that area. I developed a questionnaire of 85 questions related to different aspects of household life such as education, health, employment and income, among other issues. The initial ethnographic fieldwork was very useful for the questionnaire survey that took place later on. This initial fieldwork established a database for data-collectors.[9] My knowledge of the area and work with the NGO helped me to classify the area into specific sub-groups and streets, and this helped to make the sample as representative as possible. The results of this survey were used only for generating statistics about the number of FHHs and their different sub-categories.

Concerns Regarding Feminist Research

In trying to apply feminist research, as I understand it, several questions concerned me throughout my fieldwork:

1. Can feminist research really lead to the empowerment of the women being researched?
2. Can the power relationship between the researcher and the subjects ever be equalised?
3. What is the impact of the research on these women and do we, the feminist researchers, consider how we affect the lives of the subjects and how we are affected by the research?

In other words, my basic concerns revolve around questions about the inevitability of a power dimension in the relationship between the researcher and the subjects, the ethics of research practices, the impact of the research process on the researched, and matters of exploitation and control even within a feminist methodology.

In answering the first question one has to define what one means by feminist research. Feminism is an ideology, which seeks to bring women out of private seclusion and silence and into public dialogue. Feminists argue that women's oppression is not inevitable or natural, but that it can and must be changed (Stanley and Wise 1983; Roberts 1995). In response to conventional research methods, feminist research is concerned with removing male biases from the social sciences and social reality (Hartung et al. 1988: 1–22). Traditional research has never problematised the constant generalisations taken from the experience of 'males' and then imposed on all people, a situation that would not occur with an all-female research population. In social sciences it is rare for generalisations to be derived from research on women (Stanley and Wise 1983: 27–9). Feminist research fills in some of the gaps left by the traditional social sciences because most previous research was influenced by the predominant male ideology where the unit of study was the man (Moore 1988).

Nevertheless, there is no definite consensus on what constitutes feminist research. Most researchers agree that it involves, at its most basic level, a minimum amount of deconstruction of the implicit ideas of the male as the norm and the female as the other (de Beauvoir 1972). Feminist research is meant to be conducted for and not on women. Feminist research insists on the importance of highlighting the experiences and very existence of women. Indeed, its main concern has been the method and process of conducting research.

An important dimension to feminist research is the need to ensure that the power relationship between the researcher and the subjects should be different from that in traditional research, which is embedded with masculine and patriarchal norms. The researcher must realise that she is not better or more experienced than the subjects. It must also be clear to the researcher that the women being researched are not objects for scientific study. She must realise that both must benefit and learn from their relationship.[10] This ideology emphasises partnership, which involves treating the researched as subjects without exploiting them. However, I believe that the power dimension exists in some academic feminist research as well. Although there is a call to learn from and share with the researched women, the elitist notion of us being the theorising researching elite persists in some circles. We use their stories and experiences to develop abstract theories that rationalise what we believe and seek to prove (Stanley and Wise 1983: 7).

Another unique dimension of feminist research is its empowering and emancipatory project. Women should directly use the product of feminist research in order to formulate policies and provisions necessary for feminist activities (Stanley and Wise 1983; Maguire 1987). The feminist research project must lead to the empowerment of the researched and the transformation of their lives (Maguire 1987: 28–31). However, feminists argue that unless the research process is participatory it will not be an emancipatory project and will therefore fail to be feminist. Stanley and Wise (1983) argue that unless the researched participate in developing the methodology and the research questions then an incomplete feminist approach is being adopted. The purpose of participatory research is not merely to describe and interpret social reality, but to change it radically. Furthermore, the intent is to transform reality with, rather than for, oppressed people (Maguire 1987: 28). Thus what differentiates feminist research from qualitative and anthropological research is that it calls for the empowerment and liberation of the subjects to be researched. There is a claim that participatory research is not gender-specific and that all those who work with oppressed groups seek a more egalitarian and equal relationship with their subjects.[11] What is unique about feminist research is that it focuses on the experience of oppressed women regardless of race or class.

Yet to be as participatory as Maguire (1987) and Stanley and Wise (1983) call for means that the research subjects should be the ones initiating the process. They must, as a group, have identified their problems and should begin the process of action research to reach a solution to their problems. This is not the case in academic research. In academic feminist research the topic and tools have already been chosen prior to commencing a particular study. While it is true that being a feminist makes one more gender-sensitive to the needs and experiences of the participating subjects, the subjects of the research have neither called for help nor chosen the methods and tools of the research.

In my research I tried to apply the ethics of feminism and feminist research. I hoped to empower the women whom I chose to study. But in choosing and defining the research problematic, I did not work with the researched women and we did not generate the research problematic together. I had chosen the geographic area of research and the major questions before I even met any of the women I interviewed. In addition, the general guidelines and framework of the research methodology were established before I started my fieldwork. However, the assumptions I reached and wanted to investigate prior to the research came as a result of my work with poor women in rural and urban areas and my encounters with FHHs through the NGO ADEW for the last eleven years. So, on one hand, commencing the process was not as participatory as feminist research calls for and, on the other, it was not as divorced from actual life experiences as traditional research.

The subjects of my research were not involved in the choice of the topic or in the choice of methodology. They were informed about my research topic but were not involved in developing the general plan of research. I introduced them to the general theme, but not to my assumptions, in order to avoid influencing their opinions or their perception of their roles, status and relationships with the government, their community and the NGOs in the area.

As a feminist I respected the women's experiences, built very trusting and warm relationships with them and made a conscious effort to break class and cultural barriers. I did not come to the areas with any preconceived ideas about my future findings. On the contrary, I was surprised enough by many of my observations that they affected the flow of my research and redirected me towards areas of inquiry that had not previously occurred to me. My checklist for the interviews changed during the first month in response to the women's and key informants' suggestions as well as to some of my early observations.

My own social identity, my class position, lifestyle and work experience affected my relationship with the researched women. I tried to overcome all barriers between the researched and myself, especially the class barrier. My moral dilemma about Shadia, whose story I will recount later, is a clear example of how my middle-class values influenced my neutrality as a researcher.[12] Shadia's rebellion against her situation, her attempt to defy traditional patriarchy by having affairs with several men and by leaving her husband could be interpreted as a form of empowerment, a form of empowerment that is rejected in my middle-class morality. My middle-class values and ideas were challenged by the more realistic and adaptive value systems of the poor women whom I met.

However, I also found that the desired equality in power relations between the researcher and the researched subjects, in its ideal form, is hard to achieve. They were my source of information for my research and I believe I was their source of information on the outside world and a different class. This difference in the kinds of knowledge in itself positioned us differently, as one researcher argues:

> The researcher and the researched are positioned differently in relation to both the production of knowledge and the kinds and range of knowledge they possess. (Maynard and Purvis 1994: 6)

Finally, how do we affect the researched and how are we as researchers affected by the research process? I believe that I have changed and have become more tolerant of conduct and value systems that transcend middle-class morality. The women in the field and their survival mechanisms for maintaining their families in the very worst of conditions made me change my priorities and value my family more. Ironically, my conservative reaction to Shadia's sexual acts forced me to rethink my own values about sexuality.

The question of empowerment remains elusive and it would be disingenuous to pretend that our encounters brought power to these women. I do not think that I affected U'm Saber as much as she affected me.[13] She has maintained her traditional beliefs and continued to impose oppressive rituals on other women. A month after I left her area, U'm Saber's niece married and U'm Saber insisted that they carry out the traditional deflowering ritual on her wedding night.[14] She also accepted a suitor for her 15-year-old daughter. I was very disappointed, for U'm Saber and I had spent many evenings on the roof of her house discussing the negative impact of such oppressive traditions. I believed that I was able to influence her and that she, as a community leader, might play an important role in helping women resist and reject such oppressive rituals. I found later that I had failed. U'm Saber's perception of her status, her role in the community and the role of women had not changed.

In short, although the feminist research approach is the most appropriate for listening to and understanding the voices of oppressed women, its empowering and emancipatory project is difficult to achieve in an academic setting.

The Research Sites

I worked in seven low-income urban areas in Cairo and Alexandria. For this study any urban area could have been selected, but since population density and concentration is high in capital cites and, moreover, because their slums and squatter areas exhibit all types of poverty, I decided to select pockets of poverty from Cairo and Egypt's second largest city, Alexandria. Since they contain innumerable low-income marginalised areas – 68 squatter areas in Cairo and 56 squatter areas in Alexandria – I relied on my contacts and experience in low-income neighbourhoods to select the precise areas of study.

The selection was based on certain criteria, such as the presence of a well-established, community-based NGO in the area and cooperation from respondents and key figures. Other selection factors included accessibility to the area and the fact that no other studies were being undertaken at the same location either at the time of my research or in the recent past.

Four of the seven low-income urban areas in which I worked were clear-cut squatter areas. They were either unplanned areas, illegal housing, or temporary government shelters that had mutated into squatter areas as the families expanded and started building rooms for offspring during their wait of twenty years or more for government housing. In these areas, people from different districts were gathered and thus constituted a community only in the geographic sense. They had no traditional or kinship ties.

Two of my research communities were relatively old, traditional and well-established areas. Safety networks and kinship ties linked these communities together. They tended to be more conservative, and the information system and networks among its women and men were better established.

The last community was a cross between a squatter area and a traditional slum. On the one hand, it was a new resettlement area for people who were scattered due to the 1992 earthquake. In that sense, they shared the uprooted feelings of squatter area inhabitants, and they also did not have well-established networks or ties. On the other hand, they were resettled at a very new and much cleaner and more organised location. Many basic services were provided and a major development project was implemented in that sub-district. Five years after resettlement and the beginning of the project, the lives and habits of these people had changed and common interests between them had emerged.

Consistent and reliable data on population size, average incomes, occupational profiles of inhabitants, health and education status and place of origin were difficult if not impossible to obtain. Since it is not possible to provide a common and therefore comparable set of data on the social, economic or cultural profile of each community, I describe, in the sections that follow, different aspects of each community that were salient for my research, and, in part, shaped the decision on the inclusion of each community as a research site.

'The Shelters' 'The Shelters' is a sub-district in south Cairo. It is an area of extreme poverty that has been neglected by the government since its foundation in the early 1960s. A sanctioned and continuing government policy is to resettle people who lose their homes – due to natural reasons such as earthquakes or due to demolition – in temporary shelters until they are provided with public housing. However, most people spend at least twenty years in these temporary shelters before acquiring any government housing. For all intents and purposes, such shelters consequently cease to be temporary. This research site is one of those camps recognised by the state as a sub-district. Families of seven people or more share one-room apartments with no water service or sanitation and sometimes without electricity. The inhabitants of this area are mainly lower middle-class. Most of the educated men and women have not gone to university, and most of the women above the age of 40 were illiterate.

My first observation of the area was that a large number of the women walked around the area in their night-gowns. Many of these night-gowns were short sleeved and thus the women's arms, necks and sometimes a bit of chest were uncovered. Since most of the poor who live in the squatter areas are relatively new immigrants from villages and Upper Egypt, it is believed among the middle class that they wear conservative dress.[15] I was surprised to find that their dress code was more liberal than I had expected within the geographic zone of 'The Shelters'. Those who covered their hair did so only when they left the zone of 'The Shelters'. They wore a *khemar* (a scarf that covers the hair, neck, bust and back) only when they were outside their secure or safe zone. The conception of such a zone differed from one woman to another.

Samah, a student at the nursing school, surprised me one day in an area outside 'The Shelters' because she was wearing a *khemar*, long sleeves and an ankle-length dress. The several times I saw her – in her house, on her street and talking to both male and female neighbours in 'The Shelters' – she did not cover her hair and was usually dressed in jeans and a T-shirt. When I asked her if she considered herself a veiled (*mohagaba*) person, she said yes, and that she only took it off at home. She either did not understand or chose to ignore the meaning of *hegab* as taught by '*ulama*' or religious leaders: A woman should not be seen without a hair covering by any male who could be an eligible husband. Samah only covered when she was not at home, and home to her meant much more than her family house; it included her community.

Elderly women usually wear a small scarf over part of their heads as well, which is a rural habit and not considered Islamic dress, for their hair and neck are left uncovered. The women of 'The Shelters' made no attempt to use the Islamic uniform to improve their image within their area. The Islamic dress code was used more as a protective shield in the outside world. It was as if the slum-dwellers were different within their own space, adhering to and confirming the expectations of others, be that the government or the upper middle class, only when they were outside their own geographical area.

A major socialising activity is the 2.00–3.00 p.m. lunch. Several women sit in front of their doorsteps during the day, to cook, chat and gossip. One woman, the leader of the street, puts a *tablia* (traditional Egyptian table) in front of her doorstep and invites the neighbours to come and join her, each with her own dish. Not participating can put some women in jeopardy. When U'm Samah, one of my key informants, stopped participating, she was labelled a snob. However, when the time of her daughters' weddings comes, a woman must re-join her street group. These gatherings are not only opportunities for women to show off their cooking or the cooking of marriageable daughters, but are also a milieu for gossip. The lunches are used to spread around very particular bits of information. A girl's reputation could be ruined or saved during one of these gatherings. Thus the leaders of the gatherings are very important women who are sought for their good opinion of any marriageable daughter. The consequences can be dire if they are offended. That is why, when a girl is to be married, she and her family usually ask such a group leader to witness the deflowering ritual, in order to spread the word that the bride was a virgin and that she shed blood on her wedding night.

Another socialising activity among the women is the Friday 'clothes washing' ritual. Washing clothes is an important and regular ceremony. It is a collective activity, in which several women put their washing machines in the space between the rooms and do the washing together. By participating in several of these parties, I came to know much about the women of this area and they also began to accept me.

'The Tombs' This area is located on Cairo's periphery, and was originally allocated to a particular group as a cemetery. However, since the 1960s the government has used the empty space around it to build shelters to resettle people who have lost their homes. These were supposedly temporary shelters but, as in the case of 'The Shelters', people still live there and have not yet been transferred to permanent government housing. The area is very poor, the streets are not paved, and basic services such as health clinics, hospitals and schools are several miles away. Electricity, water and telephones are connected in only 20 per cent of the houses and workshops.

Organised Islamic groups and the mosque and its services were more evident in this area than in the others. This is not merely because I gained access to this area through the private Islamic sponsorship programme, Haj, and through its veiled women administrators.[16] By observation alone I noticed more young men wearing Islamic dress (white *jalabia* and Sunni beards) and more veiled women than in any of the other research areas. The lifestyle, in general, was more religious: men, children and women prayed in the mosque, and on Fridays one could not walk around in the area of the mosque for most of the small unpaved streets surrounding it were covered with prayer mats (*keleem*).

It was not clear how many Islamic groups were active there, but there certainly was more than one and each provided different services. There was *A'l Jami'iya Shari'iyya*, which sent its administrator to provide jobs and training for women and men in the area. There was the Zakat Committee, which was registered with the Nasser Social Bank and provided youths and widows with zero-interest loans from the *zakat* money.[17] In addition to these two official Islamic organisations, there was a subtle presence of other, more clandestine groups, as the following story reveals.

An 18-year-old girl once told me that her brother had started to yell at her and her mother, ordering them to wear the veil. Although they wore scarves on their hair, he wanted them to wear a complete veil, black stockings and black gloves.

> It is this group he is hanging around with. Since he became their friend he started wearing a white *jalabia* and a white hat and a he has grown a Sunni beard. I am afraid he will not let me out of the house in the near future. (Bothayna, 18, 'The Tombs')

'Alexandria' This is one of the oldest and most established slum areas of Alexandria and, although services and utilities exist, they are deteriorating and over-used. The area is overcrowded, with extended families occupying small apartments due to the housing crisis. The houses are run down, although the general living conditions here are much better than in the other research sites. Social and economic networks are well established and people follow traditional norms of behaviour and self-presentation. Although the majority of the women interviewed were very poor, the overall socio-economic status of the area is not as depressed as in the other research sites.

The dress code is more conservative and there is a more commercial and cosmopolitan environment than at the other research sites. Families are conservative and thus restrict the mobility of their daughters and their women. This affects their relationship to the state and its services. Most of the women I met refused to approach MOSA or the state for welfare benefits, as they did not want to be seen as beggars. So, while the people of 'The Shelters' and 'The Tombs' portrayed themselves as beggars even if they did not need the financial assistance, the people in Alexandria portrayed themselves as middle-class even when they were in dire need of such assistance. A large number of people refused any assistance from the local mosque.

'The Resettlement' 'The Resettlement' is 30 kilometres outside the city of Cairo and is surrounded by five squatter neighbourhoods and seven factories. It is isolated from urban facilities and other opportunities in general. This area was originally planned as a low-cost rental-housing neighbourhood for newly wed couples without children. However, as the result of the 1992 earthquake, which destroyed thousands of houses overnight, the state changed the area's original purpose. It resettled approximately 2,300 earthquake victims here.[18]

The area's inhabitants were all uprooted from their original communities and lost their social networks and safety-nets. According to data compiled by NGO staff, poverty and unemployment are the major problems facing

Victims and Heroines

the people. Poverty is conspicuous, with 91 per cent of families coming from low-income brackets. Most families – approximately 87 per cent of the population – have irregular sources of income due to employment in the informal sector. Most people lost access to the job market after they were resettled. The percentage of FHHs reached 24 per cent in 1993 because working-age men left their families and remarried in central Cairo to be closer to the job markets.[19]

'The Ezba' Thirty-five years ago this was a tiny rural hamlet on the outskirts of Cairo. When the state built several factories here in the 1960s, the lives of the original inhabitants changed. Many people came here from adjacent rural villages and shantytowns, and in the last 20 years this hamlet has mushroomed into an overpopulated, run-down, industrial, low-income urban area. Although high-rise buildings have been erected, families – regardless of size – live in one-room apartments and all the inhabitants of one building share a bathroom. Basic services are run down and it is common to see young children playing in streets overflowing with sewage and to hear that the sewage has penetrated the potable water pipes.

The women in the area are generally conservative in their dress codes because most of the inhabitants are still closely tied to their rural origins. Unlike the other areas, the majority of the population come from Lower and not Upper Egypt. Thus their villages of origin are physically closer to them, as are the supervising eyes of their extended families.

Two ideological groups theoretically control the area. The first, the fundamental Islamists, are gaining ground with the youth every day; they have been growing in terms of size and area of hegemony during the last ten to fifteen years. The second, workers' movement, includes among its members different ideological stands, communist and Nasserite. This group also includes remnants of the student movement of the 1970s. Both groups compete for recruits and, in their rivalry, offer different basic services to the community. In the meantime, the state and its official party are withdrawing from the provision of basic services. Thus the level of political and social awareness of the women of this area, whether educated or not, is high.

'The Bedouins' Until the 1950s this area was neither part of the urban governorate nor was it a rural town. It was one among many sites that the Bedouin tribes settled in during the winter months. After the revolution, the state built several factories and 'The Bedouins' were officially encouraged to settle down. Some 40 years later, one of the groups of people in this area, whom I called 'The Bedouins', still dress and act like desert nomads. These natives, as they like to present themselves, belong to one tribe composed of two large families, which have been intermarrying. The second group living in this area consists of peasants who came from the adjacent rural belt. The area itself is neither completely urban nor rural. The roads remain unpaved and basic infrastructure is not officially provided to all houses. The limited two- or three-storey buildings belong to men who have returned from the Gulf after working there for many years.

The two big families still hold true to their traditions and customary laws and are very proud of their heritage. Members of these families refer to the other inhabitants as peasants, connoting a lower status. It is common for a male from 'The Bedouins' to marry a peasant but it is not acceptable for the women of the main tribe to marry from among the peasants.

A large number of the divorcees and deserted women I interviewed were peasant women who were left by a Bedouin husband after some years of marriage in order to return to their first wives, who were also their cousins. A large number of the co-wives were Bedouin women whose husbands had decided to marry a younger peasant girl who would cost them much less than any Bedouin woman.

While the peasants felt discriminated against by the Bedouins, the Bedouins felt neglected by and discriminated against by the state. However, the educated youth, especially among Bedouins, have formed a very active and influential community development association (CDA), which has helped improve the quality of life for many of the inhabitants, both peasant and Bedouin. This CDA is a true community-based organisation that has identified the needs of the people and lobbied the state on many fronts to respond to the community's different needs.

'The Squatters' I chose this site primarily because it is a squatter area. Indeed, it is one of the largest squatter areas in Egypt and one that the government has decided to recognise. Its inhabitants are mainly migrants from Upper Egypt and many still speak in their original dialect. It is a conservative society in its dress code and in its scrutiny and informal monitoring systems of women's conduct.

One mosque in the area is a centre for religious, cultural and social assistance. Through this mosque, different welfare programmes are provided to the poor in general and women in particular. Conditions for eligibility for these programmes include adhering to the Islamic dress code and attending religious classes. Considering the large number of poor in the area, this religious welfare system has had a strong hold on the behaviour of the majority of the population. Hence it was not surprising that the percentage of veiled women and female children was high.

Notes

1. I worked with the Catholic Relief Services and later with UNICEF for many years and therefore had been in contact with these people.
2. Those who administer the state social assistance programmes at the district level.
3. Those who administer the aid programme known as the Sadat Pension.
4. Although I covered my hair when I visited the offices of this NGO, the male administrators were unfriendly towards me. Even the two who agreed to be interviewed threatened me later and asked me to be very careful with what I wrote.
5. Although the same checklist was used with all these women, and all of them were interviewed several times in order to verify the information and my interpretation, the interviewees' concerns varied. For example, some women talked more about their lives with their husbands, others talked more about their relationship with their family and community, and still others focused more on their relationship with the government. Some women depended on stating facts and chronological events, while others preferred to speak about their feelings and expectations.
6. In all the areas except 'The Shelters', 'The Tombs' and 'The Squatters' my entry points were local community development associations, which are people's organisations. I cannot mention their names as this would disclose the real identity of the district. In 'The Shelters', The Coptic Evangelical Organisation for Social Services (CEOSS) was the NGO. In 'The Squatters' and 'The Tombs' the Haj, an individually run Islamic sponsorship programme for orphans, was my entry point.
7. Men who have no regular jobs.
8. According to the state, Islam and the Arabic language, an 'orphan' is a child who lost his/her father.
9. There were seven data-collectors in addition to myself: five women and two men, who were trained on the questionnaire.
10. On the rules and ethics of feminist research and the relationship between the researcher and the subjects of research see Gluck and Patai 1991.
11. Personal communication with Dr Archie Mafeje, a former anthropology professor at the American University in Cairo (AUC).
12. Shadia is a case who engaged in sexual acts that challenged my conservatism.
13. U'm Saber is one of the women whose story is recounted in Chapter 7, and was also one of my key informants in 'The Shelters'.
14. Manual breaking of the hymen of the bride, see Chapter 7.
15. Upper Egypt is a rural region in the south, known to be very conservative.
16. An orphan sponsorship programme run by an individual whom I call the Haj, i.e. a man who has made the pilgrimage to Mecca.
17. The money collected as a tax from the rich to be given to the poor, similar to the tithe.
18. Bazoglou 1997; Project Document, UNICEF 1993.
19. Bazoglou 1997.

3
Defining Female Headship

The female-headed household is a relatively new phenomenon that has stirred up debates in the current development literature. These debates centre around three main research problematics. The first is the definition of headship, and female headship in particular. The second is the issue of the stigmatisation of female-headed households. The third problematic focuses on the association of female headship with poverty and whether FHHs should be a priority target group in development projects and welfare programmes.

In this chapter, I describe and analyse the difficulties researchers face in defining female headship and examine the complexity of such a concept. The prevalence of FHHs in Egypt and the profile of FHHs at the research sites are then briefly described. I next address the issue of stigmatisation. I report how these women are perceived by society and how they perceive themselves. I pay particular attention to the role of official social policies in defining the salient aspects of FHHs' needs, and how, in the process, these policies contribute to their marginal social status. I argue that social policies and programmes reflect society's perception of a household, and that the prevailing culture and ideology respects only one form of family structure, headed by a man. Women on their own are marginalised by society and man-less families are considered dysfunctional. The issue of the feminisation of poverty is then discussed briefly. Debates around FHHs' over- or under-representation in poor segments of societies and whether they are more deserving target groups for anti-poverty assistance are discussed. I also highlight that although not all FHHs are poor, research in the USA, Egypt and the Arab World shows that FHHs tend to be poorer and more vulnerable than male-headed households (MHHs). In particular, women's lack of skills and education push them into the informal sector, which provides them with no health or social services or care. Finally, the chapter highlights that FHHs suffer from their double burdens as carers at home and workers outside the home, that their vulnerability is not only economic but social and legal, and concludes that the state in Egypt should be more sensitive to the needs and vulnerability of FHHs.

Definitions

When I started this research I wanted to study the impact of social policies on women who head their households, and I defined them as those women who bear the financial, social and legal burdens of the household. My main concern was with women who are left to fend for themselves in a society that does not recognise any type of household other than those headed by men.

I found that there are two main objections in the literature regarding the concept and definition of household and female headship. The first objection is related to the cultural specificity of the term. It is claimed that female headship is treated as a dysfunctional form of family in the West due to the prevalence of the Western patriarchal male headship model. The male headship model is seen as an imposition on other cultures (Baden and Milward 1995; Buvinic and Gupta 1997). I disagree with this argument because whether the male model is Western or not, it has spread through colonisation and has become the norm in most, if not all, countries. In many other cultures, such as the Arab culture, female headship *de facto* or *de jure* was also denied, rejected and stigmatised long before colonisation due to a traditional and intrinsic patriarchal tradition. The second objection is related to the characteristics of female headship. Proponents of this objection argue that there cannot be a universal meaning and definition of headship. Kabeer distinguishes between female headship, where women maintain the house and are its key decision-makers and economic managers, and female-managed households, where women manage household economies on behalf of an absent male head (Kabeer 1992). In other words the concept of FHHs has proved to be not only controversial but also complex.

A woman-headed household, in most national and international data, is described as a unit where an adult woman lives without an adult male co-resident, whether he be the legal or common-law spouse, brother, in-law, father, grandfather or son. A male-headed household, however, is described as a unit where an adult male resides with a female spouse or children alone.[1] Thus conventional terminology defines a household as female-headed only if there is no adult male residing there, while a male-headed household applies whether there is an adult female or not. This reflects the traditional belief that women's domestic role and position in the house are unimportant in determining household headship (Folbre 1991: 92).

Debates in the literature are concerned not only with what is and who defines headship but also with what a household is. Before we probe into the different definitions of female headship, it is critical to agree on what we mean in this study when we use the term 'household'.

Defining households To define what household means is important in any feminist analysis because both the organisation and composition of the household have a direct impact on women's lives. A large part of a woman's domestic and reproductive labour is directly related to her position and role in a household. However, the definition of a household is not necessarily the same universally, and its meaning and composition can differ from one culture to another (Moore 1988: 55 in Kabeer 1991: 7). Households are not always residential units. In some societies they are economic or kinship units. In other cases, households could consist of individuals who are not related by blood or marriage but are colleagues, lodgers or friends. This is more common in the developed countries (Kabeer 1991: 7–9).[2]

Researchers agree that households could have different meanings to different people, depending on race, geographical location, tradition, habit and culture. The definition a researcher chooses depends largely on the subject being studied and the cultural context of her or his research.[3] As Kabeer notes:

> The notion of the household is an analytical construct and its boundaries may have to be drawn pragmatically, in response to the concrete research questions being investigated. The nuclear family, centred on the conjugal relationship, might be a useful unit for analysing production, consumption or reproductive behaviour in many parts of south Asia, the extent to which the extended family is considered relevant would largely depend on the nature of the precise research question. (Kabeer 1991: 9)

I have used the most common and accepted definition of household, in which one or more adult(s) and/or children live together and share domestic and reproductive tasks in the same unit. In contrast, the concept of headship is much more complex and not easy to define.

Defining headship I initially thought that the concept of headship was a descriptive term with its origins in family law, where one person is assigned responsibility and power over the rest of the household members. Traditionally, that family member was the eldest male, who exerted considerable power over the members of his family because he was the only economic provider and thus the head of the household (Folbre 1991). Consequently, I assumed that female headship becomes a fact once a woman takes over the financial responsibility of the household. But I found that this is not always the case. I also discovered that there is no simple criterion by which to define household head. Accordingly, a methodological question arose during my fieldwork regarding the parameters for defining female headship. Is it based on decision-making power, relative contribution to household income, control over expenditures, physical presence in the home, or marital status?

The household – according to my findings throughout the survey and ethnographic fieldwork – could be headed by the husband, wife or son, or by one of the relatives, such as the grandfather or uncle. The physical presence of the male was no criterion for describing the household as maintained by a man, since a large number of the women interviewed were wives of men who were physically present but did not provide for the family. The woman did. In addition, among the households where the husband had a full-time job and was physically present, there were several cases where women contributed equally or more than their spouses to the family's livelihood. In that sense, the definition of the type of household became complicated. Moreover, the ability to earn a living or to be the breadwinner was no indication of who was the head of the household. There were many cases where women worked and men took the major decisions regarding household expenses, and other cases where women were housewives but controlled the income their husbands brought in.

Although headship is problematic, three criteria have been used traditionally. The first is self-reporting or reporting by proxy. This means that the interviewee officially identifies himself or herself as the head of the household, or identifies another member of the family as such. The second and third criteria focus on breadwinning and decision-making, whereby the head of the household is the person earning the major income or is the main decision-maker (Chant 1997: 8).[4]

Each of the three criteria is problematic. Identification by proxy or self-reporting can be misleading due to cultural and traditional norms and habits. Although women could be the main providers and heads of a particular family, in traditional and conservative societies women would never identify themselves as such. In the Middle East and the Arab societies, the term 'head' itself, '*rab*', is masculine and is actually derived from the word 'God'. It is believed that the man of the house is the god of the family. Men are seen as the protectors and providers of the family and thus, in the absence of the father, it is assumed that his eldest son, brother or another male in the family will become the surrogate protector.[5]

Breadwinning as a criterion for defining headship was used to describe the head as the person who made more money (Chant, 1997). However, I used the breadwinning criterion to define which of the spouses contributed more to family expenses. In many situations, the man might make more money but spends it on drugs, drinking or another wife. From the fieldwork, it was clear that a large number of the married women studied were the major contributors to family expenses.

Decision-making is the most problematic of the three criteria. First

Defining Female Headship

and foremost, it was the most difficult criterion to assess during my research since there were many types of decisions made. In some cases, certain decisions were taken jointly by the spouses, although others were taken independently by outsiders who had power over the family for one reason or another.[6] The presence or absence of the man was not necessarily correlated to women taking decisions for the family. The type of decision also differed, and thus the person with the power to make such a decision changed. There were decisions that were taken by the paternal mother-in-law even if she was not living with the nuclear family, such as the circumcision of the young girls. In traditional societies in the Arab world and elsewhere, the elderly grandparents join in the decision-making process although they do not necessarily contribute economically to the family (Shanthi 1996: 311). Women took other decisions pertaining to food and daily expenses. It is true that women's ability to earn a steady income has given them more leeway and increased their power of negotiation over some decisions, such as buying the household equipment and tools — washing machines and stoves, for example — that would facilitate housework. However, in several cases men took a large sum of their women's income to spend on drugs and alcohol.

In spite of the controversy over the definitions of female headship, various categorisations are being used by different researchers. In Egypt, Bahie el-Din (1994) defines families supported by women as those families where the main breadwinner is the woman. These are divided into two categories. The first is when the husband is physically absent and thus does not provide any financial assistance to the family. This could be due to his death or to divorce, remarriage, or abandonment. The second category is when the husband is present but disabled, unemployed or simply refuses to work (Bahie el-Din 1994a: 2).[7]

To Moser, there are two types of women-headed households. First, there are *de jure* women-headed households, in which the male partner is permanently absent and the woman is legally single or divorced or widowed. Second, there are the *de facto* women-headed households in which the male is temporarily absent due, for instance, to long-term work migration or refugee status. In this case the woman is not legally the head of the household. She is often perceived as a dependant despite the fact that she may, for the majority of her adult life, have primary, if not complete, responsibility for the financial as well as the organisational aspects of the household (Moser 1989: 1802). In my work, I have come across many types of *de facto* heads of households, though my definition differs slightly from Moser's. According to my findings, a large number of women were *de facto* heads of the household, although their spouses were not temporarily absent. In most of the cases, these men were physically present, but were unemployed or had refused to work and enjoyed living off their wives. These men were labelled 'useless' by their wives.[8]

Youssef and Hetler (1983: 10) developed the broadest and most comprehensive of definitions, which includes five types of female heads of households with the following characteristics:

1. Households with no male partner at any time: *de jure* female-headed households. These include divorcees, widows, single mothers, and separated and deserted women.
2. Households where the spouse is a transient resident, and where women cannot count on the male partner for regular economic support: *de jure* FHH.
3. Households where husbands are away for temporary reasons, i.e. migrant husbands: *de facto* FHH.
4. Households where the male partner is present but is either not contributing economically or making a marginal contribution: *de facto* FHH.
5. Households were there is one or more males resident but not the male spouse. These households are a mixture of *de jure* and *de facto* FHH.

From the above, it is clear that defining and measuring female headship has proved to be problematic to the degree that experts recommend the use of more specific terms in order to capture the wide spectrum of different family structures that are economically dependent on women. The terms recommended include 'mother-centred', 'single-parent', 'male-absent', 'women-maintained', and 'female-led' households, among others.

Since I relied on the economic factor and a woman's economic contribution to a household's livelihood to determine headship, I originally preferred using female-headed and women-maintained households interchangeably. However, I met an ideological obstacle. Chant argues that using the term 'women-maintained' instead of 'women-headed' shows that although women carry the same burdens and responsibilities as men, they lack the same recognition and respect (1997: 9). This is indeed the situation I found in my interviews with government officials. They refused to refer to widows, divorcees or deserted women as female heads (in Egyptian Arabic they would never say '*Mara'a taru's a'l u'sra*' – 'a woman who heads her family'), but would call them '*Mara'a ta'aool a'l u'sra*' – 'a woman who supports and maintains the household'. As a senior district official explained: 'The man is the God (*rab*) or the head of the family. The woman is the mother. She is responsible as a housewife to keep the home a paradise for her husband and children' (Mr M., 49, head of social unit, 'The Squatters', MOSA).[9]

Defining Female Headship

Taking Chant's position into consideration and observing resistance to calling women heads of households, even when they bear the same burden as men in male-headed households, I decided to use the term women heads of households (FHHs). Thus in this study I define FHHs as:

1. Women who are the sole or major source of income to the family and who are the sole or major members of the family responsible for its livelihood. (By major we mean that her direct financial contribution to the household income exceeds any other by at least 30%).
2. Women who represent the family members *vis-à-vis* the community legally and socially.
3. Women who carry the main family responsibilities inside the household and outside it.

Apart from the *de jure* FHHs such as divorcees, never-married women and widows, this study includes women who are separated, who are co-wives[10] (but left to fend for themselves), and who have disabled or unemployed husbands in its definition of women heads of households. It also includes women married to imprisoned men, women married to men with no regular jobs (*u'rzu'i* men), and women married to drug addicts. These are women who have become the sole or major breadwinners of their families. Thus the head of the household, as I define it, is the chief provider who bears the main economic responsibility for the management and maintenance of the household. I chose this indicator because economic contribution and breadwinning have been the main reasons for describing men as heads of their families. Women held secondary and dependent positions within their families because of their inability to contribute financially. One of the issues investigated in this research was whether, as the new breadwinners, women managed to gain the same power and authority as the male economic providers. On the other hand, if any of the above categories of FHHs is supported financially by her sons or relatives, she is no longer defined or recognised as a female head in this study.

Typologies of Women Heads of Households

It has been shown that there are different types of female headship in different parts of the world. Chant (1997) describes different types of female households: the lone-mother household, female-headed extended households, lone-female households, single-sex female-only households, female-dominant/predominant households, grandmother households and embedded female-headed households. Chant's main argument is that female headship is not static but dynamic and that the economic and social status of women heads of households (FHHs) differ among these types. Chant used the structure and combination of members in a household to deter-mine the types of female-headed households. In my work, I have used the reasons for female headship, mainly marital status and economic contribution, as the main criteria for classifying the different types of FHHs that I encountered.

From my fieldwork I have identified ten types of women heads of households. Some of these are traditionally accepted women heads of families, while others are not recognised by the state, NGOs or religious groups as such.

Widows Widows are women who have lost their husbands due to death. In my definition these women are the heads of their households if they rely solely or mainly on their own income and not that of their children, relatives or parents for survival. Even in cases where they rely on a pension left by a husband but are still on their own, they are considered heads of households. In short, they are left to fend for themselves and are solely responsible for their livelihoods and their families. It is customary that widows, especially if they originally come from rural areas, do not remarry unless they are in dire financial need. In most cases they do not remarry from fear of losing their children to their old in-laws as the law stipulates. In addition it gives a widow a higher status among family and her community if she refrains from marriage in order to raise her children. Widows are expected to make this sacrifice because it is believed they have 'tried their luck' in the first marriage and it was God's will that they were widowed.

Divorcees Divorcees are generally perceived negatively by the community at large, particularly by other women. Unlike a widow, whose husband's absence is due to the will of God, a divorcee is seen to have brought her situation on herself. Unlike widows, divorcees can and actually do remarry. They are usually urged by their families and friends to remarry to protect their reputation, but also for economic reasons (EQI 1988: 24).

Deserted wives Deserted women have been abandoned by their men temporarily or permanently. This category of women is increasing due to the increasing economic burden on men. As job opportunities decrease, poor men in slum areas are increasingly deserting their wives without providing them with financial support.

Wives of unemployed men A large number of these women were the wives of men on pension, sick men, or old men who could no longer work.

Defining Female Headship

The latter situation occurs because it is common for families to marry their young daughters to elderly men. In most of the cases interviewed, the young wife had to work in order to provide for her young children. However, there were also cases where the husband had been laid off from a private business. Few, if any, businesses in the informal sector offer unemployment insurance.

Wives of u'rzu'i men *U'rzu'i* is a slang term referring to any person who has no regular job and thus no regular and predictable income. *U'rzu'i* men are usually the skilled and unskilled manual labourers who work when there is a specific task for them to perform. They are never offered any contract or steady assignments. *U'rzu'i* is an Arabic term derived from the word *rizk*, which means the income or wealth that is determined for the individual by God. A 1998 study in a low-income squatter area was the first to identify such heads of households:

> This is perhaps the most ambiguous and most difficult type of female household to identify. However, it may be the most common ... Its existence is a real challenge to the widespread belief that it is men who provide the main or only source of income for their families. We came across many married women who were working in various fields and whose income was sometimes supplementary but was also often crucial for the survival of the family. These women are married to men with unstable jobs, '*U'rzu'i* or casual labourers. General unemployment, underemployment or irresponsibility of the husband are the main reasons for the prevalence of these types of households. (EQI 1988: 27)

Wives of drunks or addicts These are women whose husbands do not provide for them because they spend all their income, and, sometimes their wives' income, on drugs or drinking. These women are pitied by the community but are usually looked at with suspicion by government officials, who believe that they could be drug addicts as well.

Co-wives It is not as common as might be expected in an Islamic society to encounter a man married to more than one woman. However, I encountered several scattered cases in the seven urban areas. Among the few cases I identified and interviewed, the co-wife did not live in the same household as the husband, nor did she have any contact with her husband or his other wife (wives). The co-wife is considered a head of a household in this study when she has to work to sustain herself and her family, as her husband is either unable or refuses to provide for her and her children which he has fathered.

Wives who contribute more to the family income Some of the women I met were married to husbands with regular incomes and steady jobs although their salaries were so low that they could not keep up with the needs of their household. Several of these women worked and made more money, which they spent on the household's needs. This gave them more power to determine what household appliances to purchase and empowered some of them to take decisions pertaining to the education and marriage of their daughters. They worked longer hours outside the home than their husbands and they continued to be responsible for domestic chores and child-rearing.

Never-married women (spinsters) Never-married women constituted the smallest percentage of women who headed their households. To be a spinster in Egypt, and especially in low-income urban areas where a woman's main role in life is to be a wife and a mother, has serious negative implications. A young woman is considered at the gates of spinstership if she approaches 20 years of age without any prospect of marriage. She is pitied if she is still single in her 20s, and the family considers her a lost cause if she reaches 30 and remains unmarried. According to the law, however, a woman is not a spinster until she reaches her 48th birthday, when she becomes eligible for the spinster's pension.

Even if the reason behind remaining single was family pressures or economic conditions, society at large blames the woman who remains single for failing to conform and act 'normally'. Her *unwomanly* behaviour towards men is the main reason given for this status. Poverty and lack of beauty are also mentioned for this unpopular status. Women who lack money and looks are encouraged to marry anyone, be second wives, marry a widower with children, or endure any type of hardship in order to avoid the destiny of being an old maid. Because it is expected that never-married women remain virgins, the welfare pension for spinsters furthers a single woman's humiliation by requiring a certificate from a doctor or a Ministry of Social Affairs employee stating that the woman is a virgin. Feminists in Egypt refer to this pension as the 'chastity pension' since the state is thus ensuring women's purity and chastity.

Women married to sick or disabled husbands It was not uncommon to find women who were the sole breadwinners in their families because their husbands were seriously sick or disabled. In most of the cases interviewed, the situation occurred because of the tradition of marrying girls in their teens to men many years older. By the time women reach their late twenties or early thirties, their husbands have become old, sometimes senile and unable to work. Such women are usually left with a number

Defining Female Headship

of young children whom they have to maintain, in addition to an invalid husband. Like widows, these women are pitied by the community at large. It is socially unacceptable for them to seek a divorce due to their husbands' disability and so they are forced to stay with them. Although *Shari'a* (Islamic law) grants women the right to divorce on the grounds of a husband's disability, it is extremely shameful to do so in Egypt (EQI 1987: 27–8).

Factors Affecting the Status of Women Heads of Households

Among the different categories of women heads of households mentioned above, the status, economic situation and autonomy of the women who head their households differ. This difference could be related to the marital status of each category, to the stage in the course of life, class, or the presence or absence of the spouse. It could also be related to who decides on the separation, whether it was due to what Chant calls a 'positive decision' i.e. the woman chose to be alone without a man and became the main provider, or whether she was left and abandoned by the husband (Chant 1997: 11–19). According to Chant, there are five factors that affect the status of FHHs, as follows. I have used them to describe the situation in Egypt.

Marital status This is the route by which women entered into the category of household heads. It influences how they fare economically and how they are perceived by society and policy-makers, and how they perceive themselves. In Egypt, state policies respond differently according to the marital status of the FHHs. The state's welfare programmes target widows, divorcees and deserted women, but not co-wives, wives of the unemployed or wives of *u'rzu'i* men. State officials refuse to recognise families where women are the heads of the family and its main providers as long as an adult male is either residing with or legally related to the family. This view is unambiguously expressed by a MOSA employee:

> Women who maintain their families are those women who are all alone, without any man to support them. But a co-wife has a husband and she is his responsibility. (Mr M., 49, head of social unit, 'The Squatters', MOSA)

In addition, the social standing and self-image of widows are better than those of divorcees and deserted women, not only in Egypt but in other developing countries as well.[11] In my work and especially with the Islamic NGO's welfare programme, divorcees and deserted women were seen as failures who could not save their homes and keep their men. This was stated clearly by a staff member of the Shari'iyya NGO

Victims and Heroines

No, we give grants only to widows but not to divorcees. They should have stayed in their homes and protected their family. A woman who cannot keep her husband is a failure. (Mr A., 57, administrator from the orphan sponsorship programme, 'The Tombs', Jam'iyya Shari'iyya)

Society tends to be more suspicious of divorcees and deserted women than of widows. In society's eyes, the divorcee chose her situation and was unable to protect her marriage, while a widow was forced into her situation. Younger women heads of households have their movements restricted and their actions scrutinised much more than older ones. In other countries, 'single women may also be the objects of social suspicion and butts of sexual innuendo' (Chandler 1991: 6 in Chant 1997: 63). In many societies, including Egypt, a woman outside the institution of marriage is seen as a threat by other women and as a temptation and danger to men.

In my sample, widows also fared better depending on whether they had access to a husband's pension or were on their own. They were also most likely to receive aid from the state, NGOs and Islamic groups. Divorcees have a much tougher time getting assistance from the state and religious groups, as well as the alimony or child support due to them from their former husbands.[12]

Stages in the course of life The status of being a woman head is not static. Several of the widows who were taken care of by sons or relatives at the time of my study had been the main source of income only a couple of years earlier. They had to fend for their families until their children graduated or worked and took over. In other words, the static picture that I present here is by no means final. Any number of women presented as female heads in this study could cease to be so next year due to remarriage or the fact that their children start taking care of them.

Class Although my work concentrated mainly on the low-middle and lower working classes of slum areas, class remains an important factor for determining the experience of female household heads. It is assumed that the better the socio-economic class of a female head of household, the better her economic and social situation, and perhaps her status in society's eyes. However, this is not always the case. In Egypt, the economic situation of widows and divorcees could be better the higher up they are on the social ladder, although mobility and flexibility of movement decreases among middle-class women, and is greater among the lower classes.

The physical presence of the male partner As mentioned earlier, the physical presence of the male partner is no guarantee that he will provide or be responsible for the family. Households with disabled or unemployed adult males are often described as male-headed households even though women are the major, if not the only, contributors to their livelihood (Folbre 1991: 94). Similarly, I came across cases where the male had no regular job and no longer provided for the family, and even though the women had become its major source of income, the family was described as male-headed.

Chant (1997) argues that one cannot assume which of the *de facto* or *de jure* women heads of households are better off than the other. In some cases, as in Malawi, a *de facto* FHH is richer due to more generous and regular remittance. However, especially in rural areas, it has been found that *de facto* women are very poor due to their lack of access to resources, whether land, sheep or cattle.[13] They are restricted from working in the fields without a male protector, as in southern Egypt, known as Upper Egypt, which is a very conservative and isolated rural community (Khattab 1976).[14]

Several studies show that the poverty of *de facto* women heads of households is mitigated by their increasing power of negotiation and decision-making within their household.[15] Nevertheless, it is difficult to make comparisons between *de facto* and *de jure* women heads of households. *De facto* women heads of households are in a midway position: their men are still present yet the women bear all the responsibilities. A large number of the women I interviewed were *de facto* women heads of households in the economic and social sense, even though their husbands resided with them.

One of the major concerns of this study is with the *de facto* women heads of households, who are not recognised officially or by the community as the heads of their families, and are thus left to fend for themselves. They are also excluded from the state's and other welfare programmes, which furthers their moral, social and psychological dependence on men. In fact the presence of a male partner who is an *u'rzu'i* or a drunkard erodes women's material social welfare almost more than if he were not there. As long as the man is legally tied to the woman or physically around, she is not eligible for many of the state's social services.

Chose or forced into female headship A final element of differentiation among women heads of households that may influence their economic and social situation and how they perceive themselves is the reason for their aloneness and state of being man-less. Whether they reached this stage by choice, through what Chant calls 'positive decisions', or because their husbands abandoned them determines how they perceive themselves afterwards and how they are perceived by their community (1997: 19). In this part of the world, where the man is seen as the protector of women's honour and as the provider and where women have limited powers to act independently, female headship is more often the result of men's actions through desertion, divorce or death.[16] As demonstrated in the fieldwork, those women who took the initiative and divorced their husbands fared much better than those who were abandoned by their men. The former group, in spite of the social stigma of divorce, had their families' moral and financial support. In a large number of cases, they enjoyed their single status and preferred to be in control of their own lives. On the other hand, those who were left by their husbands felt cheated and helpless and were unable to cope. They felt ashamed, resented their single status and remarried when the opportunity presented itself.

Prevalence

The rising phenomenon of women heads of households has been well documented in developed countries since the 1960s.[17] In most developing countries, however, the inadequacy of national data has made it difficult to study and plan for this category of women. Youssef and Hetler concluded that the estimates and figures about women heads of households published by the national census organisations of Third World countries were not accurate for two main reasons: first because the national census was not designed to measure this phenomenon, and second because there is no single and agreed definition of the headship of a family or a household (1983). Rosenhouse and Fergany reached the same conclusion. Rosenhouse argues that these census figures should be taken only to reflect patterns (1989). Regarding the general information from the national census, Fergany states that: 'Official statistics from censuses and surveys did not cater to the need of studying WHH [FHH]. Indeed, there has not been great concern for studying characteristics of heads of households in general' (1993: 1).

The prevalence of women heads of households has been increasing throughout the developed and developing countries. Kamerman and Kahn (1988), Millar et al. (1992) and Moser and Levy (1986) have all agreed that the phenomenon of female-headed households is on the rise in both developed and developing countries. Varely (1996) shows that the highest proportion of FHHs is in the developed world (24.5%), followed by Africa (19.1%), Latin America and the Caribbean (18.2%) and, finally, Asia and the Pacific (13%) (Chant 1997: 70). Although Folbre (1991) also used UN data from the early 1980s, she presented a different and more disaggregated regional breakdown. She calculated that the highest rate of FHHs was in the non-European English-speaking countries (26.6%)

Defining Female Headship

such as Australia, New Zealand, Canada and the USA. This was followed by 22% in northwest Europe, 19.5% in Eastern Europe and 16.9% in southern Europe. The figures were lower in the developing countries: 17.7% in the Caribbean, 14.5% in Latin America, 14% in east Asia, 13.6% in sub-Saharan Africa and 5.7% in south Asia (Folbre 1991: 95–8 and Chant 1997: 70).

Statistical data on the industrialised countries show that female-headed households, especially those of lone mothers, are on the increase. In the USA, single-parent families rose from 12.9% in 1970 to 26% in 1985, with 90% of such families headed by women. In Britain, the rate of single-parent families – 92.1% of which are headed by women – increased from 13% in 1981 to 19% in 1991.[18] Data on the developing countries demonstrate a similar increase. 'In Guyana, for example, the increase was from 22.4 to 35 percent between 1970 and 1987 (Patterson 1994: 122), in Puerto Rico from 16 to 23.2 percent between 1970 and 1990 (Safa, 1995: 17), and in Argentina from 16.5 to 19.2 percent between 1970 and 1980' (Chant, 1997: 73).

What, then, are the factors that led to this increase, especially since it is becoming a global phenomenon? One of the main reasons is sex-specific migration resulting in *de facto* female heads who might become *de jure* heads after some time. The death of elderly husbands of young wives, especially in contexts where poor families marry off their daughters at an early age, is another reason. Marital disruption, the erosion of extended family systems and traditional support networks are also important factors resulting in the relatively new phenomenon of women being left to manage and head their own families (Buvinic and Gupta 1997: 261).

In the latest census in Egypt (1986), information on the sex of the head of the household was collected but not published. Most of the information gathered to date is from smaller surveys. When the Central Authority for Population Mobilisation and Statistics (CAPMAS) census information is used, it should be taken with caution, as the definitions of household headship by bureaucrats are gender-biased. Women in low-income areas will identify their young sons as the head of the household to avoid the condescension of the government bureaucrat from the census team.[19]

Female-headed households constitute a significant proportion of rural and urban households in Egypt. They were estimated to total a minimum of 16% (Handoussa 1994) of all households. A 1988 study claimed that the incidence of female-headed households reached 18% throughout Egypt, with slightly higher than average (approximately 18.3%) rates in the urban areas (Fergany 1993). In 1994, yet another study estimated that the percentage of female-headed households stood nationally at 17.2% of all households.

As shown in Table 3.1, the rate reaches 17.8% in urban governorates,

Victims and Heroines

16.9% in Lower Egypt (the north) and 17.8% in Upper Egypt (the south) (Farah 1997: 12). Some recent research has demonstrated that in the lower-income urban areas of Cairo, the percentage of female-headed households reached 30% (Farah 1997; Fergany 1994a).

TABLE 3.1 Women-headed households in Egypt by region (%), 1993

Governorate	Total	Urban	Rural
Cairo	18.5		
Alexandria	16.5		
Urban governorates	17.8		
Lower Egypt	16.9	18.4	14.3
Upper Egypt	17.8	18.4	17.6

Source: Summary of a table calculated by Farah (1997: 12) from the Labour Force Sample Survey of 1993.

Classification of Women Heads of Households

The variation in the official statistics on FHHs in Egypt is not significant, as their classification is limited mainly to divorcees, widows and never-married women. Co-wives, wives of *u'rzu'i* men and other categories mentioned in this study were not considered statistically in Egypt to be women heads of households.

According to the CAPMAS labour sample survey of 1988, the majority of FHHs were widows (60%), while 4% of all FHHs were divorcees. It was also shown that termination of marriage was the major reason behind the majority FHHs cases (Fergany 1994: 2). According to an integrated empirical study carried out in 1993 in low-income communities, 68% or the majority of FHHs were widows, followed by divorcees (11%). Married women who headed their families constituted 20% of FHHs (Farah 1997: 11–13). In a 1994 survey on access to primary education in rural and urban Egypt, it was found that 79% of FHHs were widows, 13% were married, 4% were divorcees, and 4% were women who had never married (Fergany 1994a: 1–2).

Findings of the Fieldwork

Here I turn to analysing the types of FHHs I found in the seven research sites. This is not a representative sample, rather a purposive one, since I met and interviewed mainly FHHs. As mentioned earlier,

444 women were interviewed. Sixty-seven women were interviewed in 'The Shelters', 100 in 'Alexandria', and 129 in 'The Resettlement'. In 'The Tombs' I interviewed 43 women and 36 were interviewed in 'The Ezba'. Twenty-nine women were interviewed in 'The Squatters' and 40 in 'The Bedouins'.

Classification of FHHs according to marital status The majority (88%) of the women I met in 'The Tombs' were widows. In 'The Shelters', widows also constituted the highest percentage (34.3%) among FHHs in the sample in that area. In Alexandria, they constituted 25% of those interviewed. The majority of the sample met through the Islamic orphan sponsorship programme were widows, since the target group of the Islamic programme is really the orphaned child.[20]

In three of the areas studied, 'The Shelters', 'Alexandria' and 'The Resettlement', the high percentage of wives of *u'rzu'i* and unemployed men was surprising. In addition, the percentage of women married to *u'rzu'i* men reached 20.9% in 'The Shelters', 18% in Alexandria and 10% in 'The Resettlement'.

The wives of *u'rzu'i* men have had to rely on their own resources and work in order to provide for their families. The deteriorating economic conditions since the Gulf War have pushed men out of the informal sector to be replaced by lower-paid women. Many of these *u'rzu'i* men were skilled in construction work and car mechanics and were well paid in the 1980s and earlier. Since 1990 many of them had been laid off from the privately owned small workshops and no longer held regular jobs but worked when ever needed.

Unlike the other areas, the percentage of deserted wives in my sample from 'The Resettlement' was very high, reaching 26% based on the sample of women I met and interviewed. On the other hand, although 'The Ezba' is a very traditional old slum area, the percentage of deserted wives was relatively high there as well, reaching 17%.

I also found that the percentage of divorced women was high (18.6%) among those interviewed in 'The Resettlement' and reached 12.5% in 'The Bedouins'. Although the number of divorcees and deserted wives is relatively high, not all of them are considered heads of households in this study. The majority of the divorcees and deserted women go back to live with their parents or in-laws and are not allowed to remarry.

The percentage of co-wives reached 17% in the sample from 'The Squatters' because the majority of the male inhabitants are rural migrants who left their first wives in the countryside and remarried in the city after they settled down. In 'The Bedouins', the percentage of co-wives was also relatively very high (7.5%).

On the other hand, there were not too many unmarried women, which is to be expected given the pressures put on women since childhood to get married. In addition, the sample did not include significant numbers of wives of imprisoned, old or unemployed men.

Classification of FHHs in the research sites based on their economic contribution to family expenses Not all women who are man-less or who work are described here as heads of their families. As explained earlier, a woman is the head of the family if she is the only or major economic provider (contributing 30% more than any other member of the family) to the family expenses. In several cases, widows, divorcees or other categories of FHHs are taken care of financially by their sons, relatives or in-laws.

The majority of the divorcees and deserted women were the main economic providers for their families. This is a serious finding, especially since the state and NGOs do not provide adequately for this type of female headship.

In addition, all unmarried women and the majority of the wives of the unemployed were left to fend for themselves. Although these numbers are insignificant statistically, these findings show a growing trend for women being economically responsible for themselves, which is a relatively new and officially unrecognised phenomenon in Egypt.

Findings The findings of the survey and the ethnographic work show that new family structures, especially those headed by women, are no longer a minor issue to be ignored by policy and decision-makers. These findings also direct our attention to the increasing burden on and responsibilities of women at a time when there is no recognition of women's efforts, workload or economic contribution. These findings must alert policy-makers and urge them to review their traditional assumptions about household headship, which are at the base of social welfare policies targeting the poor and ignore and marginalise these new family structures.

The Perception and Status of Women who Head their Households

There has been a trend in the current environment of neo-liberalism and efforts to cut back on state expenditure to blame FHHs for bloating the welfare system. Single mothers – unmarried mothers in the West – are seen to epitomise a culture of dependency on the state that has become a drain on the state's resources and an obstacle to productivity (Baden and Milward 1995: 16, 6). The recipients of welfare systems are usually

Defining Female Headship

single and their singleness stigmatises them (Gordon 1990: 12). Chester asserts that families with only the mother as the head (referring to lone mothers or female single parents) are stigmatised and dishonoured in the UK (1977: 151).

Societies in both developed and developing countries have resisted any recognition of the existence and rising phenomenon of female headship because this new phenomenon constitutes an affront to established beliefs about family life (Collins 1991: 159; Chant 1997: 2). In many developing countries, especially in this part of the world, a male-headed household is seen and presented as 'normal', which renders female-headed households 'an anomalous isolated and disadvantaged category' (Chant 1997: 3).[21]

Most of the studies on this problematic and the discrimination of the welfare system against women heads of households concentrate largely on the developed countries. Indeed, very few studies have explored this issue in the developing countries. The situation in Egypt is not different. According to the Islamic groups and some Islamic NGOs, families maintained by women are dysfunctional units warranting immediate remedy by the remarriage of the woman if she is a young divorcee or widow. They also resent the term 'female-headed households' and argue that it is a Western concept that aims to disrupt the traditional family ethos of the East. They prefer to call it a male-absent family.[22]

In Egypt, women and men are seen as biologically different. Women especially are cast into two main positions as related to the family: those inside and those outside the family. Women are defined and define themselves in terms of their relationship with and place in the family. The family provides a sense of belonging and identity and is a source of financial and personal support. Relations with family members are the strongest links in women's lives (Macleod 1991: 37–8). Thus an adult woman inside the family borders is either a wife or a mother, and mothers are more respected and idolised than single women. As outsiders, women are a potential threat as temptresses and seductresses (ibid.: 1991: 83–4). Accordingly, the position of a single woman is precarious, and any suspicion or mistrust of her moral conduct can stigmatise her and her family. A divorcee is a potential threat to other women and a source of concern for her family (Smock and Youssef 1977: 46–8).

In the eyes of others in the community The community plays as important a role as the family and extended kin in controlling and shaping the lives of women in general, and women heads of households in particular. The community is the mediator between the state and the individual, especially in terms of enforcing conformity to specific traditional modes of behaviour and action. In that sense, it is logical to assume that the state's

Victims and Heroines

social and legal policies are a reflection of the community's perceptions and positioning of women in general, and women heads of households in particular (Agarwal 1988: 22).

Mr Antaar from 'The Shelters' was very suspicious of divorcees and more sympathetic towards widows:

> Why should a woman leave her husband except if she has her eyes on another man who promised her more money? A divorcee is a greedy woman who either wants more money or is seeking sinful sexual pleasures. She should be monitored carefully. (Antaar, male, 55, 'The Shelters')

Other women were not more sympathetic, especially if they were in stable marriages:

> One has to endure, that is why we are women. If one of us rebels, then she has something wicked on her mind. I personally never befriend a divorcee, she is for sure after one's husband. (U'm Tafida, 43, an abused wife, 'The Tombs')

The attitudes of women towards widows were better than towards divorcees, as clearly stated by one woman in 'The Shelters':

> A widow is a fact of life and a result of God testing his people and I am against any widow who remarries for she should not be seeking bodily pleasures after her first husband and her first luck. (Hoda, 66, married to an invalid husband, 'The Shelters')

Women 'on their own' are regarded with fear by other women and with disdain and disrespect by the men and the elderly. Widows are expected to return to their parents and stay single to take care of children (Smock and Youssef 1977: 46). Divorced women are also expected to return to their parents and are subjected to the same family controls imposed on younger and unmarried women and are placed back on the marriage market (ibid.: 1970: 46–8). Divorcees are always the topic of extensive gossip among women and are avoided for fear of jeopardising the reputation of other 'good' and married women.

Self-perceptions Many of the women interviewed, especially the divorcees and deserted wives, felt that they were regarded as deviant and as a source of trouble. They believed that others looked at them as immature and irresponsible failures who were unable to keep their men. This led them to feel insecure, unable to cope, and unsure of how to behave in different situations. Consequently, they isolated themselves and withdrew from the social networks of their communities. These feelings were relayed to me by the women I studied in the different communities,

Defining Female Headship

but are also common among women in similar conditions in other parts of the world.[23]

Afaf, a 35-year-old divorcee, felt that her neighbours were gossiping about her and that every step and move she made was scrutinised. She quit two jobs because she used to come home late and her neighbours taunted her about the nature of the job. She also stopped socialising with any of them lest they think she was after their husbands.

Safaa, a 42-year-old divorcee, on the other hand, does not feel hurt by the gossip any more. She feels that the others are jealous of her and that is why they gossip about her. She said:

> I know that I do not do anything wrong. I work hard to educate my children and I will not let these old witches force me into a marriage. I do not want to have to do anything with men.

Chant (1997: 199) carried out her study on FHHs in three countries – Costa Rica, Mexico and the Philippines – and arrived at findings similar to the situation in the seven low-income urban areas I studied. In her study and mine, FHHs knew that they were continuously under scrutiny, felt different than other women, and felt that they were at a disadvantage. As Hend from 'The Tombs' put it:

> It was tough to be a divorcee. I was young and pretty and all women in the street stopped dealing with me. I felt bad, neglected, isolated. I wanted to kill myself, and then I married the first suitor and accepted my fate. To be with a man, as our proverb says, is better than the shadow of the wall (*dil ragil wala dil hitta*) A man protects you. (Hend, 44, remarried divorcee, 'The Tombs')

The Experience of Being a Female Head

The social stigma associated with being a man-less woman has grave implications not only for a woman's status within her society, but also for how she experiences and copes with her situation. Such subjective experience has not been the subject of enough study. Little has been written about women who passed through the experience of becoming a female head of household, which is an experience of watching one's social standing in the community deteriorate. In developed countries, Hardey and Crow (1991) and Dallos and Spasford (1995) showed that the personal experience of being a female head was tough at the beginning but that women learned how to adapt and cope with their new situation (Chant 1997: 200).

Most of the women interviewed stated that they passed through several stages after being left on their own. These stages began with a sense of

Victims and Heroines

total bereavement and fear of being alone and ended with a sense of relief that they had gained control over their lives. However, not all women were able to cope and some of them opted to remarry and conform to the accepted mode of behaviour.[24]

First reactions to being alone As the citations below reveal, these women were shocked and scared during their first moments of being man-less. They had been the responsibility of their fathers and then their husbands for all their lives, and were neither prepared nor trained for this new role. This is how one woman explained her reaction to widowhood:

> After so many years with my husband, I felt naked being alone, with no support, defenceless. It is true that he used to beat me but so did my father before him. He was the only man I knew. (Sabah, 55, a widow, 'The Squatters')

Poor women in Egypt rarely initiate divorce even if they are miserable, as one woman from 'The Shelters' explained:

> I hated my life with him, daydreamed many times of gaining my freedom, but I was too scared to ask for it. But he divorced me to marry another woman. I cried and felt so frightened. My parents are poor and live in a village in Upper Egypt. I am all alone here. (Set el-Banat, 47, divorcee, 'The Shelters')

The head of any household usually represents the family in the outside world and mediates between his household and the different community agencies. Such two-way mediation is difficult for women who, historically and traditionally, have had less status and standing in the community than men. Since single women without a husband are seen as deviants anyway, their households tend to lose their bargaining power and standing with outside institutions (Chester 1997: 157). Women in Egypt are told throughout their lives that they need the presence of a man to gain the respect of their family and community. They are told that a woman alone is helpless, defenceless, an easy target. As they are never given the opportunity to be on their own, they come to believe what they are told and actually feel helpless in the early stages of being alone.

Coping with being on one's own Not all women were able to cope with the state of aloneness and many had to remarry in response to family pressure, economic need, or the fear of being on their own. Hanem, a 36-year-old woman with six children, returned to her husband begging him for forgiveness and accepted all his conditions six months after he divorced her, because she could not cope on her own. She said:

Defining Female Headship

> My husband remarried because all my offspring are girls. I was angry and went to live with my father. To punish me he divorced me. People were talking about me, and I feared for my reputation and the reputation of my girls. I went back to him and accepted all his conditions. This is my destiny, I cannot change it. (Hanem, 36, co-wife, 'The Shelters')

Most of the difficult and marginalised positions that women who head their households find themselves in, especially those women without a co-residing adult male, are due to social and economic factors and the absence of appropriate and sufficient social provisions. The precarious state of lone mothers is a result of the general situation of women in society. Their poverty stems from their lack of training and access to economic opportunities. The labour market cannot absorb women heads of households because of a lack of job opportunities, women's lack of skills, and the costs of childcare. Because the state and the society do not recognise the unpaid work and economic contribution of women as childcarers, they do not offer any social insurance against broken marriages, thus furthering women's marginalisation and dependence on men (Harris 1993: 324). Therefore, poor illiterate women in Egypt cannot risk leaving a providing, albeit abusive, husband for a low-paid and humiliating job.

The majority of the women interviewed, whether widows, deserted women, co-wives, or abused wives of unemployed or *u'rzu'i* men, opted to stay with their spouses. Ibtsam, a 24-year-old woman from 'The Tombs', chose to stay in an abusive relationship because she was unable to become financially independent. She said:

> I have six children and my father is dead and my mother lives with my elder brother and his wife. Who will feed my children and me if I get a divorce? Who will take seven mouths extra to feed? I have to stay. (Ibtsam, 29, wife of an abusive *u'rzu'i* husband, 'The Tombs')

A woman from 'The Ezba' had a similar story to tell:

> My parents are very poor, and they cannot feed me and my children. Where can I go with them? I work and I can feed them but I cannot afford a room of my own. My parents live in one room and my younger brother lives with them. (U'm Adel, 43, wife of an *u'rzu'i*, 'The Ezba')

Economic need, social attitudes and the lack of institutional support are the major reasons for many women staying in abusive relationships. There are no shelters for battered or abused wives in Egypt.[25] Housing has become a very serious and expensive problem. Furthermore, it is not acceptable for a young woman, with or without children, to live on her own. Some landlords will refuse to rent her a room. Only if a woman owns a flat can she survive, and this is very expensive. Buying or renting a flat is far too expensive for women who work as maids or in the informal sector. Many of these women cannot afford to work full-time for they have young children and cannot afford childcare, even if it exists. The above points are confirmed by this story:

> My husband beat us and was very mean to my children and me. So I ran away, but after two days I went back to him and tolerated all his insults and beating. There was nowhere for me to go, no one wanted to rent me a small room. I was also unable to work because no one wanted my children at the workplace and I have no one to leave my children with. (Amal, 27, co-wife, 'The Shelters')

Women in Egypt, especially divorcees, deserted women and young widows, find themselves having to cope with protecting their sexual reputation in addition to financial austerity and the inability to get a permanent job because of their childcare responsibilities. They thus tend to seek the only alternative available: remarriage.

Fear for one's reputation as a divorcee, especially if one has to work long hours, is another reason for remarriage, as in the case of U'm Ali. She said:

> People, relatives and others told me that my working hours are negatively affecting my children's reputation. I worked as a cook and I used to leave here at six in the morning and come back by seven or so in the evening. So I remarried to protect our reputation, but I continued to work. I have three boys and he, the new husband, will not spend money on them. (U'm Ali, divorcee who remarried, 31, 'The Squatters')

Although remarriage was seen by the families of these women and some of the women themselves as easing the financial burden, in reality remarrying is a refuge and a protection mechanism against society's low regard for and demeaning treatment of women, especially those women who do not get their family's full support. All these conditions push women into remarriage, not only because the institution of marriage is the only accepted and respected status for women but also because women do not find any other alternatives.

Some other women felt differently. U'm Sherif is a 50-year-old widow with five children. She was married when she was 15 years old and, after 20 years of marriage, her husband wanted to remarry. She said that she was happy to help him marry the other woman.

> I was relieved when he wanted to marry this other woman. I did not want to have sex with him anymore and I wanted him to be occupied with someone

else. We all lived in the same house. When he died, I was happy and felt strong and that my life was again in my own hands. I got control of my life and myself. No one can talk about me for I am a good woman and, to tell you the truth, I do not care. I know myself and I am happy without a man.

From the above, it is clear that women heads of households – more than other women in society – are put under a social microscope and monitored carefully because of their status. The ideological and social dimension of female headship may differ from one culture to the other, but it nevertheless helps to shape the images and self-images of these women (Chant 1997: 62).

Should Women Heads of Households be a Priority Target Group?

The issue of targeting women heads of households as a priority group among the poor, whether in developed or developing countries, is controversial. One argument is that female heads should be a priority target since they are at several disadvantages. They tend to be poor, are discriminated against as women, and lack the necessary skills needed in the labour market. As they cannot be selective in their employment, this makes them vulnerable and they are easily exploited by their employers. They also lack the support of their partners in managing their households. In addition, they are doubly burdened with working outside and inside the home. The argument goes that in view of their growing numbers and because of the type of problems they face, it has become imperative that women who head their households be treated as a separate category for policy formulations (Shanthi 1996: 312; Buvinic 1993).

The arguments that link female headship and poverty depend on whether FHHs are seen to be over-represented or under-represented in the poor segments of society (Ross and Sawhill 1976; Garfinkel and McLanahan 1986). In the 1980s, a new phenomenon, the 'feminisation of poverty', was linked to the rise of female-headed households in the poorest segments of Western society. It has been suggested that this is the case in the Third World too, although this has never been accurately documented (Buvinic 1993: 1).

Some studies conclude that female-headed households worldwide are poverty-stricken and extremely disadvantaged (Merrick and Schmink 1983; Buvinic and Youssef 1978). Buvinic (1993) argues that the studies of the last decade have established that women-headed households are over-represented in the poor echelons of society. From 60 empirical studies that examined the association between poverty and female headship, 44 concluded that women-headed households were poorer than male-headed households. In Brazil, Merrick and Schmink found that 53% of FHHs held low-paying jobs in the informal sector, against 30% of the male heads (Merrick and Schmink 1983: 244–71).

Studies carried out in India reached the conclusion that the majority of households headed by women are either close to the poverty line or below it (Shanthi 1996: 312). Another study in the USA argued that the phenomenon of FHHs has been increasing and that they constituted 53% of all poor families. Once poor, women-headed households are ten times as likely to stay poor as male-headed families. In comparison to men, female-headed households are in much worse economic conditions: 44.7% of female-headed households with children less than 18 years old live in poverty, as compared to 7.7% of male-headed households who also have children (Pearce 1990: 266).[26]

Other studies highlight other disadvantageous situations of poor women, especially women who head their households. Leslie states that poor women tend to work longer hours than men and to have less leisure time (Leslie et al. 1988: 1341–62). Some studies show that women who are single parents not only experience more stress than married women, but have less social and psychological support, experience downward social mobility, have lower income and educational levels and a poorer self-image, and raise children who are more likely to be poor adults and become single parents themselves.[27]

Therefore, research has found that the gender of a household head is not a useful indicator of poverty if economic indicators are the only tools used for measurement. The access to and extension of welfare measures is an important factor where there is more deprivation in FHHs than in MHHs (Appleton 1995: 1). Popkin demonstrates that in developing countries, poor women trade off leisure time with market work rather than reduce their childcare time and home production (Popkin et al. 1983). Kabeer argues that insofar as FHHs are not poorer than MHHs in terms of consumption or income, this is the result of more and greater work and effort (Kabeer 1992: 23–5). In other words, the welfare of the head of the household should be an additional tool with which to measure the poverty and disadvantageous conditions of households, especially those headed by women.

The opposite argument is that not all FHHs are poor and that one should not correlate poverty with female headship. This argument follows the logic that targeting benefits to FHHs could be an incentive to making single parenting or female headship more appealing than the institution of marriage (Buvinic and Gupta 1997: 259). Critics of the association of female headship with poverty argue that there is a danger in this associ-

Defining Female Headship

ation because it directs attention away from larger issues of poverty, gender and inequality. In addition, it is argued that other studies show ambiguous relationships between female headship and poverty. Studies in five countries – Ghana, Zambia, Uganda, Brazil and Bangladesh – where the link between female headship and poverty was examined showed that FHHs are not a homogeneous group and that their characteristics are not universal. However, even the worst-off types of FHHs are different from one country to the other (Baden and Milward 1995: 19). What these studies are saying is that not all FHHs are poor. This does not contradict the fact that the number of FHHs among the poor and the poorer sections of society is increasing and that they, as a group – whether heterogeneous or not – are more vulnerable and face more discrimination because they are poor and also because they are man-less women on their own.

Another argument against making FHHs a priority group is that free and unconditional assistance increases their numbers and encourages them to relax and not work. This distrustful, punitive and contemptuous attitude towards FHHs and the poor in general has been growing in Egypt during the last several years. The new trend is to stop charity and welfare programmes, and instead provide credit for the poor to make them productive citizens. A high-ranking MOSA official stated that: 'We are now trying to encourage the people to depend on themselves. Charity produces dependency and encourages people to be lazy.' Another government official at the office of the Cairo Governor stated: 'The new Mubarak solidarity programme will transform the dependent and lazy poor into productive and hard-working women and men. This complete reliance on the state must be stopped and not encouraged.' Yet a large number of these FHHs are old and illiterate and unable to work. Some administrators cannot see that providing credit to women without providing vocational skills and childcare facilities will only increase their burden (Bibars 1998).

In most studies on poverty in the Arab countries, the gender dimensions of poverty are not adequately addressed, if they are addressed at all. The linkages between economic poverty, food insecurity and population expansion on the one hand, and gender inequality on the other are ignored (el-Solh 1994: 3). Recent studies, however, point out that the number of poor people in the Middle East and North Africa has increased significantly, from an estimated 60 million in 1985 to 73 million by 1990 (World Bank 1993: 5 in el-Solh 1994: 6).[28] Case-studies and surveys have revealed that poverty in the Arab world has been increasing in the population in general and among women in particular, which has resulted in a significant increase in the number of FHHs. The available published information suggests that there is a link between poverty, female headship and the informal sector. These studies find: that there are more women than men who are poor, and that the poor female population will be more disadvantaged due to cultural and ideological constraints related to their female gender role. Research in rural Egypt confirms these findings, especially with regard to the poorest of the poor. It was found that this group tends to consist of females without male kin who are socially and economically marginalised in society (el-Solh 1994: 17).

The Labour Force Sample Survey (LFSS), a large labour market study carried out in Egypt under the auspices of CAPMAS in 1988, revealed that women who head their households are more concentrated in lower-income brackets than male heads of households. A 1993 study that covered 600 households in the Bulaq district found that the monthly income of a female-headed household is 48% of the monthly income of a male-headed household. Furthermore, income generated was less than expenditure in about half of the FHHs studied as compared to 16% of MHHs. FHHs lived in worse and poorer housing units than MHHs. The study also showed that FHHs are considerably less educated than MHHs. More than three-quarters of FHHs were illiterate compared to 43% of MHHs (Fergany 1994a: 3).

According to the National Health Expenditure Survey, a survey conducted by the Data for Decision Making Bureau in the Ministry of Health and the Cairo Demographic Centre in 1994/1995, in the lowest expenditure bracket in both urban and rural areas the ratio of FHHs is higher than the ratio of MHHs. On the other hand the ratio of FHHs to total households in the higher expenditure brackets is lower than the ratio of MHHs to total households in that bracket (Nassar 1997: 12).

> On average 62.6% of the female-headed households in rural Egypt are in the expenditure bracket below 20%. This ratio is 35.4% on average of all households and 31.4% for the male-headed households. In addition the ratio of the female-headed households in the expenditure bracket below 20% is higher in all regions than the similar ratio for the male-headed households and for all households. (ibid.: 13)

Kabeer argues that female headship has been used as an indicator of women's poverty because it was the only visible indicator for some time in the household-based approaches to poverty (1992: 23–5). She concludes that subsequent research showed that households recorded as female-headed encompass a wide variety of household economies and family structures. The issue is not headship *per se*, but how this headship came about and what the process implies about women's detachment from the economic support of other adults, especially that of the spouse. Lloyd and Brandon (1994) conclude that headship alone is not a sufficient indicator of poverty in all contexts. A study by the Population Council and ICRW shows that

Defining Female Headship

the issue of who maintains the family is critical for poverty, especially if dependants are involved (Kabeer 1992: 22–3). Whatever the methodology and the differences between the writers, they all agree that single and especially female parenthood is a powerful predictor of vulnerability.

I tend to agree with Buvinic and Gupta (1994), who argue that the association between female headship and poverty might not be perfect, but that it is strong enough to call for specific social policy interventions. Women-headed households are more vulnerable than male-headed households because they suffer higher dependency ratios; lower average earnings among the main earners; fewer assets; and less access to resources, credit, and full-time and secure employment. In short, it is argued that not all FHHs are poor and that they are not necessarily worse off than many of the poor women who reside with their spouses (Kabeer 1991).[29] I cannot argue for all FHHs, but the main focus in my work is on women who undertake the major share of the family's economic responsibility, whether or not the man is physically present. In Egypt, women (especially the illiterate and poor) have not been trained to be the main providers for the household; they have been limited to their private realm for a long time. They are not experienced in dealing with the public sphere and they do not know how to search for gainful employment that is not exploitative because they lack the skills and necessary education to compete in the formal labour market. In addition, they are usually constrained when pursuing such employment by the fact that they must also be the caretakers of their children and the elderly, so they find themselves in low-paid jobs that involve a great deal of drudgery. If they sought self-employment, they would then need credit, which is difficult to access for lack of collateral and a guarantor on their part (Farah 1997: 3–4).

A great institutional obstacle to poor FHHs in Egypt, and indeed to most poor women, to the benefits from state programmes is that many women do not have identity cards (IDs). This limits their chances not only for credit but also for regular and respectable employment.[30]

Similar constraining conditions face FHHs in obtaining housing in Egypt and in other countries. Women heads of households usually have limited or no access to housing because they cannot afford it financially and it is not acceptable socially for a man-less woman to live on her own.[31] In Egypt, a man-less woman cannot apply for some subsidised government housing projects because the rent must be in the name of a man. This is illustrated by the following quote from an interviewee:

> When I got a divorce, my husband kicked me out of our home because I was childless and therefore by law I had no right to the marriage house. I had nowhere to go. I sold all my gold and borrowed from my brothers and

applied to the public subsidised housing scheme. They refused to write the new flat in my name and asked for my brother, father or husband. I am not good enough for the government because I am a woman. (Mariam, 45, divorcee, 'The Resettlement')

And in the cases where women are allowed to apply, they usually cannot do so because they have no IDs.

These are the kinds of conditions awaiting women who find themselves, without warning, responsible for themselves and their families in an environment that is dominated by men and in which men are still seen as the only and most appropriate providers and heads of families.

Notes

1. On different definitions of male-headed and female-headed households in the developed and developing countries see Bruce and Lloyd 1992: 3; Rosenhouse 1989: 4 in Chant 1997: 5.

2. On different definitions of households see Winchester 1990; Brydon and Chant 1989; Thorner and Ranadive 1992 in Kabeer and Joekes 1991: 4–5.

3. For debates on definitions of household, see Harris 1981; Kabeer and Joekes 1991; Roberts 1981; Kabeer 1991: 5; Baden and Milward 1995.

4. See also Shanthi 1986: 310.

5. Chant (1997) also found that in Mexico, in the absence of the father, any male in the family is reported as the head regardless of his age, as males are considered the family's protectors.

6. Gardner 1995 discusses similar findings in relation to Bangladesh.

7. On definitions of FHHs in Egypt see also Nawar 1994; Badran 1994.

8. Many women described their husbands as 'useless'. They meant that their husbands no longer provided for the family and that they, as women, had to bear the extra burden of working outside and bringing in an income in addition to their domestic tasks. 'Useless' is a derogatory term, especially when used to describe 'the man' of the house in such a traditional society as Egypt. It connotes loss of respect and disappointment in the male partner. It also signifies how women define gender roles within the family. These men were labelled 'useless' by their wives because they no longer supported their families financially. As will be explained later, at the basis of any conjugal relationship lies a customary contract whereby women provide care and obedience and men are required to provide protection and financial support. Therefore, a man's role as protector also diminishes with his shrinking capacity to provide for his family.

9. The citation system followed for quotations of government or NGO officials will be as follows: initials of the person, job title, area and the name of the programme or the ministry.

10. A co-wife is a woman whose husband has one or more wives in addition to herself. This is allowed in Islam.

11. See Folbre 1991; Lewis 1993; Chandler 1991. On images of lone mothers in the UK see Chester 1977: 156.

12. For more detail on the subject of divorcees and social assistance of the state or NGOs see Chapters 4 and 6.

Defining Female Headship

13. For the economic and social conditions of FHHs in rural areas in the developing countries see Johnson 1992; Dreze 1990.

14. Gardner (1995) has made similar observations on Bangladesh.

15. Khattab and El Daief 1976 and Khafagy 1986 reached similar observations about the wives of migrants in Egypt.

16. Chant makes similar observations about the situation in Latin America. See Chant 1997: 19.

17. There are a number of studies on this issue. The following are particularly comprehensive: Chandler 1991; Hardey and Crow 1991; Hobson 1994; Chester 1977.

18. For more information on the prevalence of FHHs in developed and developing countries see Kamerman and Kahn 1988: 7; Burghes 1994: 7; Duncan and Edwards 1996; Chant 1997: 72.

19. On the problems in the definitions of female headship in the Egyptian census see Zaki 1993.

20. Here meaning a child who has lost his/her father.

21. On the negative perceptions of female heads of households in the advanced and developing countries see Collins 1991; Brydon and Chant 1989; Moore 1994; Hardey and Crow 1991; Dallos and Spasford 1995.

22. This term was used by Heba Raouf, a female Islamic activist, in a speech to the Labour Party's preparatory meetings for the Fourth UN World Conference on Women in Beijing, 1995.

23. See Chester (1977: 154) on lone parents in the UK.

24. Chant (Chant 1997: 200) found similar results in Mexico and Costa Rica.

25. Of the women interviewed 96% were battered wives.

26. For more studies reaching similar conclusions on the rise of FHHs in the USA, see Lindsey 1997.

27. See Grella 1990; Gimenez 1994; and Lindsey 1997: 218.

28. It is estimated that the population of the Arab world is 120 million.

29. For more arguments on the under- or over-representation of FHHs in the poorest sectors of different societies see Grosh in Chant 1997 and Lewis 1995.

30. The issue of lack of IDs for women was briefly discussed in Chapter 1 and will be dealt with again throughout the remaining chapters.

31. Moser (1987) and Brydon and Chant (1989) also found that FHHs are constrained in obtaining housing in some Latin American countries.

4
Women, Welfare and the State

As noted in Chapter 1, Western feminists argue that the state plays an important role in reinforcing the subordination of women and supporting the social advantages of men. They also argue that one of the major causes of women's marginalisation is the implementation of gendered policies infused with 'male' norms in specific institutions such as welfare bureaucracies.[1] There is therefore a need to analyse the tacit norms and implicit assumptions about gender roles that are prevalent in the different bureaucracies that form and administer the social welfare programmes.

The main issues investigated in this chapter are related to the impact of the state's social policies on the status and autonomy of FHHs. One major question is whether the state's welfare system is gendered in the sense that it promotes a male bias that furthers women's marginalisation and oppression. In this chapter I also argue that systems of social protection and welfare in Egypt justify describing it as a welfare state.

This chapter analyses the sexist nature of the Egyptian welfare system. It shows that this system is divided into two gender-linked sub-systems. The 'mainstream' social insurance sub-system is tied to full-time waged labour-force participation and geared to the breadwinner – most often the man. The secondary 'relief' sub-system is tied to the household and geared to mothers and their dysfunctional families. My findings show that these social and welfare policies are imbued with gendered interpretations of women's needs based on the underlying assumption that men are the 'normal' heads of households, with no substantial recognition paid to new family structures, especially those headed by women.

This chapter borrows Fraser's concept of 'institutionalised patterns of needs interpretation' to explain and analyse the impact of the state's social welfare programmes on women. These programmes provide a powerful interpretative map of accepted gender roles and gendered needs (1989: 7–9). They adopt a sexist interpretation of women's needs based on ideological and gender-linked dichotomies such as private versus public, mother versus breadwinner, and home versus work. Such a sexist interpretation of women's needs is institutionally sanctioned by the state and society because both are infused with a masculine and patriarchal gendered ideology. To prove these points, I will describe the structure of the Egyptian welfare system in order to identify the assumptions that are at the basis of these programmes and practices. Then I will examine the ways in which women's needs are interpreted in these programmes in order to clarify the processes by which the programmes construct those needs based on specific gendered interpretations.

Social Security and the Welfare State

Before examining Egypt's welfare system there are various questions and points that should be answered and clarified. First, if Egypt describes itself as a welfare state there is a need to agree on what we mean by a welfare state. Second, what are the main welfare state types or regimes and, finally, under which type does Egypt fall?

The Egyptian state has defined itself as a welfare state and as a comprehensive system that addresses the productive and reproductive aspects of its citizens' lives. Within this context it becomes legitimate to analyse the underlying assumptions it makes about gender roles, and to question the impact of its policies on gender relations. It also becomes legitimate to question the intentions behind its different social policies. In this chapter I review the available literature in order to understand social policy in the context of a developing country that sees and defines itself as a welfare state. In other words, I assess the most relevant works of the Western literature and apply them to the Egyptian situation.

What is a Welfare State?

Defining a welfare state has proved to be complex. There are various definitions and different criteria given to describe it by different Western social scientists. One definition stresses the fact that the main aim of a welfare state is to reduce the negative impact of social divisions and mitigate social inequalities (Ginsburg 1992: 2). Another definition emphasises the state's responsibilities for securing a basic level of welfare for its citizens (Esping-Andersen 1990: 18).

Studies carried out by Wilensky (1975), Korpi (1985) and Esping-Andersen (1985) focus on spending as a criterion for defining a welfare state. They assume that the level of social expenditure reflects a state's commitment to welfare. Yet emphasising expenditure as a measurement tool can be misleading. Not all spending carries the same weight or counts equally. Some welfare states spend a large share on benefits to privileged civil servants while other states spend on means-tested programmes. Still other nations focus on tax privileges for private insurance plans that are beneficial to the middle classes only. Under Britain's Prime Minister Margaret Thatcher, for example, total social expenditure seemed very high, but this was due not to expansion in social benefits but to the rise in the number of unemployed. Thus expenditure is not the most appropriate criterion by which to define a welfare state (Esping-Andersen 1990: 19–20).

Researchers since Alexis de Tocqueville have correlated the welfare state with the expansion of democracy. They argued that welfare states would develop parallel to the expansion of democratic rights. It was claimed that the majorities would favour social distribution to compensate for market risks. Within the institution of democracy, it was argued, wage-earners would demand social wages and capitalists would need protection in the form of subsidies. However, this argument confronts a historical challenge because the first welfare state initiatives took place in countries that were not only not democracies, but also more on the side of autocracies, such as France under Napoleon III and Germany under Bismarck. Furthermore, although the USA has a highly developed and sophisticated democratic system, it has the most underdeveloped welfare policies – when compared to many European states – to mitigate inequality. In that sense, the Western claim that a welfare state must also be a liberal democracy has proved to be inaccurate (Esping-Andersen 1990: 15). Therefore it is no longer accurate to define a welfare state in terms of its spending a particular percentage of its GDP on social provisions or in terms of its democratic institutions.

None of the above definitions or criteria for describing the welfare state directly responds to the initial questions: if welfare states differ, then how do they differ, and when indeed can a state be described as a welfare state and what criteria should be used to define it as such?

Two conceptual approaches have contributed answers to these questions. The first conceptual approach derives from Therborn (1980) who focuses on the state's daily routine activities. He claims that the state should be devoted to servicing the welfare needs of the family. This criterion would disqualify most states, since most, if not all, devote their attention to defence and the armed services, political debate, economic growth, law and order, and administration (Esping-Andersen 1990: 18–20). The second conceptual approach was proposed by Richard Titmuss. His proposal distinguishes between residual and institutional welfare states. In the residual model, the state assumes responsibility only when the market fails. The institutional model addresses the entire population. The residual model directs welfare to marginal and deserving groups, while in the institutional model, welfare is extended to all areas of distribution vital for social welfare (ibid.: 19–20).

The Different Types of Welfare State

Titmuss' 1958 approach helped researchers concentrate on the 'content' rather than the expenditure of the welfare state as a criterion for definition. This 'content' included targets of the welfare programmes, conditions of eligibility, quality of benefits and services and, finally, extension of citizen's rights, when defining, comparing and studying the different types of welfare states. After Titmuss, it became clear that there are different types of welfare state, to the extent that not all of them can be directly compared to each other (ibid.: 1990: 20).

Three types of welfare state regimes are identified by Esping-Anderson. The first is the liberal welfare state, which includes countries such as the USA, Canada and Australia. The second type is the conservative and strongly corporatist welfare state, which includes countries such as Germany and Austria. Finally, the third type of welfare state is the social democratic regime: the Scandinavian countries are the main examples in this category. These modern welfare state regime types are designed around three basic models: the liberal welfare regimes, which adopt the residual social assistance model of means-tested benefits for the poor; the conservative and corporate regimes, which adopt the industrial achievement model of social insurance based on encouraging the optimum performance of the labour market; and the social democratic regimes, which implement the citizenship model of universal social benefits (Myles 1995: 3).

Liberal welfare states apply means-tested assistance and modest universal and social assistance plans. The state and its public interventions step in only when the market and the family fail and breakdown. Such residual (means-tested) programmes are short-term and limited in scope and coverage, and often stigmatise their clients (ibid.: 7). In this type, the state works to protect the market and therefore attempts to reduce the bargaining power of the workers *vis-à-vis* the capital-owners. Thus insurance programmes are privately run, are not administered by the state, and are limited to those people who have contributed and were part of the labour market (Esping-Andersen 1990: 26–7). In the conservative and strongly corporatist welfare state, which implements the industrial achievement model, the state is ready to replace the market as a provider of welfare, but mainly to maintain the status differentials and rights attached to class and status. Such a welfare state's ideology is often shaped by the Church, which aims to maintain and preserve the traditional family structure (ibid.: 27). In the social democratic regime type, welfare programmes promote equality of the highest standard: services are upgraded to meet new middle-class demands and all are given a chance to participate, regardless of class. All members of the state benefit from these programmes and thus all feel obliged to pay. The success of this type of approach depends on the employment of all citizens. To ensure that the state does not wait until the family fails, the state pays for the cost of family preservation and gives women the choice of working, and so contributing to the system in a direct financial way. The social democratic welfare state thus takes direct responsibility for caring for children, the aged and the helpless. In that sense, it takes over women's reproductive role and allows them to work or, at least to have the choice of working (ibid.: 28).

These models are transformed into policies intended to mitigate inequality in different ways. Some policies aim at the individual's income needs, including the public provision or subsidy of services such as health, education, childcare and housing. Other policies aim at maintaining or complementing family income via unemployment insurance, maternity benefits and pension plans. And finally, another set of policies seeks to improve an individual's ability to earn or produce, which includes minimum wages, maternity leave provisions, childcare, anti-discrimination injunctions, and access to land and credit (MacDonald 1994: 1).

Contemporary debates, particularly in the USA, on welfare policies in neo-liberal contexts have challenged these models. The residual social assistance model is seen as a welfare trap that encourages people to stay on welfare and discourages them from working. Even the social assistance programme that provides security for middle-income workers is currently viewed as a waste of scarce dollars because workers are now living to a very old age (Myles 1995: 3–4).

Feminists have also been critical of the different models and their impact on gender relations and women's status. Means-tested programmes that define needs based on family income have been found to reinforce the economic dependence of women, chiefly on men. According to this definition, women whose husbands earn a good income are not considered poor, regardless of who happens to be the actual economic contributor to the family's livelihood. It also means that women are not given an institutional alternative to the male provider (MacDonald 1994: 4). Likewise, women are also excluded under the industrial achievement model because they are restricted from participation in many social insurance programmes. Women do not have equal access to paid work due to the use of male work norms. Such prohibitive work norms include continuous employment and full-time work. Part-time and temporary jobs do not provide any advantages for women, such as pensions or maternity leave. Thus, although social insurance programmes are presented in a gender-neutral discourse, they mainly target men. Such inequalities are more pronounced in Third World countries as more women are employed in the informal sector, which is, by definition, excluded from social insurance programmes (ibid.: 9–11). The citizenship model appears to be the most woman-friendly system, since it provides women with the opportunity to join the formal labour market by providing accessible day-care centres and other support systems. Given equal chances for work, women are able to survive independently of men and are able to maintain a household. Sweden is among the few states applying the citizenship model.

Is Egypt a Welfare State?

According to Western theorists, contemporary European and North American states are welfare states. They are capable of and committed to improving the socio-economic welfare of their respective populations. Western welfare states have a tradition of civil rights, parliamentary democracy and competitive political parties (Charlton et al. 1989: 22–3). Western theorists use 'size of expenditure' and 'type of political system' as the two main criteria for describing Western states as welfare states. As has been argued above, this should not always be the case.

In contrast, in communist and socialist countries the state assumes direct control and responsibility for many aspects of an individual's life, such as the economy, culture, social and family life and leisure. The state is also responsible for the health, education and employment of its women and men (ibid.: 45). In many communist countries the mutual dependency between the state and its people constitutes a welfare state, for the state, in theory, becomes committed to and guarantees the welfare of its citizens. To Egyptians, whether socialists, Nasserites or *laisser-faire* anti-Nasserite economists, until the 1980s and the adoption of structural adjustment policies, Egypt was a welfare state. Azer (1995) and Handoussa (1994) argue that the destitute are becoming more vulnerable because funding for Egypt's welfare programmes was reduced dramatically in the last decade. However, some remnants of the Nasserite bureaucracy still exist, such as the Ministry of Social Affairs with its programmes for the destitute and the commitment – although it is decreasing dramatically – by the government to guarantee free and subsidised education and health services.

The Egyptian welfare state was developed in the late 1950s and 1960s. It was committed to improving the living standards of the people, as the state identified itself then as a social and economic agent of change (Hatem 1992: 233). The government guaranteed free education, free health services, and employment to men and women in rural and urban Egypt until the 1980s (Nassar 1995; Handoussa 1994; Hatem 1992). For women in particular, education developed into a valued opportunity, for it guaranteed them a secure government job and provided them with a regular, albeit small, income. The 1956 and 1963 constitutions recognised the equality of all individuals, regardless of gender, and forbade any kind of discrimination (Hatem 1992: 232). The government guaranteed a job to all high school and university graduates, which gave equal opportunities to women. Women from working-class and lower middle-class families were granted education and employment opportunities (Moghadam 1992a: 41), especially in the government sector. In the 1970s, the percentage of working women in the government and public sector in relation to the total female labour force was 39.4%, while that of men was 23.9%. The government sector was attractive to women because it offered secure wages, non-discriminatory employment regulations and policies, and comfortable working hours (Nassar 1996: 22–3).

Since Nasser's time and until the new labour law is put into effect, women working in the public sector have been assured a 50-day paid maternity leave.[2] Both public and private sector employers were forbidden to fire pregnant women, and employers who had more than one hundred female workers were required to establish day-care centres. Since 1964, the Ministry of Social Affairs has maintained a network of subsidised low-cost day-care centres throughout Egypt. According to articles 10 and 11 of the current labour law, a female employee has the right to take two years of unpaid leave to look after her child up to three times during her employment years. During these absences, the state covers the social insurance of the woman, ensuring that she receives her full pension after retirement and that she is not discriminated against for her absence due to childcare. The law also grants the female employee two fully paid half-hour breaks for breastfeeding daily for the first 18 months after her return to work. In addition, all employees, whether male or female, are covered by the social insurance law if they work in the formal sector (el-Safty 1996: 15). In that sense, like the citizenship model, the Egyptian state has attempted to pay for the cost of family reproduction. By guaranteeing government employment to all university and high school graduates, establishing public and subsided day-care centres, and using woman-friendly labour laws, the government provided women with the choice of working. The role of women thus became a public concern (Hatem 1992: 233–4).[3]

Under Sadat, economic liberalisation created new forms of management that affected the demand for women's labour, essentially reducing women's opportunities for employment. The progressive laws of the 1950s and 1960s were ignored and inequality of opportunity in the labour force was introduced in its most explicit form – advertising for male-only jobs in the private sector (ibid.: 231–4). In a study carried out in 1995, it was discovered that during periods of personnel reduction accompanying privatisation, women were the first employees to leave. At the Principal Bank for Development and Agricultural Credit, 11.7% of the total number of female employees and 6.4% of males left in 1993–94 (INP 1996: 100). With privatisation and the ensuing exodus of women from the formal and state-owned labour market, the main resource for women became the informal and agricultural sectors. In the informal sector, women have no unions or legal protection and do not enjoy labour rights such as paid holidays, fixed working hours, healthcare or day-care for their children. Thus, not only is women's share in the public and formal labour market decreasing but their exodus to the informal sector is depriving them of many social benefits (Farah 1997; Nassar 1997).

This study will not rely on the Western criteria of expenditure or the presence of a democratic system to define a welfare state. Based entirely on the Western experience, these criteria are ethnocentric. This study will use Third World criteria. My study borrows from Nassar's (1995) work on the economic and social impact of structural adjustment on the destitute and the poor in Egypt. In her work she developed three main characteristics for defining and analysing the Egyptian welfare state, namely: the adoption by the state of the human capital approach, an economic approach and a welfare approach.

The human capital approach According to Nassar (1995) the human capital approach means that the state improves the productivity of its population through available and accessible healthcare, education and better employment opportunities. Egypt's 1962 Charter and 1971 Constitution specified that healthcare and services must be provided and accessible to all citizens, in rural and urban Egypt, irrespective of their ability to pay. Government expenditure on health in 1965 constituted 5% of total government expenditure. However, this trend decreased in the 1990s with structural adjustment (Badran 1995: 8–9). In addition to the largely subsidised health services offered to the public, social health insurance provided medical care to those insured in both the public and private sectors. This insurance covered injuries caused by work or accident and included periodic medical check-ups (ibid.: 9).

During Egypt's last three five-year development plans, the percentage of the government's expenditure in the social sector increased from 5% in the first five-year plan under Mubarak to 11.8% in the plan of 1992–97.

The economic approach The economic approach attempts to increase the income-earning possibilities of the population, especially the poor, through easier access to paid work and access to credit and by improving conditions in the labour market. The economic approach was reflected in the employment guarantee policies as a response to the educational policies adopted in Egypt. Since 1952 education has been free to all Egyptians. Employment policies – which continued until the end of the 1980s – guaranteed employment opportunities and a fixed income for all graduates.[4]

The welfare approach The welfare approach entails direct transfers to the poor to increase their income and improve their standard of living. Transfers take the form of either cash payments or subsidised goods and services, in particular subsidised foods. The welfare approach was reflected in the food security system and the social assistance schemes.

i. The Egyptian food subsidy system covered approximately 93% of the population in 1989. The majority of these people received the full ration (green card: 47,085,001) and the rest (1,416,013) received the partial subsidy (red card). To reduce the cost of the food subsidy programme, the government adopted several cost containment measures. The cost to the government of the 1989/90 ration programme decreased to approximately half that of the years 1984/5.

ii. The social security schemes include the social insurance contributory programme and the social assistance non-contributory programmes. 27.1% of the population were covered by the social assistance scheme in 1992/3 while 10.2% of the population were covered by the social insurance scheme in the same fiscal year. (Nassar 1995: 17)

Egypt has applied all three approaches since the 1960s with varying degrees of success, especially in terms of coverage and targeting. The question was not whether Egypt, as a welfare state, was committed to the above goals, but whether it was able to achieve the goals it set for itself. In that context, Egypt is considered a welfare state in this study. According to the definition cited earlier, the Egyptian state is committed to securing 'the basic modicum of welfare for all its citizens'. It does, however, have problems of management, finance and efficiency.[5] These are some of the issues that I raised and examined in my fieldwork, focusing on the state's relationship towards poor women, especially those who head their households.

Egypt under Nasser adopted the – very popular at that period – socialist reform approach, and followed the model of the Soviet Union welfare state. As a self-defined welfare state, Egypt sought to bring society together for better production, better standards of living and social welfare during this period. This modernisation project might have been too ambitious for and did not fit with the existing social reality, although the intention to modernise Egypt according to a vision of social equality was genuine. It is within this context that I try to investigate the hidden assumptions and biases that might have distorted the actual implementation of the state's plan for social modernisation.

The Egyptian Welfare System and Women Heads of Households

In this section I will investigate whether Egypt's welfare system is two-tiered, with one mainstream system favouring men and another secondary system that increases the subordination of women. For the purposes of this study, I examined two programmes of the welfare bureaucracy in Egypt:

1. the Social Insurance Contributory System, which targets mainly full-time workers; and
2. the Social Aid and Assistance Non-contributory System, which targets the destitute (non-working poor).

The Ministry of Social Insurance is in charge of the social insurance programme, which includes old age, disability and death insurance, work injury and unemployment insurance. Social insurance schemes are administered by two organisations: the Insurance and Pension Organisation (IPO) and the Social Insurance Organisation (SIO). The Health Insurance Organisation Programme (HIOP) is responsible for providing medical benefits (Kashef 1987: 10–11).

The Ministry of Social Affairs plays the leading role in running the social aid programmes. MOSA provides social aid and cash transfer services directly, through its social unit offices all over the country and through the various NGOs that fall under its jurisdiction. These are the most prominent welfare programmes of the Egyptian welfare system.

Egypt's welfare system is generally inadequate and does not address the needs of the poor. In its current structure, it is divided into two sets of gendered programmes. The *mainstream* set of programmes targets the individual, and its benefits are tied to active participation in the paid workforce. Unemployment insurance and social insurance in Egypt are its main schemes. The *secondary* set of programmes is geared towards the household or family, and its benefits are tied to the lack of an adequate household income and to the absence or disability of a male breadwinner. In Egypt, pensions for widows, divorcees or deserted women and assistance for the disabled, sick and completely disabled heads of households fall under this set of programmes.

The mainstream contributory sub-system This sub-system includes the workers' insurance scheme, unemployment insurance and the universal social security scheme.

The workers' social insurance scheme is tied to individuals, especially those in the paid workforce (whether the public or private sector). The ratio of men to women under this scheme depends greatly on the percentage of women who are in the formal sector, i.e. those who work for the government in full-time jobs.

The unemployment insurance scheme provides social insurance to private sector employees covered by the labour law, but excludes those approaching 60 years of age and construction workers.[6] This scheme is irrelevant to the majority of the unemployed who are, in reality, job-seekers and have never been employed, and are therefore ineligible for this type of insurance. In other words, because most of the unemployed are new entrants they do not benefit from this scheme (Nassar 1998: 11; Assad and Rouchdy 1998).

The Universal Social Security scheme of law 112 (1980) covers those who do not benefit from the workers' insurance scheme. These include temporary and casual workers in agriculture, small artisans, the self-employed, domestic servants and others working in similar jobs.

All the above schemes target those engaged in full-time paid labour. According to the Ministry of Insurance's annual report for the fiscal year 1994–95, only 12.7% of those insured in the public sector were women, as opposed to 22.4% in the private sector (Ministry of Insurance 1997). The majority of the direct beneficiaries are men. These beneficiaries are considered rights-bearers and customers who have paid for their services. They do not apply for their pension but receive it automatically upon retirement. Their heirs fill in one application form and produce the necessary documents to be eligible for the pension. In recent years, the state has further simplified the procedures for collecting the pension. People no longer wait in queues: their cheques are either transferred to their bank accounts or sent to the post office nearest to their home. In other words these customers, the majority of whom are men, are treated with respect and concern for their comfort. The beneficiaries of the secondary non-contributory sub-system are not treated with such deference. They endure a long process of screening by officials to ensure the weeding out of ineligible clients.

The secondary non-contributory programmes: social aid, Social Security Act no. 30 (1977) MOSA's main safety-net arrangement for the poor is the social aid set of programmes (il Daman il Ijtimaii), issued as law 30 for 1977. This non-contributory set of programmes is means-tested and targets the destitute and vulnerable. It targets families and not individuals, and covers those who do not fall under any other insurance scheme. The beneficiaries include the unemployed and the non-contributing clients of the aid and welfare system, such as the elderly, the totally handicapped, widows, divorcees and children of divorcees, orphans, and the families of imprisoned persons. Its monthly value is estimated to be LE10 for orphans[7] and up to LE33 for the elderly and prisoners' families. The 'chastity pension' for never-married women falls under this programme (INP 1996: 93).[8] No in-depth study of this system has ever been undertaken. Descriptions of the system and of its coverage and economic values have been carried out on a small scale. No gender analysis of the impact of the system on women – whether it discriminates against them or institutionalises their stigma and poverty – has been carried out so far (see Handoussa 1994; Nassar 1996; Azer 1995; Nagi 1995).

In addition to the above there are two other traditional welfare schemes. The first is known as the winter assistance or *Maoonet el shetaa*. This assistance is described as follows by one MOSA official:

> This is a quick, one-time remedy. A palliative until the family finishes the procedures for any other type of social aid. This is for men and women who are destitute and needy. It is usually distributed during religious and national occasions. (Mr D., head of the social unit of 'The Squatters', MOSA)

The second scheme is a type of emergency assistance. It is given in cases of death and need for funeral expenses, relief and compensation for loss of life, and natural disasters.

There is also another non-contributory scheme that has exceptional origins. The Sadat pension was established in 1980 and was closely tied to law 112. It was created as a temporary mechanism to address the immediate needs of the working poor (those covered by law 112) until they are legally entitled to their pensions from the universal social security scheme. This programme – designed to cover widows, orphans, the totally disabled, the elderly and divorcees – was conceived to be phased out once those working in the informal sector were covered by the insurance law 112. According to the World Bank, the ratio of beneficiaries was as follows: widows 23%, divorced women 20%, the disabled 29%, the elderly 19%, and children of divorced women 1.5% (World Bank 1991: 63–6; HDR 1996: 93). The ratio of female to male beneficiaries in this scheme is 1.0 to 0.53. In contrast, the ratio of all beneficiaries in the other insurance schemes is, on average, 1 female to 12.5 males. (Ministry of Insurance 1992/93 in Nassar 1995: 25). The Sadat pension was LE10 per month in 1980; it was then raised to LE30 and one study claims that it reached LE50 in 1996–97 (Farah 1997: 14). The Sadat pension's beneficiaries constituted 15.9% of all pension beneficiaries in 1994/95 (Nassar 1997: 7). However, there has been a 34.8% decline in its number of beneficiaries during the period 1987/88 to 1994/95. This is mainly because beneficiaries who drop out, usually because of death, are not replaced (ibid.: 2).

The beneficiaries of these non-contributory programmes are described by officials as beneficiaries of the state's largess. They are not considered rights-bearers but are viewed as charity-receivers. As will be shown in the next chapter and through the case-studies in Chapter 7, the application process is both lengthy and complex. The state and its bureaucracies have established difficult screening mechanisms to weed out those who are not needy or destitute. Furthermore, a stigma is associated with these applicants because of the general official attitude and image. State bureaucrats and society at large perceive recipients of these non-contributory programmes in a negative and condescending manner. As one MOSA employee stated:

> These people are lazy and unwilling to do one day's honest work. They prefer to be a burden on the state. (Mrs H., former under-secretary, MOSA headquarters)

These programmes also provide a gendered interpretation of roles and needs. In both sub-systems, divorcees are not welcomed and are even punished for initiating the divorce and not enduring an abusive relationship. As will be shown in Chapter 5, a divorcee who initiates divorce is not eligible for her husband's pension after his death: only a woman whose husband divorced her is eligible. The 'chastity pension' is yet another mechanism by which these programmes meet women's needs only if they conform to specific gendered roles.

In October 1995, MOSA announced the inception of the Mubarak solidarity programme, or Takful Ijtimai. Its main declared aim was to alleviate poverty and integrate the poor into the development process through the direct provision of financial aid and the establishment of income generating projects (Farah 1997: 15).

According to the Alexandria Directorate of Social Affairs, there is no special regulatory decree for the Mubarak programme, although some recommendations have been issued by the Minister's office. There is no specified budget line item for this programme other than those already designated for the existing welfare programmes. In reality, there is no specific Mubarak programme with a new or more sophisticated and accurate targeting system. From what I found, the proclaimed achievements of the Mubarak programme are in fact the accumulation of the achievements of all MOSA social aid programmes during one year.

In 1996, MOSA officials at Governorate and central levels announced the specific achievements of the Mubarak programme for political reasons. Nationally, the government claimed that, since its inception in February

1996, the Mubarak programme had reached and supported 2.6 million beneficiaries. The state's concern with promoting the mythical Mubarak programme demonstrates the importance of social welfare gestures to legitimise governments and politicians.

Implicit Patriarchal Assumptions behind Needs Interpretation

Recent feminist research has been concerned with the extent of male dominance in the welfare state and the extent to which a welfare state is woman-friendly. In other words, whether women's interests and needs – as defined by women themselves – are taken into consideration determines whether a welfare state is woman-friendly or not (Hernes 1987; Orloff 1993; Gordon 1990). State social welfare programmes are, according to Fraser, sexist and gendered. They are infused with masculine and patriarchal norms. Consequently, they tend to interpret women's needs in ways that maintain the patriarchal status quo and reinforce women's subordinate position.

According to Fraser, the positions of the beneficiaries of the 'mainstream' and 'secondary sub-systems' are affected by three interlinked elements. The first is the judicial element, whereby the beneficiaries are accorded or denied rights to these services *vis-à-vis* a legal system (Fraser 1989: 150–3). The mainstream social welfare programmes are contributory and the participant is treated as a customer who has paid for the service. The participant is a rights-bearer and is seen as deserving what he receives. He is not treated as a charity-receiver and neither his behaviour nor his economic status is investigated. The bureaucratic procedures for acquiring the service are simple and less demeaning than the secondary social-welfare programmes.

The secondary social assistance programmes address their target groups differently. These programmes are non-contributory and are financed by the state's general budget. As a result the benefits are inadequate, to the extent of providing beneficiaries with resources far below what is required to cross the official poverty line. These relief programmes require a great deal of time and work on part of the applicant in order to qualify. They are screened though a long process and their personal lives and behaviour are scrutinised. As I found, the majority of these beneficiaries are women. Women, then, are caught in a dilemma. Since the state does not offer them accessible and affordable day-care centres and job training, they are unable to join the paid labour market and are accordingly pushed towards welfare programmes. Furthermore, the state positions them as mothers and caretakers and thus interprets their needs as maternal needs only (ibid.: 150–2).

The second element deals with administration. In order to qualify for and receive benefits from a bureaucratic apparatus, participants must meet bureaucratically defined criteria. In the 'mainstream' sub-system, applicants must meet such criteria as having reached the age of 60 or becoming invalids or, in the worst of cases, death and bereavement. Applicants in the secondary sub-system must conform to a process that has been defined by the bureaucratic apparatus and that is infused with patriarchal values. They have to prove that they are destitute and man-less, for example, as in the case of MOSA's aid programmes. The beneficiaries of the secondary sub-system are perceived as deviant by the administrators and this directly affects how their needs are interpreted. In the USA and according to Fraser, a third element that affects the positions of the beneficiaries is the therapeutic one. Especially in the secondary sub-system, clients are assumed to be deviant and in need of different types of counselling (ibid.: 155). This element, however, is not present in the Egyptian system.

To demonstrate how the welfare programmes reinterpret women's needs in a gendered manner, we must consider the size and type of benefits they receive. To see how these programmes position women as subjects, we have to study the associated administrative practices.

The serious problems with the secondary non-contributory social aid programme are the limited size of its benefits and its coverage. Handoussa argues that both the social security system and the Sadat pension schemes are deficient in terms of the average cash payment per household. The benefits for an average recipient – assuming she has no dependants – would cover only one-quarter of her expenditure level if she were to stay at the poverty line (Handoussa 1994: 5–6). A study carried out by the World Bank and the Ministry of Insurance and Social Affairs (MOISA) estimated that the lowest expenditure rate per person should be between LE50.3 – LE67.8 per person per month. This is much higher than the monthly assistance provided by the social assistance programmes or the Sadat pension, which range from LE14 per month to LE46 per family per month. There remains a huge gap between the benefits of social assistance and the minimum amount required to survive (Mansi 1995: 4–5).

Policy-makers and scholars agree that MOSA has not made any serious assessment of the national need for any type of social assistance. Since the assumption is that women are a secondary source of income for the family and that families are supported by men, social assistance benefits are considered supplementary. The state has not provided women with an institutional alternative to the male provider.

In addition, the non-contributory programmes have established gendered and humiliating criteria for eligibility. The most extreme expression of this is the spinster's 'chastity pension', where a woman must conform to conservative modes of behaviour and prove with a doctor's certificate that

Women, Welfare and the State

she is a virgin to be eligible for the benefits of this programme.[9] The beneficiaries of the other non-contributory social aid programmes also have to prove that they are 'destitute' and in dire need. They endure public humiliation when social workers visit them to verify their status through their neighbours. There is an element of surveillance not only in monitoring their economic conditions but also in demanding their conformity to pre-defined gendered roles. By enforcing these conditions for eligibility, these programmes reassert and reinforce women's subordinate position. The following chapters give more empirical detail regarding such experiences.

Notes

1. For more on the state, welfare and aid bureaucracies and gendered policies see Wilson 1977; Piven 1985; Sassoon 1987; Gordon 1988; Skocpol, 1992; Goetz 1991a, 1992.

2. The new law will limit women's ability to take childcare leave and will put restrictions on working women's maternal rights. This new law has provoked many debates among feminists and politicians and the final law has not yet been issued publicly.

3. It is important to note that women's rights in theory were equal to those of men except when it came to laws governing marriage and divorce. In addition, in many instances discrimination against women was in the implementation rather than in the content of some of the laws.

4. These policies resulted in a huge bureaucracy composed of unmotivated and low-paid civil servants. Such a bureaucracy became a cover for disguised unemployment, which later affected the efficiency and effectiveness of the Egyptian civil service.

5. It is vital to highlight that the system is currently heavily dependent on foreign aid. The health sector and especially its preventive services are financed mainly by donor funds. However, most of this money does not trickle down to the beneficiaries, in contrast to the huge amounts that are being spent effectively by the Islamists. In Chapter 6 I will describe the Islamic programmes and compare them to the programmes run by the state.

6. Since construction work is irregular and periods of unemployment are numerous.

7. Since law 12 of 1996, the benefit for orphans and sons of imprisoned and dead divorcees increased to LE20 per month. In July 1997, it reached LE25 per child.

8. Women over 48 years old who have never been married are entitled to the spinster's pension; however, they have to prove that they have never been married and that they are still virgins.

9. MOSA officials claim that what is needed is an official paper stating that the woman has not been married, but women claim the need for a certificate stating that they are still virgins.

5
The Politics of Exclusion

This chapter describes how the state marginalises women and excludes certain types of FHHs from its welfare programmes. The underlying assumptions and the relationship of patronage between the concerned officials and these women are examined. The aim of this chapter is to demonstrate how the state's social policies are implemented on the ground and to assess their impact on women, especially women heads of households.

I will highlight the main causes for the exclusion of different types of FHHs from the state's welfare programmes. The problems I address here have to do with the hidden assumptions and obstacles in programme design and application requirements, which exclude and push away poor women, especially those who head their households. I will also show how even 'inclusion' in these programmes affects the status of women negatively. This is demonstrated through stories about the attitudes and practices of fieldworkers and bureaucrats who stigmatise women and put them in a supplicant relationship with the state.[1] The following stories highlight some of the issues that are addressed in this chapter. As one MOSA official said:

> I totally refused to help her before and will insist on not helping her, so please do not interfere. This is a loose woman; she was married twice and was divorced both times. To apply now for assistance is uncalled for. She came before and I told her that she is a troublemaker and since she does not want to live like a respectable woman, the state will not help her. (Mr M., general-director, 'The Ezba', MOSA)

This was Mr M.'s angry response to a schoolteacher regarding the case of Elham. Elham is an intelligent and ambitious 29-year-old woman who finished high school with high grades, although her family did not let her continue her education. Instead, they forced her to marry Adham, a plumber who was 20 years her senior. According to Elham, Adham used to beat her every night and then force her to sleep with him. She complained to her family and to the Sheikh at the local mosque, but to no avail. 'Marital rape' is not recognised by the state's legal system, by Islam or in

The Politics of Exclusion

the community. After breaking her ribs and nearly killing her, Elham went back to her parents and insisted on divorce. Within the same year, Elham's elder brother forced her to marry his supervisor at work and threatened to put her child in an orphanage if she refused. The new husband had another wife who made him divorce Elham only four months after the marriage. Consequently, Elham became a woman twice divorced and thus labelled as loose by state officials and also by other members in the community. She was refused state assistance because she did not live up to the 'conservative' and acceptable stereotype of a wife.

Hind, on the other hand, decided that she would not apply to the MOSA programme because she did not want her neighbours to know she was a divorcee. She complained that MOSA employees were not discreet and that they 'humiliated' applicants to their programmes by going publicly to their neighbours and asking about the economic conditions of the applicants. She also added that these social workers sometimes gossiped about their clients with others in the area. This is her story:

> I was married for 14 years and lived with him in Fayoum. We had four children. All of them are girls and that is why he married another woman to get a boy. I accepted the new situation because I had nowhere to go. However, once she bore him a boy, she asked him to divorce me. He kicked me out of the house and I came to live here with my sister in Alexandria. We told the neighbours that my husband was in Libya. I have four girls and we live with my widowed sister. If it becomes known that I am a divorcee we will lose our reputation. I heard about the MOSA programmes but I didn't apply. They are known to be nosy and ask about you in your area. They also do not keep your secrets and sometimes gossip about their applicants. I cannot take this chance. I do not want anyone to know about my real situation. (Hind, 39, divorcee, Alexandria)

These stories show how the state's social welfare programmes do two things:

1. They virtually dictate a particular family form and a particular form of acceptable female behaviour by virtue of their conditions for access, as they exclude all those who do not conform to the socially constructed role of the 'enduring' housewife.
2. They adopt a condescending attitude towards women who do not conform and thus push them away. The stigma associated with being seen as coming from a dysfunctional family makes many women exclude themselves from such programmes.

In looking at the state's welfare system, I discovered that specific groups of women heads of households are excluded from both its major programmes;

contributory and non-contributory. Investigating the issue of exclusion, I adopted Martin Greeley's 'exclusion dimensions', which he used to assess women's access to rural credit programmes in Bangladesh. According to Greeley one must differentiate between programme-driven exclusion and self-driven exclusion. There are two types of programme-driven exclusion. It might result from conditions and regulations that hinder the access of specific groups to a particular service. A pertinent example of this kind of exclusion in Egypt is the requirement to procure an identity card, which is a major problem for many women, especially women heads of households. The second type of programme-driven exclusion could be due to the bureaucracy's perception of the target group, which can deviate from official definitions of programme beneficiaries and affects the way service-providers define and treat the beneficiaries of a particular service. Self-driven exclusion, on the other hand, is the result of the individual's desire and decision to exclude herself from joining a particular service. A pertinent example of this kind of exclusion is when some women decide not to join the social assistance programme because society stigmatises its beneficiaries and they decide that they do not want to be associated with the needy and the poor.

The Mainstream Contributory Programme: Social Insurance Programmes

Programme-driven exclusion In the mainstream programmes there are certain inherent rules and regulations that exclude certain types of FHHs, such as divorcees. In addition, hidden assumptions and perceptions of what a normal family structure should be serves as another programme-driven dimension for excluding 'non-traditional' types of FHHs.

Conditions and procedures for eligibility According to the social insurance policy of law 79 (1975), a divorcee is eligible to receive her deceased husband's pension if she meets the following stipulations:

1. That she was not the initiator of the divorce and that the divorce was against her will.
2. That she was married to the participant for at least 20 years.
3. That she has not remarried since the divorce.
4. That she has no other source of income.

The following case of Khadiga is an example of how this law discriminates against women.

> I am a divorcee. We were married for 24 years. I am the one who asked for

divorce because he was always insulting me and treating me very badly. I tried to be a good wife but I just could not take it any more. He died within six months of the divorce, and I found out that I have no right to the pension. According to the law, because I asked for the divorce I do not deserve my share in his pension. (Khadiga, 43, divorcee, 'The Squatters')

Women are thus being punished for initiating divorce procedures and for demanding a way out of an abusive relationship. This law reinforces the submission of women by encouraging them to endure abuse in order to ensure a source of income.

Definitions, perceptions of and hidden assumptions of family structures Public, government and private sector employees, whether men or women, pay a percentage of their monthly salary to cover their pension, which will be used after they reach 60 or upon their death. Hence the social insurance scheme is a contributory system whereby individuals and their employers have contributed amounts of money to cover the financial needs of the future. The pension is disbursed to the family of the deceased, his wife and children. The pension of the children is stopped once the son works or reaches 26 years of age, and once the daughter marries or begins to work. However, the husband does not receive a share of his wife's pension when she dies because the law does not consider her to be the head of the household.

Husbands complain that after their wives' deaths they do not collect a pension on behalf of their wives. As stated by the head of public and external relations at MOISA, a man will receive his deceased wife's pension only if he is unemployed and cannot find a job, or is at least 50% incapacitated.[2]

'We give pensions to the family of the maintainer and keeper when he dies and that is usually the man, for the man is the keeper and head of the family.' He continues: 'The pension is like the *nafaqa* [alimony] in the *Sharia'a*: it is only payable to those maintained by the maintainer. There is no *nafaqa* from wife to husband.'

This means that her contribution is lost. (el-Damarani 1997)

The following unusual admission by an Egyptian man shows the growing trend of spouses sharing in household expenses in Egypt now:

My wife and I were married for 24 years and we have been law-abiding citizens. We had four children and both of us worked hard to educate them. We were real partners in this marriage. She worked and her salary contributed to the family income and, now that she has died, I have no right to her pension. Well, this is affecting our budget and style of living and I think this is unfair. (ibid.)

This quote, in addition to my research findings on the great variety of situations in which women are *de facto* heads of households, and the major economic providers, suggests that it is time to question the accuracy of assumptions about men being the sole providers.

Dr Ahysa Rateb, former MOSA minister and professor of international law at Cairo University's School of Law, stated:

> The law of social insurance is based on the belief and assumption that the man is the head of the household and maintains the family. Thus we deprived him of his wife's pension which was deducted from her salary. Life has changed; men and women now share in the household expenses and in maintaining the families, yet the law has not yet internalised that. (ibid.)

This assumption that the man is by default the head of the household also governs how young female children are treated regarding their father's pension. Once a daughter is married it is automatically assumed that she has become the responsibility of her husband and thus her part of the pension (30%) is withdrawn. This not only shows bias and prejudice in describing the gender roles within the family, but is no longer realistic. Traditionally, Muslim couples get married in two stages. The marriage is first registered with the *ma'zun* (*sheikh* registrar), the second stage is the actual consummation of marriage. The first step, known as *katb el-ketab*, could last for a long period because of the economic situation of many couples who are new graduates. They wait until they find a place to live and then furnish it. In reality, although many of these girls have registered their marriages, they could still be living with their parents and be responsible for themselves. By cutting her out of the pension, the law has increased the financial burden on both the family and the girl. Furthermore, it is no longer common for the man alone to provide for the home. Egypt's legislators should come to understand this reality. As one interviewee recounts:

> I have been married at the registrar (*Maktub ketabi*) without consummation for the last four years. I still have not bought all my necessities and we are both working to furnish the flat we rented. My brothers insist that we will not consummate the marriage until the flat is finished. However, since I registered my marriage my share in my father's pension has been cut. My father's pension really helped and I feel it is unfair. I am responsible for myself, none of my brothers or even my husband spends money on me. (Doreya, 22, civil servant, 'The Bedouins')

Perception of state officials The above summarised the problems with the laws governing social insurance. These policies and regulations marginalise certain groups because the laws were built on assumptions that were either originally flawed or are no longer valid. Another dimension to programme-driven exclusion is how the staff perceives and treats the beneficiaries.

The role of the bureaucrat in interpreting and implementing policy is as important as the policy itself and the attitude of the policy-maker. It has been argued that if policies challenge conventional beliefs or run against the values and norms of the bureaucrat, they can be translated into something far from what they were intended to be.[3] Goetz (1996) argues that lower-level bureaucrats are *de facto* policy-makers as they may reinterpret and implement policies for different programmes. Her description of the attitude and behaviour of the fieldworkers in the rural credit programmes in Bangladesh is very similar to how lower-level bureaucrats act in Egypt. Bureaucrats in Bangladesh found themselves delivering programmes that challenged how traditions and the local system organised gender relations. Their attitudes and practice had a great impact upon the success of these programmes, which purported to challenge gender inequality. In many cases the biases, beliefs and values of the fieldworkers could undermine the desired outcome of the programmes and reinforce conventional interpretations of women's needs (ibid.: i). Similarly, in Egypt, the lower-level front-line bureaucrats are central to how social policies are interpreted and implemented at the local level and are critical to how women's and especially FHHs' needs are perceived and met.

In one insurance office I witnessed the tensions and hostility between the employees and the public. I observed that all the members of the public who came to ask for a service were treated unprofessionally, and that the poorer and the less well-presented the person, the worse the treatment. There was no differentiation between men and women. All the poor were looked down on and discouraged from asking for clarifications about what was required of them regarding papers.[4] There was a deliberate effort on the part of the government officials to cultivate an attitude of deference, subservience and gratitude on the part of the public. The state officials – of the contributory programmes in this case – resented having to serve people they believed to be lower than them, such as the petty vendors or maids, and tried all means to push them away. The following dialogue illustrates my point:

> MOSA employee 1: Why do you want to be insured? You will only get LE60 a month, while you are making more money now.
> Sayyeda: I have three children and my husband died five years ago. They will need every penny for school and I am not getting any younger.

MOSA employee 1: Why send them to school? Maids like you clean houses and make a lot of money without having to endure school and all that headache.

MOSA employee 2 (addressing her colleague): In addition to what they make on the side out of stealing. I had a maid who stole the gold earrings belonging to my child. They never appreciate how good we are to them and end up always betraying us.

Sayyeda: I am not a thief and all I want is to apply for the social insurance.

MOSA employee 1: Don't you dare raise your voice. Never forget who you are. Anyway we have no application forms today, so come another time.

The Social Aid Programmes: Il Daman il Ijtimaii and FHHs

Programme-driven exclusion

Conditions and procedures for eligibility   By law, all applicants should receive the monthly social aid pension immediately or within 15 days of the day of application. However, this is constrained by the budget and the size of the waiting list. The central MOSA directorate distributes the budget it procures from the central government to every social unit in a particular governorate according not to the demand or need of the social unit but to the availability of funds. Each social unit then disburses the money it gets according to the budget line allocated to it. According to a high-ranking official at MOSA, the size of the beneficiaries is determined annually based on the funds allocated to the ministry. Planning and targeting are carried out by the head of the social unit in every district according to the number of beneficiaries who were supported the previous year. Newcomers are added only to replace those who have dropped out due to death or re-marriage.[5] In addition, receipt of the pension order by the applicant does not necessarily mean that she will start receiving payment. There could be a long wait, sometimes up to three months, before cash disbursement.

Because the application process requires proof of age, marital status and address, women were usually asked to present their identity cards. Yet a large number of these women did not have identity cards. In several research sites the head of the social unit depended on his personal knowledge of some participants to exempt them from producing an ID. It was left to personal contacts and also to more flexible officials to determine whether a woman was eligible, even if, in some cases, her documents were not complete. This condition excluded a large number of women from the service.

The procedures were lengthy and not clear to many of the participants. Several of the women interviewed waited a long time for assistance. Others

The Politics of Exclusion

found the transportation and wasted time too expensive, and so stopped enquiring and dropped the whole thing. According to the 'Shelters' survey, 59% of the women who obtained assistance stated that they had waited several months before receiving a pension or assistance. Thirteen per cent stated that it took a year, and 7% said more than a year. In my fieldwork, I found that women dreaded going to the MOSA offices because of the time it took them to reach the appropriate employee, unless they had already established personal connections with them. The officials claimed that the two main reasons for delay were that the woman did not complete the required documents or that the social unit did not have enough funds in its allocated budget.

Applications were collected by social workers and handed to the head of the unit, who screened them. He would then assign one of his social workers to visit the applicant at her home to check the information. Due to a general shortage of social workers, lack of time and lack of financial resources to carry out these visits, it sometimes took the social worker months before visiting the applicant.

The applicant must prove not only her marital status – whether she is a divorcee, widow or deserted – but also that she is destitute. To be considered destitute an applicant must prove that she has no other source of income and owns no property, even if it is the room or house where she lives. She must also prove that she is not a beneficiary of any other welfare programme and that she does not take any pension from the insurance authorities or from any other public or private agency. Applicants are consequently required to go to the insurance authorities with a letter from the social unit to check if their names are in the computer database of the insurance organisation. Then they must obtain a letter from that office confirming the fact that they receive no insurance. In several cases, due to mistakes in data entry or to similarities in names, women were given letters stating that they were receiving a pension even though they were not. In such cases the computer employees did not bother to re-check the information, even in cases when it was clearly a mistake, as in the following story.

Hamida is a 64-year-old widow who has never worked in her life for a wage and is illiterate. She is childless and her husband used to work as a peasant on a relative's land. When he died, Hamida depended on the generosity of her neighbours and lived on charity. Four years ago she applied to MOSA. She followed all the procedures and when she went for the routine check-up at the insurance database, they told her that she was already receiving a pension from her previous job in a big public sector factory. Her alleged pension was more than LE200, which meant that her job was managerial. She tried to explain that she was illiterate and that she had never worked and never left her village except in the last five years

Victims and Heroines

when her husband got very sick and came to the hospital in the city. But no one listened to her and the social unit refused to grant her the old-age or the widows' pension. They even acknowledged that she might be right, but said that without a letter from the insurance authority's database they could not help her.

Divorcees, deserted women, and to some degree young widows are required to prove their marital status annually to the social unit by providing documents stating that their situation has not changed. Once they remarry the assistance is withdrawn as they then become the responsibility of the 'male provider' and no longer the responsibility of the state.

Definitions, perceptions of and hidden assumptions about family structures
The underlying assumptions of these programmes ignore and marginalise a large percentage of *de facto* FHHs whom they do not consider to be heads of households. Government officials and the law are oblivious to the fact that, particularly in low-income communities, many men are no longer responsible for their families and women are the *de facto* maintainers of the household.

The following two citations from my interviews with MOSA officials show their attitude towards female headship:

> The woman who maintains her family is the woman who has no man in her life to take care of her. She has no one to help her with family care and responsibility. No, the co-wife is not one of these women, she has a husband. (Mr M., general-director, 'The Ezba', MOSA)

> No, we do not support the co-wife, she is still the responsibility of her husband. No, she is not eligible for any of our aid programmes. She can sue him if he does not support her. This is her legal right and there are regulations governing that. (Mr I., under-secretary, central ministry, MOSA)

A large number of welfare programmes in Egypt target the head of the household, who is usually the man, as U'm Attiat demonstrated when she recounted the following story:

> I was burned and since then I cannot use my hands and cannot walk long distances. So I stopped going to the market to sell ghee and cheese. When I went to the MOSA office Mr Mohammed told me that my husband receives the old-age pension and that I am his responsibility. My husband is a useless drunk. He takes the money and spends it on his own whims. That is why I used to work. But I am not good enough for the government law, I do not deserve their money. (U'm Attiat, 59, wife of an elderly man, 'The Shelters')

The Politics of Exclusion

Mr D. from the social unit of 'The Squatters' told me:

> This pension is to substitute for the lack of income of the provider of the household, who is the man. In most cases it is men who receive it. The woman is the responsibility of the man: this is the law. If the woman is unmarried, or her husband is either dead or absent, then she is eligible.

Thus a large number of families are excluded from these programmes because the state and its bureaucrats insist that the normal and most common family structure is that headed and maintained by a male.

Perceptions of state officials As shown earlier, the way in which these bureaucrats perceive women, especially FHHs, in low-income urban Egypt affects the accessibility of different services and welfare programmes for these women. In addition, how the bureaucrat interprets and implements the different decrees and regulations leads to the inclusion or exclusion of different categories of the poor. As mentioned above, some social unit heads are flexible about IDs, while others insist on them and thus exclude a large number of needy women who head their households. Another example of personalised interpretation is related to age and marital status. According to the law, the social aid programmes mainly target the non-working poor, i.e. those who cannot work. Many of the divorced and deserted women I met claimed that the officials had refused to enrol them in the programme because they were young and thus able to work. They considered them to be part of the working poor, although similar women in the same age category were enrolled in other areas because the MOSA officials there interpreted the rules differently.

The attitude of government officials towards the poor in general and women in particular is patronising and condescending. They look at man-less women as helpless, as one official clearly stated:

> We try our best to help these poor widows, for they become helpless after the death of their provider. (Mr A., head of social unit, 'The Tombs', MOSA)

Throughout my fieldwork and my interviews with different people, the attitudes of the communities, the officials and the FHHs themselves were very revealing. In many cases, the perceptions of government officials were very similar to those held by men and women in the community, regardless of level of education. The different categories of FHHs were grouped by government officials and community members alike under certain labels. Divorcees and deserted women were seen as either failures or temptresses. Widows and spinsters or unmarried (but still virgin) women were seen as victims and helpless women. Wives of the unemployed and *u'rzu'i* were seen as hardworking and resourceful women. Co-wives were either seen as ungrateful women if they were complaining or were pitied for the abuse they received from their husbands. Finally, wives of imprisoned men or drug addicts were thought to be as bad as their husbands.

The elaborate screening systems to keep out cheaters stemmed from the overriding lack of trust by government officials towards the inhabitants of the poor areas studied. Government officials described poor illiterate women as ignorant, and as lacking a value system. They were more wary of divorcees and women who had to live on their own as they saw them as loose women with no value system, no integrity due to their ignorance, and no clear understanding of religion.[6] Nevertheless, whether the attitudes of both sides were friendly or resentful, a particular relationship was established in which the expected roles and positions of both were preserved. The government official was positioned by women and by himself or herself as the patron and the giver. The women, especially the women heads of households, were the receivers and the beneficiaries. The relationship was one not of equality but of patronage.

Outreach The social aid programmes are administered by the Ministry of Social Affairs through what is known as social units at the sub-district levels. These offices are located all over the country in urban and rural areas. The World Bank report of 1991 recorded that MOSA programmes are well known among the different populations through this intensive network of offices. However, in the fieldwork I found that both the coverage and scope of the programmes are small.

According to the survey carried out in 'The Shelters', 48% of the women knew about the MOSA services and welfare programmes through people they labelled *ahl el kheir* (good and kind people), 27% from relatives and neighbours, 11% through inherited pensions, and 10% from government employees. In Alexandria, 75% of the women knew nothing about MOSA services to the destitute, especially those for women. In 'The Ezba' not all the women interviewed knew about the services, but 75% of those who knew had found out from *ahl el kheir*, neighbours and relatives, but not from MOSA employees. In short, the majority of my sample knew about the state programmes through informal channels, and there was no official mechanism for advertising the services or for outreach programmes to increase the coverage.

The fact that knowledge about the programmes is an informal occurrence and depends on personal contacts affects the inclusion of many others who might not have access to government employees, Community Development Associations (CDA) employees, or good neighbours who would inform them.[7]

The Politics of Exclusion

Self-driven exclusion: fear of the state On another level, women knew how the state officials perceived them and this affected their relationship with and attitudes towards the state and its employees. Many women dreaded applying to the welfare programmes out of fear of humiliation. Women tended to portray the government as a foreign or alien entity. The government was seen as an entity in itself that controlled the lives of the poor and that had the power to improve their lives if it wanted to. This mistrust of government and the feeling of alienation make people feel that it is acceptable to try to abuse the system whenever possible. It is common for Egyptians to evade taxes and boast about it, for there is no confidence about where the money will go (Singerman 1989: 215).

Similarly, the women interviewed also boasted that their husbands or neighbours illegally connected their homes to electricity so that they never had to pay for it. As one woman said:

> So what if our homes are connected illegally to electric power. We are poor and the government and the ministers are very rich and they will never notice the peanuts that are spent on our electricity. (Hala, 35, wife of an *u'rzu'i*, 'The Squatters')

In short, women themselves do not think very highly of the government. As a result, a gap exists between the people and the state. In some cases this alienation makes poor and marginalised groups too afraid to tap the state's programmes. It is a case of mutual distrust.

Alienation encouraged some women to seek alternative providers to the state, as these quotes show:

> I told my daughter to go to U'm Haytham at the mosque. She is a woman who knows God and is kind to the poor. Mrs S. at MOSA is a bad person; she gets paid to serve us, but she thinks we are *remama* [rubbish]. I would never go to the government for anything. These officials are stuck up and they really do not want to help us. You see, if they give us money then their salaries will not increase. (U'm Salama, 62, widow, 'The Tombs')

> Those who work in the mosque are religious people and they are giving *zakat* money. The MOSA employees are thieves; they give money to their relatives and friends only. I also heard that they take a percentage from the pensions of the poor women. I prefer to apply to the mosque. (Mona, 34, widow, 'The Squatters')

> U'm Haytham and her friends came to my house and drank tea with me and my children. She verified that I am poor in a polite manner. The wretched girl from MOSA did not bother to come in and asked about me in the area and asked my neighbours. She scandalised me. I refused their money. (Sanaa, 42, widow, 'The Tombs')

These quotes show why certain women refuse to access the state's services if they have access to the Islamic programmes. While the image of the state's bureaucrat is that of an arrogant and insensitive person, the administrators of the religious programmes are known to many of the women interviewed as more friendly and discreet.

How Women Subvert the System: Coping and Opposing Mechanisms

On the other hand, women who actually participate in the different state welfare programmes realise that government procedures are problematic, and therefore establish different techniques to subvert the system. It is true that most if not all of the women I interviewed were oppressed and marginalised in some way by the men in their lives. However, this did not mean that they were completely powerless or unresourceful women. In their relationship with the state's welfare programmes and the bureaucrats who represented the government, some of these women learned to use the system (with all its flaws) to their own advantage. From my field observation I identified three coping mechanisms, which I classified as follows:

1. negative self-representation: confirming the stereotypes about women on their own;
2. informal networking: using personal, kinship and family ties; and
3. 'log-rolling' or exchange of favours.

Negative self-representation: confirming the stereotypes Poor women, especially women heads of households, are seen and portrayed by the different male and sometimes female government officials as minors who must be protected and provided for by a male. Whether the official interviewed pitied or resented this category of women, he or she described them as helpless creatures or loose women who needed a male presence to guide and protect them. The following citations show the negative perception by officials of poor women and especially those who head their households:

> These women are ignorant and are unable to determine what is good for themselves. They are lazy and do not want to work. They need a man to take care of them. (Mrs S., social worker, 'The Tombs', MOSA)

> They are helpless on their own; they cannot manage; they were taken from their father's home to their husbands' home. We help them here and protect them from a future with no hope and we help their children too, and protect them. (Mr E., social worker, Alexandria, MOSA)

The government officials interviewed, especially the male employees, explained that the Ministry of Social Affairs' social aid programmes for widows and divorcees were designed to compensate these women for the absence of the male, who is the main provider.

The rules of eligibility for such programmes insist that the beneficiaries have no other source of income and must be destitute. This was also what the bureaucrats were looking for when selecting their clients, and the women knew that. The bureaucrats enjoyed the feeling of being benevolent givers or patrons and the women complied with the expected profile of women in their position. These women carried two stereotypical identities: that of being helpless women and that of being poor. They were thus attributed feminine qualities such as fear, submission and weakness as well as the qualities of the destitute, which included helplessness, lack of resourcefulness and, in some cases, laziness. In response, women in such situations decided to confirm this image.[8] They appealed to the chivalry in male employees and the pity or empathy in female employees. Some of the women stated that they preferred to deal with male employees because they were more sympathetic and 'easier to fool'. It was stated that men expect women on their own to be 'lost', 'helpless' and in need of guidance and protection. On the other hand, my interviewees said that the female employees were more cautious and did not believe all the women's stories, even when they were true. As one interviewee stated:

> I prefer to go to Mr E. at the social unit. He is more understanding and he believes our stories. He knows we are helpless women who need help from the government. Mrs F., on the other hand, is not very kind, and tells us that we must go to work and not beg from the government. I am ignorant, poor and with five children, and my health is very bad now. If the government does not help me, who will? (Sithom, 32, widow, Alexandria)

Many of the women of the areas I studied acted and described themselves as 'sick, poor, ignorant and in need of protection', even when I knew for certain that this was not the case. U'm Saber is a very determined and powerful woman, mother of three and married to a carpenter who has not been in regular work for the last two years. U'm Saber has learned the rules and regulations of the Ministry of Social Affairs' welfare programmes by heart. She managed to get financial assistance from the local NGOs, the local parliamentarian's office, and MOSA to build her house and educate her son and two daughters. By any standards, U'm Saber is a strong woman who knows how to survive and use any situation to her advantage. However, U'm Saber does not perceive herself as a strong woman or, at least, that is not how she describes herself:

Victims and Heroines

> I am an old woman, exhausted and tired. I have many health problems and my energy is not as it used to be. But life is difficult and we are only ignorant women, we do not know what to do with our lives. (U'm Saber, 44, wife of an *u'rzu'i*, 'The Shelters')

This is exactly the image that is presented by officials and even, in some cases, the NGOs of low-income illiterate women in urban areas. Although I know for sure that U'm Saber's description of herself is inaccurate, her perception of herself is a reflection of society's and the government's perception of her. The question is whether she is just saying what others want to hear or whether she herself believes it.

It was also common among the women to present themselves as naive and inexperienced:

> What can I do, I do not know how to go around. I barely know the main streets of my district. When I was married (or with my family and under my father's protection) I was not allowed to leave the house alone. (Sania, 44, widow, 'The Bedouins')

> Good girls are always under their families' protection until their marriage and, later, under the protection of their husbands. (Mariam, 34, widow, 'The Shelters')

> Now I am all alone, and I cannot find a job for I do not know where to look and I cannot deal with strangers. I am also sick and cannot work in a demanding job. The government must take care of us, for if they do not, who will? (Zarifa, 57, widow, 'The Ezba')

The above statements contain some elements of truth but also some misleading elements. It is true that women in Egypt, and in particular low-income illiterate women, are born into dependency on their fathers and later on their husbands. And it is true that they lack the necessary education and have no marketable skills, which leaves them at a great disadvantage once they find themselves on their own. Nevertheless, a good number of these women were survivors and had learned to cope with their circumstances.

Due to their marginalised and oppressed situation within their natal and later their conjugal families, women learn to devise mechanisms not only for survival but also for opposition. In their relationship with any source of authority, women adopt the coping mechanism of passive resistance. A large number of the women who described themselves as helpless and unresourceful were successful in gaining access to several welfare programmes run by the government and NGOs.

Informal networking: personal, family and kinship ties The web of networks that people in popular areas cultivate are a major source of their bargaining and negotiating power *vis-à-vis* the state and its bureaucrats. Informal networks are based on cooperation between different groups in the community to achieve collective goals. Informal networks are also effective mechanisms through which Egyptians influence the distribution of public resources. In other words, people influence and have access to public services through their contacts and the networks they establish (Singerman 1989). Networking in the Arab world and the Middle East has been associated by social scientists with corruption and nepotism. However, it is argued that in societies where there is no equality of opportunity and there exist under-represented and marginalised groups, informal networking and the establishing of ties with strategically positioned bureaucrats may be the only avenue not only for political participation but also for access to basic services (ibid.: 163–6).

In the research communities women formed informal networks of assistance, which helped them learn about the procedures for application and what papers were needed for each welfare programme. In every area there were several natural leaders who informed the widows or divorcees of what to do as soon as these women became female heads or were in need. These natural leaders were themselves women heads of households of one type or another. Furthermore, although they played a central networking role in their communities they continued to portray themselves to officials as helpless and in need of protection.

Several of the women I met in the different areas were able to cultivate relationships with different key people who would facilitate their access to basic services. Aziza in 'The Ezba' was connected by marriage to a civil servant at the central offices of the Ministry of Social Affairs. She persuaded him to introduce her to the employees at the social unit in her district and used this contact to provide services to her friends and neighbours.

In a society where demands on the bureaucracy are relentless, it is vital that individuals and families have connections with local politicians or state bureaucrats. Such connections help resolve problems in coping with bureaucratic demands. Illiterate people and especially women rely on their more educated neighbours or friends in their informal networks to help them fill out the various forms and direct them to the right offices. It is customary for any individual to undertake many trips to various offices (and sometimes to the same office) around the city in order to finish one kind of business. The Egyptian bureaucracy is overburdened with thousands of daily requests and outdated work processes, which exhausts the patience of the underpaid employees (not to mention the applicants). It is thus a great asset to be connected to or to know any employee at the different ministries, thus resulting in quicker services, fewer visits to the offices, and fewer delays (ibid.: 215–17).

Close ties and networks are not always developed with only low-level bureaucrats. Several women I met, one of whom was my key informant, worked as local leaders for a female politician in 'The Ezba'. The community knew her close connection with the parliamentarian and it helped lift her status among her neighbours. Through this informal political network, Gihan, the local leader, received loans, publicly subsidised goods, an apartment in one of the areas for resettling earthquake victims and, finally, assistance with bureaucratic problems. She was also able to secure the widow's pension for her mother, a productive family loan from the Ministry of Social Affairs, and some financial assistance for her sister. She used a business card signed by the female politician to open all the doors with the social unit's employees. Gihan chose her informal networks and connections cleverly. Although most of the poor cannot develop networks with political figures, most do try to establish contacts with low-level bureaucrats who manage to facilitate their daily dealings with the government.

Exchange of favours This mechanism is not unknown in higher political arenas. In fact, it is called log-rolling in parliamentary negotiations in which one MP agrees to support another in exchange for future political support. Similarly, in the relationship between the employees and the women there was an exchange of favours. The applicant provides one type of favour to the employee and, in return, she is enrolled in the welfare programme.

This mechanism was applied in three of the areas studied (whether it is applied elsewhere I do not know). I learned about it after some time spent in different government offices while women were either receiving or applying for their pensions and also from my interviews with different women. Only two officials admitted that it went on.

The most popular form of exchange of favours was the 'running of errands'. Several of the women who applied to the different MOSA welfare programmes used to shop, clean, or do some sort of work for several of the officials. The running of errands mechanism included buying and cleaning vegetables, cleaning the homes of some employees, childcare, and even helping the employee's wife or family during big parties or family gatherings. It is true that these women were paid. However, the payment was usually much lower than the market rate in similar situations. In some cases, the women were paid in kind as they were given leftovers and only the transportation money. In return, the employees included such women in all old and new social aid programmes. They informed them before

The Politics of Exclusion

anyone else about increases or new bonuses that could be incurred during feasts or special occasions. They advised them and helped them gain access to other social aid services provided by big mosques, such as the Mustafa Mahmoud mosque, or big bank programmes, such as those of the Faysal Bank or Nasser Social Bank. They also helped them apply to these services and provided them with letters of recommendation. In addition, they helped them fill out financial aid applications to exempt their children from paying school fees.

The women interviewed who actually provided such services to several MOSA officials did not resent this relationship or consider it exploitative. On the contrary, they felt at an advantage with these officials as they were guaranteed privileged treatment. Women who were unable to establish such a relationship, whether due to their pride or shyness, resented both the providers of the domestic services and their recipients (the employees). They thought it demeaning and insulting to have to work as servants to government officials just to gain access to their rights. They claimed that MOSA employees ignored them and deliberately delayed their requests for assistance because they refused to be servants to them.

The following is what U'm Sayyeda told me about her encounter with some MOSA officials in 'The Tombs':

> Each time I go they make me wait for a long time and request different and new types of documents. I wondered why until I began to notice what was going on around me. They used to send the other women to buy them their breakfast or Pepsi for their guests. I did not participate in these errands and never offered my services. However, Mrs A. once asked me to go to her house and help her clean it. I got very hurt and upset and told her that my brothers and my sons would kill me if they found out I turned into a maid. Since then she has treated me even worse and I have been waiting for more than a year for the assistance to deserted wives to no avail. They want us as servants and I will never accept that. (U'm Sayyeda, 49, deserted wife, 'The Resettlement')

The different women who applied one or more of the coping mechanisms mentioned above are actual participants in the government programmes, and have have managed to get benefits from the state despite all the constraints. They have manipulated their self-image, used log-rolling to get more out of the officials, and developed networks to circumvent the tedious application procedures. In that sense, these women are not in the least acting as helpless victims but are resourceful women who have managed to maximise their benefits from the state welfare sector even if it meant some self-degradation by creating an image of helplessness or providing services to the officials.

Notes

1. It is important to note here that we are citing cases of discrimination against women by bureaucrats to show trends and highlight the types of issue faced by FHHs. However, this is not to not deny the fact that there are other cases where officials are not as harsh or prejudiced.

2. MOISA is the Ministry of Insurance and Social Affairs but is known as MOSA by the public in general.

3. In her study of credit programmes in Bangladesh Goetz (1996) found that the front-line bureaucrats can play a major role in obstructing the policies that they do not agree with.

4. However, it is also fair to say that these employees were underpaid and that they depended largely on unofficial financial gifts – bribes – from their clients in order to survive. Moreover, their working conditions were very poor. More than three employees shared one desk and there were not always enough chairs. In addition, they had to fill all forms manually and in many cases they had to borrow – or ask beneficiaries – to get pens and papers because the state did not supply them with the necessary stationery.

5. Personal communication with the official, July 1998.

6. Personal communication with several male government officials.

7. CDAs are people's organisations.

8. Chant (1997) found that FHHs in other countries in the world are perceived in the same way.

6

Beyond the Veil: Religion and Welfare

The main reason for dedicating a chapter to religious welfare programmes is that their presence was significant at all the research sites – especially the Islamic programmes. Although the existence of this shadow and parallel welfare system is an important phenomenon with a profound ideological impact on society, it has not been studied comprehensively, and the few in-depth and descriptive studies that exist are limited in their scope.[1] As we will see in this chapter, this system is more efficient, has better outreach, and is perceived as more desirable by some women. The implications of its impact in reinforcing and reasserting a traditional pattern of gender relations are serious.[2] This parallel system has the potential to undermine and perhaps even reverse the secular gains that women have achieved. In the slums, six-year-old girls are veiling to gain access to the 'orphan's sponsorship'[3] programme, a clear sign of these programmes at work. There is a need to examine the implicit assumptions about gender roles and the family that inform these programmes. The religious programmes interpret women's needs in a way that is as sexist and gendered as the state's social welfare system.

In this chapter, I describe several private non-governmental religious welfare programmes and examine their impact on the status and autonomy of FHHs. The two Islamic programmes studied are a nationwide orphan sponsorship programme administered by a non-governmental organisation (NGO)[4] called the Al-Jami'yya al-Sharii'yya and a personally run orphan sponsorship programme completely funded by a philanthropist, referred to here as the Haj.[5] The latter is only one of many such private programmes and by no means the largest or the most impressive. It is cited here as an example of the types of informal welfare programmes that exist and how they function. Finally, in order to present a more comprehensive profile of the religious welfare system, it was imperative to compare these Islamic welfare programmes and other programmes run by the Coptic Church. For this purpose, the welfare programmes of All Saints church in Cairo and the Virgin Mary's church in Alexandria were studied.[6]

Victims and Heroines

The questions investigated in this chapter include:

1. What are the main features of the religious programmes under investigation here? To what extent are they woman-friendly and to what extent do they further the marginalisation of women, and especially FHHs? Who is excluded from these programmes and why?
2. What are the main similarities and differences between Islamic-run and Coptic-run welfare programmes, especially in their perception of women and FHHs and their impact on their status?
3. What are the underlying assumptions at the base of these programmes?
4. How do women cope and make the best use they can of these programmes – in a way, exploiting them if they can maximise personal and family benefit?

Background and Historical Context

It is not possible to understand the importance and impact of the increasing numbers of religious NGOs and their relevant welfare programmes if one does not understand the political and social environment within which they operate. Since the early 1970s, the demand to reintroduce *Sharia'a*[7] to all aspects of life has been one of the main objectives of Egypt's Islamists. The state consented because it was unleashing the Islamists to curb the power and popularity of the left and the Nasserite groups, especially in the student unions of the national universities (Abdallah 1993: 29–32; Hatem 1992: 234).

In response to pressures of the growing Islamists and in an attempt to control and co-opt these groups Sadat incorporated *Sharia'a* into the 1971 Constitution. For the first time, it was stated that women and men have equal rights as long as it does not contradict *Sharia'a*. In addition, Sadat's regime in its early years supported publicly the different symbols of the Islamic movement. He was more tolerant of the *Da'awa* magazine – the Muslim Brotherhood official paper – than he was of the Communist party's (A'l-Tagm'u) *A'l-A'hali* paper and the Nasserite elements in the state and the national university. It was argued that the Sadat regime was seeking new allies and trying to establish a different social base than that of Nasser (Abdallah 1993; Hatem 1992; Badran 1991).[8]

Even the Egyptian political parties – whether the ruling or opposition parties – have been very ambivalent in their relationship with the Islamic groups. The Labour Party is currently in a very close coalition with a fundamentalist section of the Islamic camp. The Wafd (Delegation Party), which is essentially a capitalist party, has been in coalition with them. They side with the Islamist camp, forming alliances with it and adopting

Islamic slogans. Even the Unionist Party, the communist party of Egypt, has been very hesitant in identifying its position. This party once announced that it would not form any alliance against the growing strength of political Islam because it feels that the alliance should be against the USA, Israel and the government of parasites. Compared to these enemies, Islamic extremism is seen as a secondary danger that can be dealt with only by curing the main ills of Egyptian society (Flores 1993: 32–8). Thanks to the state's mistakes and miscalculations, the socialist Labour Party, which is in close alliance with the Islamist camp, is becoming a powerful pole for the radical but non-violent Islamist alternative in Egypt (Abdallah 1993: 30).

The state is unable to compete with these groups in union and syndicate elections.[9] They are usually very organised, have a strong outreach programme and are well financed. Furthermore, the government does not seriously disagree with many of their Islamic rules and regulations as long as these groups do not threaten its existence as a ruling class. So, when it is women who are attacked, the state and its apparatuses will not waste their resources in defending them. This appeases the Islamists, whose power increases, and also appeases the masses, who are more attuned to the Islamists due to their outreach programmes. The government will fight only if its survival and the class it protects are in jeopardy (Flores 1993: 36–7). For example, several attempts in the 1970s were made to modify the personal status law of marriage and divorce in order to be more just to women. The attempts of 1974 and 1976 were met with an uproar from the Islamic and conservative groups. In these two cases the state retreated. However, in 1979 Sadat unilaterally issued a new law that gave women more rights *vis-à-vis* their spouses in matters of divorce and custody.[10] However, in 1985 the law was repealed on the basis that it was unconstitutional. Instead a more conservative law was issued. This law 100 removed many of the gains women won in the 1979 law. The state succumbed to the pressures of the Islamic groups at the time in order to appease them and appease the growing conservative masses. In other words, the state was prepared to sacrifice women's secular rights for the purpose of placating the Islamist lobby.[11]

From all the above, it becomes clear that a determinant factor in the state's attitude towards women is Islam. Although there are several progressive efforts to reinterpret the place of women and gender in Islam, there is no doubt that when Islam is used by states or religious groups as a form of political expression, it curtails women's autonomy (White 1992: 14). Despite reforms permitting educational, juridical and state institutions greater autonomy from religious authorities, *Sharia'a*-inspired legislation in family and personal status codes persists even when secular laws have been adopted in every other sphere. Women's equal citizenship rights, guaranteed by the national constitutions, are circumscribed by personal laws granting men special privileges in the areas of marriage, divorce, custody, maintenance and inheritance (Badran 1991; Baden and Byrne 1996; Kandiyoti 1991b).

All established religions call for social solidarity and for mechanisms to help those in need. Concepts of mutual responsibility – such as assisting strangers in need and ensuring that the indigent and weak have a claim on the community – are shared by the Muslims and Christians of Egypt (Habib 1990: 89).

By the mid-nineteenth century, these religious feelings had translated themselves into the formation of private voluntary organisations (NGOs), which provided the poor with material support, education and homes for orphans and the handicapped (Ibrahim 1993: 53). The first religious NGOs established in Egypt were Islamic Charity (Al-Jami'iya A'l-Khairiiya A'l Islamia) in 1878, Coptic Charity (Jami'it al-Mas'aii A'l-Khairiiya Al Keptia) in 1881, and Tawfik Coptic (Jami'it A'l-Tawfik A'l-Keptia) in 1891.[12] The role of the first Coptic NGO was to provide assistance to the poor and to organise the collection of contributions from wealthy Copts. Its major achievement was the establishment of the Coptic hospital, which provided healthcare and other services to all the Egyptian poor: Muslims, Christians and Jews alike.[13] Several other Coptic NGOs were formed to address the social, cultural and religious needs and problems of the Copts in Egypt (Habib 1992: 160–2).

The significant rise in the number of religious NGOs in the second half of the nineteenth century was a response to the encroachment of Western Catholic and Protestant missionaries who attracted the Coptic and Jewish poor through the provision of social, medical and economic services. In response, Islamic and Christian NGOs emerged and provided similar services. By the First World War there were 20 Islamic and 11 Coptic NGOs, and their activities extended into the social and economic spheres as well (Kandil and Ben Nefise-Paris 1994: 52–4).

Until the 1952 revolution, Islamic and Coptic NGOs were the main – if not the only – source for the provision of social and welfare services. With the revolution, however, autonomous philanthropic work came to an end and the role of NGOs weakened as the new state incorporated social, political, economic and cultural activities within its institutions and system.

The philosophy of the new government was to hand down more socio-economic rights and privileges to the different marginalised groups through state agencies and state departments (Ibrahim 1996: 24–5). Nevertheless, the role of religious NGOs and congregations continued, but on a much smaller scale, paling in comparison to the national social policy of the 1952 government, which adopted the concepts of social equity and democracy. The voluntary sector's activities were restricted further in the 1960s under centralised social planning and the nationalisation of the voluntary hospitals (Ibrahim 1993, 1996; Kandil and Ben Nefise-Paris 1994).

With the demise of Nasser and the Pan-Arab project, which was the basis of the regime's legitimacy, in which Egypt situated itself at the centre and projected itself as the leader of the Arab world, the state was left in an ideological void. Sadat attempted to fill this gap by embarking on the road to economic liberalisation in conjunction with efforts to strengthen Egypt's links and ties to the West. These economic reforms, which brought momentary respite and growth in the 1970s, culminated in debt and a severe economic crisis by the early 1980s (Shukrallah 1991: 17–18). The state failed in its political project after the 1967 defeat; it failed in its economic project as the open-door policy led to an economic crisis; and it failed in its social project with the state's abdication of its social responsibilities. These failures resulted in a political, economic and social vacuum. The only political and social discourse left that was not discredited was the Islamic discourse (ibid.; Ibrahim 1980, 1988).

Meanwhile, by the end of the 1970s and Sadat's liberalisation policies, NGOs were being encouraged to resume their activities. Within such a liberal atmosphere, Coptic charities and Islamic institutions increased the scope of their direct services to the poor within their religious communities (Ibrahim 1993: 53–5). In the 1960s, Islamic NGOs constituted 16.57% of all registered NGOs. In the 1970s, this increased to 30.6%, and in the 1980s, Islamic NGOs constituted 32.83% of all NGOs (Kandil and Ben Nefise-Paris 1994: 99–103). Coptic organisations constituted 12.22% of all NGOs in the 1960s and 9% in 1991 (Assad and Rouchdy 1998: 59).[14]

Such Islamic organisations play a major role in Egypt's social and economic development. They have developed efficient social, economic and cultural services that target the poor and needy (Sullivan 1994: 65). Many Egyptians look to these religious associations and not to government institutions for support and assistance. It is argued that as the Islamic NGOs, in particular, gain ground with the people, the legitimacy of the government could be discredited (ibid.: 66). In the eyes of the beneficiaries, these NGOs represent Islam and, thus, the 'Islamic alternative'[15] to the current economic and social policies of the state. This identification with the Islamic alternative poses a problem not only to the state but also to women. First, the Islamic alternative is positioned as diametrically opposed to and a substitute for the state. Hence any increase in its legitimacy means a reduction in the state's credibility. Second, the Islamic alternative is infused with traditional and patriarchal norms regarding gender relations and consequently impacts heavily on women's status and position.

On the other hand, the Coptic Church's approach to women, especially FHHs, is not any different from that of the Islamic NGOs, as will be shown later in this chapter. These religious NGOs pose no threat to the state on gender grounds. Indeed, they support a gendered ideology about the family, which furthers the marginalisation of women.

The following sections will group my findings and observations about all the religious welfare programmes studied under three main themes:

1. the main features and similarities among the studied programmes in terms of type of services offered, groups targeted, and the way they operate;
2. the underlying assumptions about the family and women's role that are the ideological cornerstone of these programmes; and
3. the impact of these programmes on women, how they exclude certain FHHs, and how women and especially FHHs subvert and exploit these programmes.

The Main Features of the Religious Programmes

While a large number of private voluntary organisations are independent, others are part of networks. The most famous of the Islamic NGOs, one that has its own widespread network throughout Egypt, is the Al-Jam'iyya al-Shari'iyya li a'l a'milin bi a'l-kitab wa a'l sunna a'l muhammadyya-Shari'iyya (the Lawful Religious Association for those who Behave According to the Book and al-Sunna). This NGO has a branch in each of Egypt's 26 governorates and 123 branches in Cairo alone. The Shari'iyya NGO owns hospitals and health clinics, libraries, and other service-oriented institutions (Sullivan 1994: 80–4).

The activities of this NGO are divided into three main categories; clear religious activities to spread the word of God; provision of basic services to the needy; and the provision of social and welfare programmes that aim at strengthening ties between Muslims (Shari'iyya Annual Report 1996).[16] These activities and services overlap in the different communities because they work, as the NGO board believes, in a comprehensive approach towards building 'the Muslim character'. The main sub-activity of this NGO that is highlighted in this chapter is the Kafalet al-Yateem (National Orphan Sponsorship Programme), which targets children who have lost their fathers. It provides them with regular financial assistance, school fees, and food and clothing during Ramadan and the feasts, among other things. This programme works through 1,129 mosques all over Egypt and reached 230,000[17] beneficiaries in 1996 alone. The programme's total cost in 1996 was LE84,042,000,[18] or approximately LE7,004,000 per month.[19]

The second Islamic programme studied is the personally run sponsorship programme for orphans. It was begun in 1993 by a wealthy man called the Haj. This programme sponsored 80 cases in 'The Squatters' and 100 cases in 'The Tombs'. Its female administrators stated that the programme operates in five other low-income urban areas that lack basic services. The Haj spends between LE 8,000 and LE10,000 every month. This programme offers the same activities and, with some exceptions, targets the same group as the Kafalet A'l Yateem programme of the Shari'iyya NGO.[20]

I also studied two Coptic welfare programmes of All Saints church in Cairo and the Virgin Mary's church in Alexandria.[21] The main reasons for selecting these two churches was accessibility. Being a Muslim woman made interviewing in the Coptic cathedral, for example, very difficult, but through my personal contacts I was able to reach these two churches.[22]

The church of All Saints is located in a poor over-populated district in Cairo and is looked after by a priest. It serves only the four streets around it or, as stated in administrative terms, the sub-district it supports. Mme Terez works under the priest as a social worker. She volunteers her time for the poor and is responsible for managing the social welfare and charity programme. Together, the priest and Mme Terez started an outreach programme that employs 55 volunteers known as *khadimat*, or servants of the church. The majority of the *khadimat* are young women, although some men also participate. The services of this church include religious and spiritual guidance and regular pensions to orphans and widows. The church also offers in-kind assistance such as food, housing needs, clothing for wives and families of men who are drug addicts, financial assistance to families of men who are very sick or invalids, school fees for orphans and very needy children, and pocket money for university students from destitute families. Mme Terez refused to tell me how much they spend. However, my Coptic contact was able to get an approximate figure of LE160,000 per month. However, according to my own calculations, the total amount spent per month was LE260,400 in one church.[23] This discrepancy is the result of the secrecy with which the churches guard their finances because they, like the Islamic groups in Egypt, feel threatened by the state and are under constant heavy scrutiny.

Situated in a slum area in Alexandria, the church of the Virgin Mary is managed by a priest who used to be a physician. This church looks after the Copts of several squatter and slum areas in the city. It has adopted an outreach type of operation, and has opened branches and outlets in the different squatter areas that are not near the church. The church's activities include spiritual services and religious preaching; health and medical services, including subsidised check-ups and medication; and emergency assistance in case of death in the family, operations, and debt leading to imprisonment (where the church pays the debt on behalf of the debtor). Financial aid and in-kind assistance – usually donations of winter and summer clothing during religious feasts such as Coptic Christmas on 7 January and Easter in April – are also available to orphans and widows. In addition, the church provides orphans, their families and widows with school uniforms at the beginning of the school year and food during feasts. This church spent an estimated total of LE70,800 in 1996.

Gender Exclusions: Assumptions Shaping Programme Design and Delivery

To understand the ideologies of these religious welfare programmes it is important to highlight the underlying assumptions that inform them. It is equally important to study how they operate and whether their internal processes, conditions and procedures result in excluding, stigmatising and furthering the marginalisation of women, and especially FHHs. In Chapter 5, Martin Greeley's 1996 framework for explaining why certain groups, especially women, are excluded from credit programmes was adapted to explain why and how women, especially FHHs, were excluded from accessing the state's social and public services. The same framework will be used in this chapter. To reiterate, Greeley has classified two forms of exclusion: programme-driven and self-driven (1996).

Programme-driven exclusion All the religious welfare programmes – whether Christian or Islamic – shared common and similar factors that constituted an obstacle for various groups, especially FHHs, and thus led to their exclusion from joining them. Through my fieldwork, I was able to identify three main factors shared by all the programmes studied that produced this result:

1. definitions and perceptions of family structures;
2. conditions and procedures for eligibility; and
3. outreach and coverage.

Definitions and perceptions of family structures In Islam, women and men are considered equal in front of God and their rewards and punishments are also equal for identical deeds. However, due to the patriarchal social system at the time of the prophet, a woman's financial survival depended on the provision of her male kin.[24] In that sense, families were considered male-headed. There was no conception of a family where the woman is the sole or main breadwinner; she was viewed as the provider of comfort and care to her husband and children. The man was seen as the only provider of financial maintenance and the representative of family needs in the outside world. These beliefs and assumptions were also shared by the male and female employees of the two Islamic-run orphan sponsorship programmes (the Shari'yya NGO and the Haj programme). As one woman said:

> No, they at the mosque refused to give me any assistance. They said that my husband is alive and that my children are his responsibility, and that I should and will soon find another man who will take care of me. No, I am not a widow, I am a divorcee. (Fathia, 28, divorcee, 'The Shelters')

As one administrator said:

> No, only very few families have a woman who is totally responsible. You do not know the real Egyptians. No man in a family will let his sister or sister-in-law work and degrade herself. There is always someone who takes care of her, even if he is her young son. (male administrator of the national programme, Kafalet al-Yateem, 'The Tombs')

This assumption of the male-headed family still persists. It is, therefore, not surprising that Islamic welfare programmes define orphans as children who have lost their fathers and not their mothers.

The story of Naglaa shows how the bias towards describing men as the main providers is no longer valid. Naglaa is 16 years old. Her mother divorced her father eleven years ago and she was brought up by a stepfather whom she considered to be more like a real father to her. She rarely sees her father, who left their district and now lives in another governorate. Naglaa has four sisters and three stepbrothers. Three years ago, Naglaa's stepfather died, followed one year later by her mother. Naglaa became responsible for a family of eight, including herself. The mosque could not help her through the Kafalet al-Yateem because her father is still alive. Only her three stepbrothers are eligible for the assistance. She was forced to leave school and go to work. She is not eligible for any assistance, either from the state or from the mosque, for she is not an orphan.

The Coptic programmes used the same definitions for orphans. In Cairo, the churches assisted families of drug addicts and sick men because it was recognised that the male provider was unable to carry out his financial responsibilities. Any church assistance to daughters or widows ceased once they married. As the social worker in the church stated:

> After she gets married she is *fi ra'abit ragil*.[25] In other words, she becomes the responsibility of a man, her husband. (Mme Terez, church of All Saints)

Officially, it is only the father who is recognised as a source of income for the family, even if this is not so in reality. In addition, although the employees and volunteers of both churches claim that they help all those in need, 85% of the recipients in Cairo and 80% of the recipients in Alexandria are widows. Further, only widows are allowed into the weekly religious classes, and the payment of their monthly financial stipend is contingent on their attendance at these classes.

The Islamic sponsorship programmes set implicit controls on women's sexuality by subtly penalising those women who seek and obtain a divorce – either through outright exclusion from benefits or through stigmatisation. Their claim is that a woman should endure any hardship to keep her family intact and that divorce is the woman's fault. Thus they exclude single and especially divorced women from their programmes. This is how one administrator from the Islamic NGO put it:

> No, this is how we think and it is right. A divorcee could have stayed to take care of the children and not get herself divorced, or she could remarry. A young widow will always find a man to marry her or male kin to take care of her ... but the children who have become orphans need protection. God advised us to take care of orphans. According to our religion and culture men take care of the women of the family. (male administrator of the national Kafalet al-Yateem, 'The Squatters')

These interpretations of women's needs are sexist and are based on the assumption that men are the heads of the households and the only financial providers. By offering a gendered reinterpretation of the needs of these women, these programmes have reinforced traditional meanings that render women secondary and dependent.

Conditions and procedures for eligibility In order to qualify for assistance from religious welfare programmes, applicants must conform to expectations about gendered roles. In the case of the Haj's personally run orphan sponsorship programme, all girls beginning at six years of age had to cover their hair and shoulders in the photographs attached to their application forms. This behaviour was encouraged in the religious classes for the young, mainly through the clothes – ankle-length dresses and a *khemar* – that this programme provided for the girls. Young recipients received three such sets of clothing during the year: one for the summer season, one for winter and one during the Bayram.[26] Given their economic situation, these were the only new clothes they received. In 'The Shelters' and 'The Bedouins' women found that condition unacceptable. They believed that they were sufficiently pious and that their traditional dress was respectable enough. They resented the insinuations made about what the administrators labelled as 'undisciplined attire', meaning anything that did not conform to the Islamic dress code.

Another condition that excluded a large number of women was the requirement that mothers hold an identity card. Women had to present their ID card, the death certificate of their husband, and the birth certificates of their children in order to be eligible for any assistance. Although this requirement was not as strictly applied in these two programmes as it was in MOSA offices, compliance varied from one area to another depending on the discretion of the social workers and administrators. In all the programmes discussed thus far – whether governmental or not – this is one basic condition for the provision of the service. However, given that a majority of illiterate single women do not posses ID cards, these programmes exclude a significant number of eligible women clients. Yet they still deal with this problem as an exception and exempt some women from such a requirement only from sympathy or because they know the woman and her situation.

Outreach Although the religious welfare programmes have successful outreach, they still do not have a regular and systematic process for women and the poor to follow to ensure easy access to their services. In other words, access is not a right, nor is coverage comprehensive for most women: it depends to some extent on the arbitrary circumstance of word of mouth. With regard to the Islamic programmes, a large number of veiled women had visitors come to their own homes to inform them about the services of the mosques. But the other 'commonly dressed women' learned about these services from a neighbour or relative, by word of mouth, or never knew about the service at all. Apparently, the outreach programme was more effective with women who conformed to the Islamic dress code. In short, programmes are selective and biased, with rules of membership that force women to conform to religious orthodoxy.

In the case of the two churches, again word of mouth, attending religious classes, family and friends were the main sources of information for FHHs about the services. Here too the degree of piety, and consistency in attending church services, were conditions for eligibility. In all the programmes, women's sexuality and their adherence to customs and traditions were factors that affected their access to the different services.[27]

Self-driven exclusion Self-exclusion occurs when the potential target person herself decides not to apply to the programme because she believes that she cannot participate. Women's reluctance to participate in such programmes could be related to a number of factors, such as how the target group perceives itself or how it thinks others will perceive it, or the women's belief that participating in these programmes will stigmatise them.

Perception of FHHs and their relationship to the religious programmes Some of the women interviewed in the different areas reported that they did not apply to any of the Islamic-run orphan sponsorship programmes and they did not want to apply. In Alexandria, in 'The Bedouins' and 'The Resettlement' areas, a large number of women stated that only beggars and the destitute go to the mosque for charity, *hassanah*, and that it is not respectable to be seen begging from the mosque. In 'The Shelters', two main reasons were mentioned for this self-driven exclusion. The first was the notion that the Sheikh and his entourage served only their own people. There were rumours that the administrator of the programme was corrupt and that only his relatives, friends and those in his good grace received any help. The second reason the women interviewed gave for refusing not only the financial assistance but also the school supplies assistance distributed by the Islamists was that they did not want to open their homes to the fundamentalists. The following two quotes show the attitude of some women towards Islamic programmes:

> Those Sunnis are widespread here and they want to recruit more youths. If I accept their help then they will begin laying down conditions and will try to recruit my son. I do not want problems with the government. (U'm Khaled, 45, widow, 'The Shelters')

> If we take their money they will ask us to pray and wear a veil. We do not want that, we want our freedom. (U'm Saber, 44, wife of an *'urzu'i*, 'The Shelters')

Some of the women refused to join the programme because they felt it was humiliating and stigmatising to be associated with it. Others feared being associated with the fundamentalists, who are considered outlaws by the state and, obviously, by some women as well.

In 'The Tombs', a large number of women joined, but those who refused to join or who dropped out were angry at the management style and the system. The following citation shows the anger of one interviewee towards some religious programmes:

> They send their people to the veiled women only, those totally covered in black or grey, and they ignore us. I have the traditional rural scarf over my head and I do not want to wear the veil. So they punish me by ignoring my application or by making me wait. (Sabah, 33, widow, 'The Tombs')

How Women Subvert the System

In spite of regulations and checks and balances, the field research showed that these women have learned to subvert the system. With regard to the Haj's personally run Islamic orphan sponsorship programme, a particular incident is selected to demonstrate how poor and illiterate women were able subvert some rules in order to access the service.

One day in May when I was in the mosque of 'The Tombs' helping one administrator, U'm Ali, count the money and keep a record of who was receiving payment, U'm Haytham came upstairs shouting and asking us to stop all payments. Three months earlier, the two administrators had begun a system of disbursing money based on a person's attire. The first to receive payments would be those who were totally veiled, followed by those wearing the *khemar* and finally those who wore only a traditional cover over their hair, whom they considered undisciplined (*ghair multazimin*). This decision was reached because one day in February many women came to get their money, creating turmoil. The payment took place at the time of the mid-day prayer. The administrators got very angry that many of the women did not pray but waited outside until the prayer was finished and then went in to collect their money. The administrators also began to notice that fewer women attended the Saturday religion classes although they were told it was a prerequisite for receiving the monthly stipend.

The women recipients did not welcome this new system because it delayed many of them. A long delay could prevent them from going to work or running an important errand, perhaps causing them to lose a day's wages. They preferred the old system whereby they were paid according to alphabetical order by name.

On that day in May, U'm Haytham noticed that many women were wearing the *khemar* and was happy about it:

> I went down to encourage these women to come to the classes and to show them how happy I am that they began wearing the *khemar*. I discovered that these women were cheating us in the home of God, in the mosque. I found that they are exchanging one head cover downstairs among themselves to ensure that they get their payments quickly.

This is a very clear example of how women were able to subvert the system and manipulate its symbols and discourse to their own end. They realised that their attire could make a difference to the administrators and decided to appease them, even if for a short while. They saw what they did not as unethical or unreligious but as a necessity to overcome an obstacle. As U'm Nagah put it clearly:

> At the beginning they used to read out our names alphabetically and give us the money and that was fair. But now it is not fair. I have a scarf over my hair and I pray. I am a good Muslim. If they chose to be unfair then they deserve to be lied to. (U'm Nagah, widow, 'The Tombs')

As for the Coptic programmes, I met only five women who were beneficiaries of the Cairo church and I met them only once. Being a Muslim from outside the area was not very helpful and I do not think that they were comfortable talking to me. However, I met 40 Christian women in the seven low-income areas of Cairo and Alexandria with whom I established very close and friendly relationships. Thirty-five of those women were widows and five were unable to locate their husbands.

I did not find any differences between the women, whether Christian or Muslim, in their perceptions and attitudes towards the different welfare programmes. They all found themselves in a situation where they were responsible for their families and had to fend for themselves. They all adopted the same coping mechanisms, not only with their husbands but also with their communities at large and the state. The oppressive rituals to contain women's sexuality and social development were applied to all women, regardless of their religion, and all had to conform to what society at large expected of them.

Like U'm Saber, U'm Nagah and other Muslim women, poor illiterate Christian women also subverted the system by adopting the required image of being poor, helpless, sick and in need of guidance. The five women I interviewed from the church of All Saints in Cairo introduced themselves to me as lonely, sick and poor women who are in need of assistance. The 40 women I knew, several of whom were quite active and strong, also presented themselves to me and to the church in the same manner.

The Politics of Needs Interpretation

When comparing the approaches, attitudes and assumptions of the different religious welfare programmes regarding women, clear similarities appear. Many traditional customs and rituals are associated with Islam and Muslims in Egypt and the Arab world. Among such rituals are the circumcision of girls and the *dukhla baladi*, or manual deflowering on the wedding night. I found that both the Muslims and the Christians (Copts) of the seven low-income areas of my research observe the same traditions and rituals regardless of their religious beliefs.

I also found that the attitudes of the social workers and administrators of the two Coptic programmes towards women and FHHs were nearly identical to those of the administrators of the Islamic programmes. Both systems have the same underlying assumptions and beliefs regarding women's role and status within their family and community. Both religious programmes hold the view that a woman is a female head only when her husband dies or is lost and she cannot reach him, i.e. when the husband is physically absent from his home and is no longer heard from. Apart from widows, neither system considers the needs of other types of FHHs identified by this study.

The religious programmes – in consonance with the state's welfare programmes – also reinterpret women's needs and define their identities and roles. Religious and state programmes also follow similar interpretations, and their definitions are gendered and reinforce women's subordinate position. Their interpretation of women's needs institutionalises patriarchal and discriminatory norms and values that give women secondary and dependent status. Because these religious programmes are non-contributory, they share many similarities to the state's 'secondary' sub-system. They target the destitute and the needy and treat the beneficiaries not as rights-bearers but as those in need of assistance or charity. The administrators pity them. Although the administrators of the religious programmes, unlike government officials, are not condescending towards their clients, they nevertheless do not show them respect or deference.

Applicants must conform to a need that is defined and interpreted by the administrators of these programmes. These programmes have established sexist criteria for eligibility. Divorced and deserted women do not qualify for these programmes as they are seen as deviant and unworthy. Both systems impose implicit (symbolic) constraints on women's sexuality: by accepting only widows and abandoned women as legitimately in need of help and by requiring conservative personal behaviour both programmes look with disdain on wives who prefer separation or divorce. To be eligible for benefits, women have to prove that they conform to a code of ethics and dress that is deemed appropriate and disciplined by the administrators of the religious programmes, Islamic or Coptic. In addition, these programmes interpret women's needs as subsumed to their families' and children's needs. While they target the children or the family with their assistance, it is the women who must comply with their constraining and gendered conditions. These programmes have positioned women as mothers only.

While bureaucracies use ostensibly rational and objective language to de-politicise and marginalise the politics of interpreting women's needs, the religious welfare programmes disguise the political implications of reinterpreting needs and identities of their subjects behind dogmatic slogans and religious misconceptions. For example, divorcees in Islam are not condemned as the two non-governmental Islamic programmes lead us to believe. Several of the prophet's sayings, the *hadith*, show that women have the right to initiate divorce if they are unhappy in their marriages. The prophet himself married a divorced woman, which is a sign that they should not be punished for their marital status.

The dogmatic and allegedly religious language of such programmes imposes an aura of legitimacy over their interpretations, which makes their assumptions seem natural and pre-given. By adhering to the belief that these interpretations are not contested, women's position and status is compromised.

The four religious programmes mentioned above are only a small example of the informal welfare systems that run parallel to the state system. Their presence and outreach in the areas of my research were much greater than I had expected and they were welcomed by the majority of the people, with rare exceptions. They are perceived as good people who volunteer their time to help others. In this context the government bureaucrat, who should be a servant of the people, being paid by the state to serve them, is perceived as abusing his or her power. When comparing the religious programmes to the state's, especially the MOSA system, people clearly appreciated and respected the efforts of the non-governmental programmes.

It is also vital to highlight that great amounts of money are being spent by these programmes and that their organisation is highly sophisticated. I was able to estimate the costs of the national Kafalet al-Yateem project, and was astounded by the amount spent. While MOSA's budget for 1996/97 for social aid and pensions was around LE32 million as per their annual report, the Shari'iyya NGO as per their annual report spent LE84,042,000 on one of its many sub-activities.[28] The estimated, though not verified, cost of the Haj programme, according to its administrator, was an average of LE8,000 per month or LE96,000 per year. This is a tremendous amount of money spent on charity by one individual. If we take into consideration that there are hundreds of similar programmes, then the amounts could be enormous.

This chapter has given only a glimpse of the activities of two Islamic and two Coptic welfare programmes. There is a need to carry out more focused and comprehensive research on the different Islamic and Coptic welfare programmes in order to demonstrate the magnitude of this shadow and parallel welfare system.

Notes

1. For the most comprehensive studies on religious and Islamic NGOs and groups in Egypt see Latowsky 1995; Sullivan 1994; Habib 1990a, 1991, 1992; Kandil and Ben Nefise-Paris 1994; Ibrahim 1988, 1980.

2. One of the programmes run by Islamic NGOs.

3. This was intensified in the 1980s, when large Islamic corporations, 'god's bankers', and owners of the Islam Investment Corporation emerged. These institutions were very influential in the Egyptian financial markets.

4. An NGO is a legal entity that is managed by a board of directors. Its funds are considered public money for which the NGO is responsible.

5. *Haj* is the term given to a man who made the pilgrimage to Mecca.

6. I have given them new names at the request of the priests in the two churches.

Beyond the Veil

7. Islamic law and regulations are known as *Sharia'a*, i.e. legislation.

8. To gain more legitimacy Sadat began a campaign known as de-Nasserisation whereby he began a process of undermining Nasser's achievements. One tactic was supporting the Islamists in University and Syndicate elections. This proved to be a detrimental policy since it was these same groups who conspired to assassinate him in 1981.

9. In the last 20 years Islamic groups have penetrated all the professional syndicates.

10. This law was labelled Gihan al-Sadat law because it was claimed that his wife pushed him to issue it. He chose the unilateral decree venue because there were many objections from the Islamic elements in the parliament and he feared they would not let the law pass, as in the earlier incidents.

11. For more on the legal rights of Egyptian women and especially with regards to the personal status law see Bibars 1988; Baden and Byrne 1996; Badran 1990.

12. *Tawfik* means success and prosperity.

13. In 1908 this NGO was renamed the Coptic Charity Organisation. It also provided free education and regular financial assistance to poor Coptic families.

14. In a study on Islamic NGOs in Egypt, Sarah Ben Nefise-Paris defined them as those that centre around a religious and Islamic activity such as Quran recital, those that centre around a mosque, and those that have the word Islamic in their name (Ben Nefise-Paris in Shukrallah 1991: 45). I have found that the same kinds of distinctions apply to Coptic and Christian NGOs.

15. This concept of the Islamic alternative was first used by Shukrallah 1991 and Sullivan 1994.

16. This is the Annual Report of the Al-Jami'iyya al-Shari'iyya li a'l a'milin bi a'l kitab wa a'l sunna a'l muhammadyya-Shari'iyya (The Lawful Religious Association for those who Behave According to the Book and al-Sunna).

17. While MOSA reached 216,000 people in 1996.

18. Exchange rate US$ 1 = LE3.42/£1 = LE5.5

19. I have not calculated the private tutoring or medical treatment costs and have used conservative estimates for all costs in general.

20. Conditions for eligibility and the procedures, activities and services of this privately run programme are based on the national Kafalet al-Yateem model, with very few exceptions..

21. In both cases my key informants, who worked for the churches, as well as my Coptic contacts asked me to keep the identity of the churches confidential.

22. I worked for an American NGO, Catholic Relief Services (CRS), for many years. Through my work there I established close friendships with high-level clergymen in the Catholic and Coptic churches.

23. This is the cost of the social welfare programme of one church.

24. There are some exceptions. Khadiga, the Prophet's first wife, is one of them, as she was a businesswoman.

25. Literally meaning 'attached to the neck of a husband'.

26. The Bayram is the Western name for the Islamic feast after the month of fasting known as Ramadan.

27. Single mothers out of wedlock are not recognised by any of the above programmes, as their situation challenges existing traditions regarding women's sexuality and proper behaviour.

28. The complete budget for MOSA for the fiscal year 1996/97 was LE113,668,000, which includes salaries for their staff all over Egypt, material, running costs, social aid and other projects.

7
Women as Victims, Women as Survivors?

This chapter gives voice to the opinions and concerns of eight women heads of households, drawing on interviews with women in the different areas of Cairo and Alexandria. The stories told to me by these women were important for my research, whether they be fact or fantasy. The stories in themselves reveal how these women perceive themselves and how they believe they are perceived by their community. However, it is important to note that what is presented here is also affected by my own perception of these women, their stories and how they affected me.

Who are these Women and Why did I Choose their Stories?

The women whose cases are presented here are the children of working-class rural immigrants, and live in low-income working-class neighbourhoods. What these case-studies and life histories reveal is that women in general face different types of oppression at different periods and stages of their lives. A woman's misery begins with female genital mutilation (FGM) which entails physical mutilation as well as an invasion of privacy. This is followed by early marriage, which entails the ritual of manual deflowering of the young bride by a third party on her wedding night (*dukhla baladi*). These stories demonstrate how women are discriminated against as young children and later as adults by their families, their spouses and society at large. They also demonstrate how society prescribes and proscribes certain roles for women in order for them to achieve respectability. Finally, the stories show how these women cope with and occasionally subvert all these conditions. This chapter is also intended to show how women experience state welfare measures, and to assess how far these measures are of any real help to them. I will highlight in the following sections and through these women's stories how their own interpretations of their own needs differ from the state's interpretations.

Similarities and Differences Between the Women

Several concepts kept reappearing during my interviews with the women, and I found that these concepts divided the women into sub-groups. There were the 'heroines' – resourceful women who managed to undermine and overcome many pressures and use the disadvantages to their benefit. They underwent the same experiences as the other women, but were able to stand up and oppose what they believed was threatening to their survival. Among this first group I have included U'm Saber, Hedeya and U'm Nagah.[1] The second group includes those young women who became the backbone of their natal families. They were women heads of households because their fathers chose to rely on them to maintain the family. These women introduced me to the concept of *a'b a'si*, the 'cruel father', who leaves his daughter to fend for herself and the family and offers no appreciation of her contribution. Both Shadia and U'lfat were exploited early on by their fathers and used as a source of income to maintain the family. Both their fathers gave up the role of protector and provider for the family. They nevertheless expected their daughters to be obedient and to comply with the family ethos. Shadia's father sent her to work as a servant when she was six years old. Later on, he wanted to marry her off to a much older man to make money out of the marriage.

U'lfat's father also exploited his daughter, not only by sending her out to work instead of working himself, but by engaging her to several men in order to use the engagement as a pretext for borrowing money and expensive gifts from the potential grooms. Normally, such behaviour is unheard of. In Egypt, a father's main concern is to protect the reputation and honour of his female family members in order to protect his family's honour. Both of these men were described by their daughters as ruthless and heartless: 'A'buuya dah ragil a'si, ma'andush a'lb', 'My father is a ruthless man who has no heart' was a sentence repeated many times by each girl as they recounted their stories to me.

Another shared situation among the interviewed women was the notion of the 'useless' husband. The women mentioned this when they were asked about their husbands' profession or job: 'lamua'khdha malush lazma', meaning 'excuse me he is useless'. Many of the interviewed women who were married to *u'rzu'i* men – those with no regular job, few skills and who are regularly unemployed – described their husbands as useless when they ceased to provide for their families.

When I probed into this description and tried to learn what it really meant to these women, I discovered that they mainly use such a term to describe men who no longer provide money for the family. Sex roles were very clearly delineated in the minds of both the women and the men interviewed. Men were expected to bear the financial responsibility of the family. They were expected to work hard, and to respond to all the financial needs and requests of their wives and children. Women were expected to take care of their husbands, their homes and their children. They were expected to keep a calm and comfortable environment for their hardworking men. This comfortable environment included not only domestic duties and childcare, but sexual duties as well.

Women saw men's value in their ability to provide for them and protect them from need: 'E'l ragil lazim yekafi baytuh wi meratuh' means 'the husband must keep his wife and family financially satisfied'. He is also expected to keep his wife sexually satisfied or content. However, in most of the cases mentioned, a man's uselessness was related to his inability or incapacity to perform his financial role rather than his sexual role. In the very few cases when women were described by their husbands as useless, it meant that the women were not always ready for their husbands' sexual advances. Women also described themselves as useless if they did not comply with their husbands' sexual requests. In that sense, women saw the primary value of men as financial, and believed that their own primary role was sexual.

I was surprised by the prevalence of instances when it was the father or husband who was exploitative and useless, especially in a culture and society where men are portrayed and like to portray themselves as 'macho', 'the masters' and 'the protectors'. It seems that men have begun to abdicate this traditional role recently. While some of the men in these case-studies were truly obliged to rely on women due to sickness or calamity, many others opted not to work and chose to live off their daughters and/or wives.

In a society where men condemn and resent women's work, where working women are looked down on and their children are pitied for being neglected, I was unprepared to discover that fathers and husbands are often the main players in encouraging their women to work. It is true that the informal labour market is pushing out men and attracting lower-paid women. However, men, at least the husbands in my sample, were not adapting themselves to the changing situation. In many of the cases studied, when the men were laid off or their salaries decreased, their egos could not tolerate this degrading treatment. In contrast, women accepted lower pay and more demeaning jobs as a matter of course. Unlike middle-class men, who may reject the idea of their wives working to avoid being seen as incapable of providing for their families, the low-income men whom I researched appeared to have no qualms about allowing their women to work.

This was a very surprising discovery. Middle-class perceptions of working-class men and the lower middle class are very different. The middle class, where I come from, is under the impression that working-class men will not allow their wives to work because it implies, in their customs, that they are not 'men enough'. My interviews with the male leaders of the different communities support this view. I interviewed 25 men in the different communities who represented different class structures and whose attitudes towards their women's work were unanimous. They all rejected the idea that their wives could work, although for different reasons. More than half of these men, especially those from the lower middle class and the rural immigrant working class, saw women's work as a potential threat to men's supremacy at home. This quote shows how certain men perceive women's work:

> If the woman goes to work she will ride on the man as she rides on a donkey (*Lau el sit kharagit lilshughul ha tirkab i'l ragil wi tidaldil rigleha*). (Iskander, mechanic, 55, 'The Shelters')

> If the woman goes out to work, she will meet other men and she will feel that her man is not man enough, and that she is equal to him and she could then answer him back in a fight. (Taha, mechanic, 49 years old, 'The Squatters')

The more educated and wealthier men and the civil servants whom I interviewed refused to let their women work for different reasons:

> *Ily yu'ozu il bayit yehram ala il gami'a*, what the house needs is forbidden to be given to the mosque. Women are needed to take care of the children. The mother's presence is better than any school. (Galal, 59, merchant, 'The Shelters')

This attitude about women's work was shared by many of the men and women interviewed. In spite of this, I was surprised to learn that a growing number of men are abdicating their traditional role. Such men were looked down upon and have lost the respect of other men and women in the community. As one male interviewee said:

> The man who stays home and lets his wife go out to the street is not a man. He is not a man. Excuse me, he is a wench ('Dah mish ragil lamukahdha dah yiba'a maraah') (Fekri, 45, policeman, 'The Shelters')

As noted earlier, I have grouped the cases to fit into the framework of this chapter. There were several women whom I perceived as resourceful and who were brave heroines in my eyes. These women included U'm Saber, U'm Nagah and Hedeya. The second sub-section tells the story of Kesma, who was pressured by her husband to play multiple roles. This is not to say that the other women were not playing such roles, but that she thought that her husband's demands, especially his sexual demands, were uncalled for. She felt that she as a woman was forced to provide for the family and thus was turned into a man. Kesma put it very well when she said, 'These men want us to be men by day and women by night.' She clearly refused, opposed and resisted the process of becoming the financial head of the household. The third sub-section is made up of women who are the wives of 'useless' men. Intisar and Hanan fall into this category. The fourth sub-section includes exploited daughters, Shadia and U'lfat, whom I call daughters of a lesser God, and who called each other daughters of 'cruel fathers with no heart' (*A'b a'si malush a'lb*).

Resourceful Women: Heroines?

U'm Saber U'm Saber sought me out and became one of my most important and reliable informants in her community. She decided that I would become a member of her family, and she involved me in their daily problems. She also involved herself, without invitation, in my life. She gave me advice about my sexual relationship with my husband, and told me what I should do and wear to become more appealing to him.

But who is U'm Saber? She is a representation of what is known in Egyptian culture as *bint al-balad*, which literally means the daughter of the country. This phrase actually refers to strong, generous, helpful and reliable Egyptian people. U'm Saber is an example of low-income urban women who control their lives as much as any poor person can. This is how she described her life:

> My real name is Hoba, though not very many women are called that. I have two sisters and a brother, but they have always relied on me. My father was a great man and, while he was alive, we never needed anyone. My mother was a traditional woman; she loved my brother more than any of us.
>
> I was married in one room with only a bed and nothing else. When we were first married, he made 50 piasters per day. It reached 20 pounds last year. However, now he works one day and then stops working for weeks at a time.
>
> I have two girls and a boy. My sister Sakina is younger than I am. My sister is very naive; she is not as practical or knowledgeable as I am; I am the one who really knows how to get around. My father trusted me and knew that I would be able to solve problems when they arose.

U'm Saber chose the role of the matriarch, the chief of her family, of her own will. She was not only responsible for her husband and children but also took care of her brother-in-law and her parents as they grew old and sick. U'm Saber has the personality of a self-taught leader who has learned to get what she wants. She is very intelligent and knows her way around.

When my brother-in-law, A'm Mustafa [Uncle Mustafa], fell sick I had to take care of him. Reda, his eldest daughter, is now 25. I decided to marry her off to the man she loves and will help them with the furniture and everything. I have asked the international NGO that works here to provide Reda with a bed and a stove. They do that for needy people. I work with them sometimes as a natural leader and they know and trust me. I also contacted Mr M. from the local NGO where you yourself work. I asked them to help Reda to build and paint the room where she will be married, and Mr M. has agreed.

U'm Saber is also very resourceful, and she has learned to take advantage of any and all situations:

I am around 44 years old and I have been married for 25 years. When we first moved here, we had a nicer flat in one of the better houses. This current house is really illegal, and we built it ourselves. We started by building one room, but now we have a kitchen, another room where Saber will be married, and we have also built a room on the roof for the girls.

U'm Saber, like many poor people, tries to utilise her scarce resources in the best way possible. Borrowing money or joining a savings scheme are two major 'crisis management techniques':

The best way around here to save is to be a member of a *gam'eyya* [a rotating savings mechanism]. We collect money daily and then each day one of us gets the entire amount. Sometimes we make it 20 piasters per day, sometimes half a pound and when the market is good we collect 75 piasters per day.

We usually join such a *gam'eyya* in order to repay a debt or to pay a down-payment on an appliance we want or to build an additional room. The people here trust me so I am usually the coordinator of such *gam'eyya* . I do not take any fee but I gain people's love and respect. Whenever anyone is in need she comes to me and asks me to organise such a scheme. I go around and arrange with several people to be members of the *gam'eyya* .

Our relationship started when I noticed in her these leadership qualities and she found in me a potential source of power and prestige in the community. She recognised that by spending time with me and being my link and contact with a number of women, she would be considered a *wastiet khier* (a source of good and benefit) for her people. By introducing me to other women and informing me about the habits and culture of the community, she gained my respect as well. It is important to note here that U'm Saber and all the researched women knew very clearly that I would not offer them any material benefit, either in the present or in the

Victims and Heroines

future. However, these women felt so marginalised and neglected that having me listen to their problems and show concern was encouraging in itself. They had no mechanisms to express their misfortunes and found in me – a stranger and hence neutral – a sympathetic listener who would not be around long enough to tarnish their reputation with any of the information they gave me. Thus U'm Saber was able to carve out for herself a central role in my research. Many women in the community sought her out in order to meet me.

This central role is not new and was not acquired by U'm Saber through my research. She has been playing this role for a long time within her family and the community at large. She has been the liaison between the NGOs in the area and the community. More than that, she was the main source of information for many widows and poor and sick people about the regular and temporary welfare programmes offered by the government, NGOs and Islamic groups. In several cases she went so far as to take a widow or needy woman by the hand to the appropriate office and introduce her to the officials or programme administrators. What she asked in return was not material gain but the recognition and acceptance of her central role and leadership status in the area. As she explained:

> I have excellent relationships with the employees of the MOSA office of this sub-district, and the employees of the two NGOs also trust me. They come to me to check if the names and addresses of the applicants to their welfare and development programmes are correct. When A'm Fahmy [Uncle Fahmy], our neighbour, died last year, leaving a wife and five children behind him, his family came to me for help. I told them what papers to get, introduced the wife to Mr M. and Ms S. from the MOSA office and also went to her children's school and convinced them to exempt the children from the school fees as they are orphans.

In return for all her efforts, U'm Saber was the largest beneficiary of all available governmental and non-governmental services and could be labelled as a 'professional assistance-seeker'. She also cultivated very strong and warm relationships with the bureaucrats who administered these programmes and they filled out all the forms for her, for U'm Saber is illiterate.

All these talents and abilities increased my respect and admiration for her. She is an example of a woman who has overcome all circumstantial obstacles facing the poor, and especially poor women, in Egypt. She was also able to turn all situations to her advantage, yet U'm Saber was no opportunist. She deserved all the assistance she got. Her husband was an *u'rzu'i*, trained as a carpenter but without any regular employment, and their three children were in school. She used her negotiation skills to build formal and informal networks with government officials in order to obtain services and maintain her family.

The following is her story of life with her husband:

> When things started to look bad for us, my husband thought of going to any Arab country to increase our income. Many people went to the Gulf countries and made a lot of money. By 1989 he thought of going to Iraq. Now just going there cost so much money. So we started selling our things, electric appliances and other things we had here.
>
> Then Aly went to Iraq and for eight months I heard nothing from him. I started borrowing money from everyone hoping that when he returned he would have money and we could repay everyone. It is very normal here to borrow from your neighbours, for we trade places. Of course, my father used to help us very much at that time, and also A'm Mostafa, the husband of my eldest sister.
>
> I was also able to go to my son's school and tell the social worker there that my husband was not around and I had no source of income, so he wrote me an application that I took to the Islamic Bank of Faysal and they gave me 30 pounds for my son. This is not an easy task. I had to fill out all the papers with the social worker at the school, and then I went to the bank in one area down-town. They said that I had to go to the other area (an hour and a half away), but of course, I had to go there another day for their working hours are very short. Then when I went to their branch in the Giza area, beside the pyramids, they gave me another paper and asked me to go the MOSA branch in my district to stamp it. I could have waited for them to use their mail, but I would have waited for ever. I have a friend who had to prepare the necessary papers three times because they were lost between all these offices. Anyway, I went to our branch maybe three times before the employee was there, and she was very nice and helpful and stamped them immediately. Now, one has to do this exercise every six months in order to get 30 pounds.

U'm Saber's story reveals that she is a resourceful woman who has learned to cope with the different pressures put on her by society. She relies on networking as a mechanism for getting through to government officials and accessing the basic social services provided by the state to the needy and destitute. Her strong relationship with the social worker at the school and the MOSA employee at the government social unit helps her and facilitates the procedures of accessing these services. The procedures are long and complex: if she had relied on the normal work processes and the flow of official paper and approvals, it would have been nearly impossible for her to get the school fee exemption for her son, financial assistance from MOSA, and free medication for her brother in-law.

Victims and Heroines

Hedeya This is the story of another strong and resourceful woman. Hedeya learned to cope with a changing situation when she became the main breadwinner for her family instead of her husband. Hedeya's life is full of examples of how women are oppressed at different stages of their lives. She was married at an early age to a man who was imposed on her by her family. The following is how she introduced herself:

> My name is Hedeya. I was born in a small village but brought up here in Cairo. I went to school but did not continue because I got married. I have been married for 15 years. My cousin proposed but my family refused because he was poor. I met my current husband through my brother who worked with him in the same factory. I was only 12 years old while my husband was 30 years old.

Hedeya's introduction to marriage was traumatic. According to Islam but more specifically to Egyptian tradition, a man and a woman are married in two stages. The first stage, *katb el-ketab*, registers the marriage with the *ma'zun*, i.e. the *Sheikh* registrar. Many people perform this procedure in a mosque, but the *ma'zun* is really an official of the government. Although men and women become legally and religiously married through this procedure, they are not expected to consummate the marriage until the wedding night. The second stage is the consummation of the marriage itself, which is called the *dukhla*, literally meaning entrance. This refers to the fact that the bride will enter into another household and another family.

In Egypt, the wedding night is expected to be the night of consummation or deflowering, since women are expected to be virgins. The virginity of the woman is not only hers; it signifies the honour of the whole family and the respect they receive.

> Virginity holds a central place in the culture of sexuality of Egyptian peasants.[2] The hymen is referred to as *wish el-bent* meaning the 'face of the girl'. The analogy with the face, which gives a girl her identity, denotes the importance of virginity for girls. A girl without a face has no identity or place in her community. (Khattab 1996: 21)

Thus sex before or outside of marriage is a taboo. Virginity is closely tied to honour, and honour, in this case, is collective. It is the honour of the whole family and not of the individual alone. Women are thus given the responsibility of maintaining the group's honour, and men hold the responsibility of protecting and monitoring its maintenance. It is a woman's fault if she loses her virginity, and because she is not trustworthy, the family takes precautions. For the family to preserve its purity, its men become the defenders of the family's honour (Pitt Rivers in Goddard 1987: 157). Closely associated with sex role segregation and the subordination

Women as Victims, Women as Survivors?

of women, the concept of *a'l-sharaf* or honour mainly refers to control over the sexuality of women. It is believed that men control women's sexuality and that their honour is established when that control is socially recognised, accepted and legitimised (Kagitcibasi 1982: 11).[3]

Rituals and regulations have been established to ensure that women maintain their purity, thus safeguarding the family honour (Goddard 1987: 167). Among these systems and rituals are two widespread and common practices that I encountered in most of the research sites. The first is female genital mutilation (girls' circumcision). The second is the *dukhla baladi*, the collective manual deflowering of a young bride to prove to her in-laws and community that she is a virgin and that she has preserved her purity and thus the family's honour.

There are various approaches to the deflowering process itself, depending on the class and the education of the families involved:

> Deflowering is defined as the rupturing of the hymen (of a virgin) by sexual intercourse. In Egyptian rural customs and traditions, deflowering is mostly done by hand and not through regular intercourse. The hymen is torn by inserting the fore-finger enfolded in a white handkerchief into the outer vagina of the bride pushing hard until the hymen is ripped off and the blood oozes out on the handkerchief. (Khattab 1996: 23)

The quote below is Hedeya's account of such an experience:

> On the wedding night they decided to get the *mashta*[5] and that I would be deflowered in the traditional way. On that terrible night, the *mashta*, my mother, my husband and two of his aunts entered our bedroom. The two aunts held my hands and my mother and husband held my thighs and the awful woman put her fingers inside of me and kept on poking until I bled enough to satisfy the required amount. I was so terrified and upset. I was also very angry and felt that they were killing me slowly and invading a very intimate part of my self and my soul. I never liked intercourse since that night. I dreaded his demands on me every time, even after 15 years of marriage. This is what is called the *dukhla baladi*.

Through the practice of *dukhla baladi*, the family's relatives and neighbours are informed that their honour remains unblemished. This is done by showing the cloth soaked with the blood of the deflowered bride.

Women's expectations in other areas of life are also submitted to similar mechanisms of control and, often, their dreams remain unfulfilled. As women, they are forced to play secondary roles. Hedeya wanted to continue her education, but first her family and then her husband prevented her from achieving this goal. She recounts sadly:

> I wanted so much to complete my education, but my husband refused and beat me hard when I insisted. This was another one of my dreams that died in me as a young girl. My mother used to scold me whenever I told her about my dreams. She said that she got me married early because she feared my inappropriate ambitions. For all these reasons, I am insisting that my children, whether boys or girls, must be educated.

Young and inexperienced, Hedeya found herself responsible for her family as her husband let her down.

> After the birth of my second child, I found out that my husband was not only a drunk but also a drug addict. He used to work in a shoe factory and was well paid, but then he started taking drugs and was forced to leave his job. After being a supervisor, he is now a mere distributor like any vendor in the street. I began to work with him to help him. I was able to learn all about the job and made the acquaintance of the retail and wholesale merchants, and all of his clients and the government officials that he had to deal with.
>
> He is now more nervous and violent. As a good wife I am standing beside him. I do my best to spare him any contact with people for he makes enemies easily. This means that I have to deal with the school and hospitals or doctors if one of our kids becomes sick. Without me, my husband and my children would be lost. I am very important for their survival.

Getting a divorce is not an easy thing for women to do for many reasons. First, a divorcee is put under the scrutiny of her family and the community at large. Her freedom is constrained. Second, to get a divorce a woman needs to hire a lawyer to prove that she has been physically and psychologically harmed, which is not easy and is very expensive for poor women. To Hedeya, getting a divorce was not an option:

> In our family and culture, once you are married you should never even dream of divorce. A divorcee is a woman looking for trouble and an ungrateful person. We have no alternative but to accept. We can suffer and endure but there is nothing else for women like us to do.

Hedeya decided to ensure a different future for her children, especially her daughter. And yet when it came to issues of honour and the protection of her daughter's reputation, she recommended the same discriminating and oppressive measures and rituals that her parents imposed on her.

> My two children are dear to me. I will do anything in the world to make them the best people. I insisted that both must continue their education and I refused all the suitors for my young girl. Her father and his family want to marry her off to get rid of her burden. As you know, girls are a

Women as Victims, Women as Survivors?

potential shame; they could dishonour the family. But I want her to be a doctor or an engineer and I want my son to be a policeman.

Never will I allow my girl to suffer as I did. Of course, she will not be married as early as I was and to a man she does not love. I will also not allow a *dukhla baladi*. My parents were ignorant peasants. However, yes, she is circumcised. This act protects girls and women from themselves. Imagine, if I was not circumcised, I would be loose. My husband has not touched me for more than three years. His drinking and drugs made him very weak in this matter as well.

The relationship between women and the different government bureaux is very tense and hostile, and women expect to be degraded and humiliated. This feeling of mistrust is not unfounded. It has led women like Hedeya to refuse any assistance from the government. Furthermore, there is a stigma attached to anyone who applies for or receives any social benefits from the government or the mosques.

No, I do not need any help from the government. I did not go to MOSA or anyone else. I am a strong woman. Only the very poor and those who have no dignity go to the Ministry of Social Affairs or the mosque asking for help. You have to be desperate to accept the way people are treated by government officials. They are rude to us because we are poor, and they are worse with women. Why should I humiliate myself and ask for money or their help if I can avoid that?

As a woman who took financial, legal and social responsibility for the family, Hedeya faced many pressures. The presence of her husband was never an asset in her struggle, and it did not help her with the outside world either. She faced obstacles with every decision she made. Chant found that women in Mexico and the Philippines pass through the same process: they were hurt and angry at their misfortune, but over time gained confidence and took control of their lives (1997: 200). The following quote shows what Hedeya experienced:

Of course, everything at the beginning was more difficult. Men in the market were not nice to me and thought that I was an easy woman because my husband was always drunk. We have to renew our licences every year and each time I wait for hours in the government office. That is because I am a woman. The employees keep on asking me why I work and if my husband is not man enough. I was so scared at the beginning. I thought we would never make it, and the distribution licence would be taken away from us, and my children would starve. Because of my children I became strong and decided to suffer for them. Now I do not care. I feel important and needed and that is enough. I am a true Hedeya [gift] to my family.

Hedeya was proud of her role and was able, through her good relationships with men and women in her area, to gain their admiration and respect. People in the area referred to her as 'better than a hundred men'. Her greatest asset, according to her neighbours, family and children, was how she stood by and supported her husband. I considered her a heroine because she was resourceful in spite of her limited experience in dealing with the outside world.

U'm Nagah Tall and generously built, U'm Nagah is never unnoticed or ignored. She usually wears a black *jalabia* and a black scarf over her hair. She is dark-skinned and still speaks in an Upper Egyptian dialect. She emphasises and exaggerates the dialect when she wants to threaten or scare someone.

When U'm Nagah, her husband and their four children reached 'The Tombs' 15 years ago, it was not as crowded as it is now and they were able to build three rooms, a kitchen and a bathroom in an empty space. Arabi, her husband, joined a gang of thieves in the area. Since his death, his two elder sons and U'm Nagah herself have become very important members of the gang.

Due to her close relationship with the criminal gangs of the area, my visits to U'm Nagah took place on special days and I limited my wandering with her to her own street. I never went to the mosque with her but I was civil when I saw her there, and as friendly with her as with everyone else. My relationship with U'm Nagah was very complex. I didn't want to offend her because she could be detrimental to my work, and yet I also genuinely liked her and enjoyed her sense of humour.

U'm Nagah had experienced her share of discrimination and oppression due to her sex. She was married to Arabi when she was 12 years old; he was 25 years older than she was. Her sexual experience was very traumatic. During her husband's lifetime, she played the expected and traditional role of a housewife. She also endured her husband's physical and sexual abuse. As far as she was concerned, divorce was unheard of and totally unacceptable in her family. When her husband died, U'm Nagah could not return to their village because she wanted to protect her children[5] and yet there was no one in Cairo to assist her. She was very young and her eldest son was in his early teens. Her husband had been a thief and a gangster and there was no source of income after his death. Her experience with MOSA was also very traumatic. This is her story:

> My neighbours told me to go and apply to the Ministry of Social Affairs. They said that they have a pension for widows and orphans. I still remember the first day I went: the employees made me and the other applicants

Women as Victims, Women as Survivors?

stand outside for more than an hour while they had their breakfast and tea. By the time they let us in, more people had come and the tiny place was full and became very noisy. People were also pushing each other. The two female employees started to shout and the man who works in the kitchen came and started organising us into queues but in a very rude way. He even pushed several women and men. He also did not respect the order of our arrival and this caused more anger among us, for some of us had been waiting for hours and newcomers were being served first. That day, I spent hours there, leaving my children with the neighbours. Finally, they gave me a form to fill out. I do not know how to read or write so the man of the kitchen helped me for 50 piasters and told me what documents to bring. By the time I finished and it was my turn for the employee to see me, office hours had ended and they asked us to come later.

Three days later, I went and submitted my application to one of the female employees, who asked me if I had brought all the necessary documents. I presented her with my husband's death certificate, his identity card and my identity card. She looked up at me angrily and told me that I also needed the children's birth certificates and a paper from their school stating that they were students there. She complained to her colleague that we only waste their time and never learn or understand anything. I told her that I had done what their messenger told me to do and he had not told me what other documents were needed. She said that the instructions are written on the board and that it was not her business that we are not only illiterate but also stupid. I endured all that humiliation and I went home that night and cried a lot. Two days later, I went and got her all the papers she needed. She took them and then made me wait for an hour while she served others who came after me. Then she told me to return after a week. A week later, I went to her office and she looked into her files and said that all the applications were sent to the central office to make sure we are not taking any assistance or insurance from any other governmental body.

For six months I went to and fro, spent money, and wasted time and effort and felt humiliated and insulted by her treatment. At the end, I found out that my papers had been lost and they wanted me to start the whole process again. That was the straw that broke the camel's back and I promised myself that I would never deal with any government office again until the day I die, or apply for the government's assistance ever again.

This experience was what introduced U'm Nagah to her profession, as she calls it. U'm Nagah's speciality is beating up people for a fee. In other words, she is a female thug. She and her colleagues are hired to start fights and beat up other women. She had resisted the offer to join her husband's gang because she wanted a different future for her children. However,

Victims and Heroines

without any source of income and distant from her family, she could no longer afford to live off the charity of her neighbours. She had also sold all the furniture and was left with an empty house. When she approached her husband's colleagues, they welcomed her. They told her that she could join the women's branch of their gang, which specialises in beatings. Being well-built was an asset for her new career. Before she joined, she asked them for a favour: to beat up the female employee who had insulted and humiliated her. They agreed to do it as a gift, free of charge.

> I decided to join this group for I had no other place to go to. I did not want to work as a maid. This is very humiliating and unacceptable and my sons would have been disgraced. This new job was fun and had no demands on my time with and for my children, except when we are needed for an operation. But I was also so angry with the woman of the Ministry of Social Affairs that I asked them to beat her up for me. I stood away and watched them beat her and I felt vindicated. Afterwards, I became a professional and people come asking for me from all over the country. I have no regrets. No one, no one will ever humiliate me the way the government did then, ever.

Why have I included U'm Nagah, the outlaw, among the strong, resourceful women I call heroines? In dealing with U'm Nagah, I had to freeze and leave aside my middle-class moral ethos and values. I had to empathise with a woman who was surrounded by an environment of crime and outlaws. She had tried a better way out by seeking state assistance through the Ministry of Social Affairs, but in her weakness and dire need she was humiliated and rejected. Although I am not condoning her profession, I cannot help but sympathise with a young mother who found her empowerment in a way that is totally unacceptable to society. She decided to subvert the system by rejecting it completely. U'm Nagah does not fool herself, and realises that she chose an illegal path. But as she put it: 'Our lives are like a big play, and only the strongest will survive. My motto in life is that might is right, whoever has power has the world in her hands.'

U'm Nagah's story is a good illustration of the burdensome and humiliating procedures of social welfare. It clearly demonstrates how the 'application ordeal' is used as a screening mechanism to weed out people. Hers is also an extraordinary story, an extreme example, if you will, of the extent to which resistance to and subversion of a system can reach.

A Man by Day and a Woman by Night: Mixed Roles and Responsibilities

Kesma, co-wife Kesma is a 32-year-old, well-built and pretty woman. She married her husband as a second wife after a great love story. She

Women as Victims, Women as Survivors?

says she married him because he promised her the world and told her that she would never have to work again. The eldest of her eight brothers and sisters, Kesma had had to work in a private garment factory since she was eleven.

> I used to make a lot of money, and I was very successful. I was the princess of my family, the breadwinner. All my sisters and brothers respected me, but I was tired and I wanted to be a respectable housewife. He promised me the moon. Nine months later, he stayed at home and I was forced to go out to work.

Women like Kesma enter into the traditional marriage arrangement. They are promised protection and care by their men and, in return, they promise obedience. They are still expected – by society and religion – to obey their husbands, but are not guaranteed similar rights. Their men no longer provide for them. On the contrary, women are forced, in many cases, to provide for their families and their husbands. They are no longer isolated in the private realm. They are forced into the public realm, but without the same rights as their spouses and male kin. The following quote shows how Kesma and her family viewed her work:

> I had to go out and work after he left me for the other woman. I had no money to go to the courts and seek my alimony. I am now too old to work at the garment factory, and I could not work in a hospital or a school as a cleaner like my sister did. I had to work as a maid. I work six days a week, cleaning a flat every day, and I take 10 pounds a day. They also give me food and rice and clothes for my kids. Without this work, I would have never been able to help my children. However, the neighbours and my relatives talk and gossip about me. If I come late one day they tell my children that I have been arrested in a brothel. My brothers had a big fight with me: they wanted me to send my children to their father and his wife and go back and live with them. They said no respectable woman works. I cannot let a stepmother treat my children badly. People talk about me because I work and go out of my house; they tell me what I should or could have done. I am a lonely and ignorant woman.

A co-wife may find herself on her own, having to take care of herself and her children. In other cases the husband may continue to provide for all his wives. In Kesma's case, her husband abandoned her and stopped any financial contribution to the household. Yet, as a co-wife who is still legally bound to her husband, she was not eligible for any financial assistance from the state or the NGOs. She was considered the responsibility of her husband. This is the story of her experience with MOSA:

I was told by neighbours about the assistance of MOSA and the mosque. I was in need of such help because after he married the other woman I stayed for months with no income. I relied on the charity given to me by kind people. So I went to apply to MOSA and to the mosque and in both cases I was rejected. I was told at the government offices that I should either produce my divorce certificate or prove beyond doubt that my husband has deserted me in order to be eligible for other programmes. To prove that my husband has deserted me, I have to go to the police station and file a case there stating that I do not know his whereabouts. That is not the case. I do know where he is, but I cannot get any rights or the rights of his children from him. I cannot file for divorce for many reasons. First of all, I have no money to pay the lawyers. Second and more importantly, I do not want to be a divorcee. A divorcee is a threat to other women. Even now they are suspicious of me and never ask me into their homes unless their husbands are not there. Also, if I get a divorce my parents will ask me to send the children to their father, and probably force me to remarry. I am desperate and there is no law or agency that will help me.

A co-wife is legally bound to her husband even when he has ceased to provide for her and her children. Furthermore, a co-wife is excluded from all welfare programmes, whether governmental or non-governmental. This is based on the underlying assumption that the man is the head of the household and only when he is no longer physically or legally responsible will his family be eligible for any type of welfare.

Kesma's story highlights several issues that concern this study. First, she is a clear example of a woman who resents and refuses to play the role of head of the household. Second, her story also demonstrates how the state's policies either ignore or refuse to recognise some different forms of female headship, in this case that of a co-wife. And finally, this story also shows that work for poor illiterate women is neither liberating nor empowering but could have terribly stigmatising effects on them.

Lamua'khdha malush lazma: Excuse me he is Useless

Intisar As mentioned earlier in this chapter, society has established rituals to control women's sexuality and bodies. The manual deflowering, *dukhla baladi*, is such a tool to ensure that the collective family honour is intact. However, some women manage to subvert this very procedure. Sometimes the *dukhla baladi* itself becomes a camouflage to hide the fact that the bride is not a virgin. The plot can include the *mashta* herself. The bride, whether in collaboration with her mother or by herself, pays the *mashta* to fake the whole process. The *mashta* wraps two pieces of cloth around

Women as Victims, Women as Survivors?

her finger, the upper one white and clean and the lower one stained with blood, from a dove, as if from a hymen breaking. There is a belief that a dove's blood resembles human blood more than chicken blood, for example. In the case of pregnant brides, the father of the child is usually the groom himself. In that case, he carries out the procedure using the same trick. Intisar recounts how her *dukhla baladi* was faked:

> I am 26 years old. I was married when I was four months pregnant. It was a crime and a mistake that I have paid for dearly. My father is a very traditional and conservative man, and he insisted on a *dukhla baladi*. My mother knew the real story and she beat me but had to protect me. If people had known, I would have been disgraced forever and my father could have killed me. My mother got a dove and killed it, and put the blood on the white handkerchief, my panties and the night-gown. She did all that in our room when people were waiting outside. We allowed only my mother and my elder sister in the room with us. The bloody pieces were all taken out and paraded in front of everyone and my father's honour was saved.
>
> I felt very ashamed and embarrassed and my mother and sister never forgave me. Neither did Abbas, my husband. He used to call me a whore and a loose woman whom he saved from scandal. They all made me feel that it was my responsibility and my mistake alone, and that I must pay for it for the rest of my life. But now, so many years later, I believe that it was the mistake of my father and mother, who were never my friends but my prison guards, and of Abbas, who took advantage of my situation and my naivety. I do not say that I did not make a mistake, but I should not be the only one to blame. They must be blamed with me.

Young single women and girls are placed under family scrutiny and their movements are curtailed by everyone, including younger brothers. In order to protect the family's honour and reputation, after adolescence, girls are not allowed out of the house without a 'chaperone' unless they are going to school. Thus, in many cases, the girls' only opportunity to meet men is during school hours or on their way to and from school. All the girls I met in the seven areas were not allowed to go shopping alone, and most never went to the cinema or only once or twice before they turned ten years old. The following quotes show how Intisar knew Abbas inspite of all restrictions:

> I knew Abbas when I was still in secondary school. He started to talk to me and he was the first young man I ever talked to alone who was not a relative or a close family friend. Abbas was so tender and kind and he used to speak nicely to me. No one had ever treated me like this.
>
> At the time we met, I was 17 years old and he was 30 years old. He was

> unemployed. He wanted to propose to me and when he met my father he was rejected. My father told me that he was irresponsible and could not be trusted.
>
> Meanwhile, I kept on seeing him. I graduated from the technical secondary school and found a job in the Food Security Bakery where we used to sell bread from kiosks. I used to make about 20 pounds a day. Abbas convinced me then that I should give him the money so that we could buy all we need for our future home.
>
> Later, I took him to work with me at the bread kiosks. But after two weeks he started to stay at home and I had to work for both of us and, as before, gave him all the money. I might have been fooling myself, telling myself that he would change after marriage. But in reality, I had nowhere to go. I had lost the most valuable thing for any girl and for her family, my virginity. No one else would have married me and my father would have killed me if he had found out. So I had to endure and wait for him.
>
> When he proposed the second time, my father refused him because he did not offer a suitable *shabka*.[6] So I joined a *gam'eyya* for 10 pounds a day and when I had 1,500 pounds in my hands I went and bought three bracelets, a ring and earrings and gave them to Abbas to present to my father. Only then did my father agree to our *katb el-ketab*. He insisted that the consummation of the marriage would not take place until he had finished furnishing our home.
>
> After marriage the nightmare began. Abbas had already beaten me twice before marriage, but after the wedding he was so mean, so insulting, so humiliating, that life became unbearable. We actually lived off my father, and I was unable to work because of my child. The situation became very bad when Abbas had a fight with my father and they nearly hit each other. I was so fed up by then, and we were also in a lot of debt.

The circumstances deteriorated even more. He sold every piece of furniture she had bought. She felt that he was no longer a responsible man or the protector she was looking for. The relationship worsened to the extent that she could no longer have sexual intercourse with him. She felt she no longer owed him this duty.

> He ceased to be the man of the house in my eyes and I lost interest in having intercourse with him. The last fight we had was because I refused to make love to him. He told me that a woman who refuses her husband is useless. She could be cursed until doomsday. I told him that he had become useless [*malush lazma*] since he no longer provided for my son and me and that I cannot live with him anymore. I need a man who takes care of me and my demands [*Yekafinii*], and whose word I obey and respect. I cannot respect a man who has become useless. He got so upset and beat me so hard

that my father heard and came up. He fought with my father and beat him too and called my mother names. My father was right. I should not have married him. He fooled me.

It is interesting to see how Intisar placed all the blame on others. First, it was her parents who controlled her so that she was naive enough to fall in love 'blindly' with Abbas. When she slept with Abbas out of wedlock, she was tricked by him. Intisar used the traditional excuse for playing the fool and the minor. If her family and society at large force women into dependency and consider them unable to think or act on their own, then why should not women use that to their advantage? Intisar decided to live up to that image. As a female, she is portrayed as unable to think, and, as is commonly known, lacks brains and religion. This judgement is taken from the *Hadith* (the prophet's sayings), in which women are described as *naqisat 'aql wa din*. Women are portrayed as emotional, and quick to lose their temper and to make hasty decisions. In that sense, they are incapable of rational thinking like men, and thus are considered *nakisat 'akl* ('*akl* here means both reason and brains). They also lack religion, *din*, because five days per month, during their periods, they cannot pray because they are considered *negseen* (impure and unclean). These cultural beliefs have their origin in Islam, though they are shared and acted upon by both the Muslims and Christians of low-income urban Egypt.

Intisar decided to play the fool in order to achieve the goals she set for herself. She wanted a husband in order to be equal to her peers, and she also wanted a son to complete the required cycle for women. After reaching her objectives, she no longer wanted the man who failed her when he did not play his expected role of protector.

Several months after the fight over *gima'a* (intercourse), Intisar and her father filed for divorce and also sued Abbas for *tabdid manqulat*. It is customary that the bride's family in low-income sectors forces the man, on marriage, to sign an inventory of actual and imaginary furniture and household appliances with inflated costs. The aim is to ensure that the man will pay the woman this amount if he divorces her or marries another woman. It is also used as a bargaining tool to protect women's rights.[7] This inventory is called the *ayma* and is seen by poor women as their weapon or insurance policy against *ghadr*[8]. Intisar's parents were able to make Abbas sign such a list of furniture and appliances worth LE2,000. Abbas had actually never bought anything. According to the law, he has to produce the items on the list or pay the amount stated if he is called on by his wife to do so. This document is legally binding. If he fails to do so, he could be sentenced to a period ranging from six months to three years in prison. Abbas divorced Intisar *ghiaby* (in her absence) and disappeared. He sent her the LE2,000 through his mother and was never located to pay her and her son alimony.

Intisar did not realise how her position and status would change within her family and community after the divorce. Her movement and activities became constrained and limited. Her family scrutinised her every move and she was not allowed to stay out after sunset. She had to go to work because her father retired and could no longer provide for her and her son, whom she wanted to educate. In spite of the fact that she had completed the public technical school several years earlier, Intisar's ability to read and write was very limited and she had no other skills. She said:

> I tried to find any job, as a cook or a maid. I worked as a maid for four months, but they asked me to leave because sometimes I was late and for several days I was unable to go at all. I have a son who is five years old. Who will stay with him? Who will take care of him? I rely on a sister or a neighbour, but sometimes they have other things to do. Then I worked at another house for three months, but the people I worked for accused me of stealing. They are so rich they feed their dogs meat every day while my son eats meat only twice a year.

While I was interviewing Intisar and later as I was transcribing the tapes, I was unable to decide whether she was a manipulator or whether she had been manipulated by her family, the man she loved, and society at large. Did Intisar break traditions and rules when she got pregnant out of wedlock or did she live up to the image and expectations that society has of girls? Society expects women to be loose and irresponsible. That is why rituals exist to control their bodies and their sexuality. Women are portrayed as cunning, deviant and mischievous: the only way to stop them is to keep them locked behind closed doors. So Intisar lived up to that stereotype and image of the irresponsible girl who has no control over her desires. In the process, she got what she wanted: a husband and a son. As mentioned earlier, she also subverted the system by, again, living up to what is expected, when she went through the charade of a *dukhla baladi*, faking the breaking of the hymen on her wedding night. In short, Intisar could be a victim of society's image and expectations.

Hanan Household organisation is a function of the expectations people hold about family roles. The expected and accepted role of a husband is that of a breadwinner: he brings in the money and the food and is expected to be aggressive, authoritarian and temperamental. His desires are to be gratified immediately in return for his breadwinning services. Traditionally, the woman is expected to be a self-denying mother who is also patient, persevering, resourceful and economical. Her main reproductive role is as a wife and a mother but, traditionally, also includes 'sexual duties' to her husband (Rugh 1984: 69–72). The following quote shows how Hanan perceived gender roles within her family:

> I married my husband when I was eleven years old. We were engaged for two years. He brought me many golden earrings and rings in addition to the *shabka*. He was 25 years older than myself. When we got married I was so terrified. He was a big, dark and hairy man. I cried for a whole week and did not let him finish his business with me. My mother had to come and talk to me, and also his mother. And only a week later did we consummate the marriage.
>
> When I was first married, my husband was very rich and we lived in a nice flat in one of the popular areas of Cairo. We were happy for the first ten years. He was a good husband, taking care of all his responsibilities and I, in return, was a good wife, keeping his home clean, taking care of his children and also being very obedient in bed.
>
> Then everything changed. My husband stopped working and became a useless bum. He refused many jobs because he felt they were beneath him. He felt that he was a big *ma'lem* [skilled labourer], and should not accept working for less than his usual fee. He did not care about us, or from where we would get our money or who would feed our kids. We were kicked out of our flat, for we could not pay the rent and we came here to live with my mother. I am now the poorest of my sisters after I was the best of them. I had to go out and work, in a club, and later in a hospital. But as you can see, I am young and pretty and I am not left alone. Men are always chasing after me but I do not want to tarnish my reputation. I am the mother of several girls.

To Hanan, her husband was useless because he was unemployed and unable to meet his financial responsibilities towards his wife and children. In return, she refused to sleep with him. Marriage for Hanan is a bargain: the man performs by providing for his family and the woman by providing sex to the man and care for his children. She expressed these sentiments clearly when she said:

> I married him so that he takes care of my demands and me. A man is only a man with what he has in his pocket and with his money (*e'l ragil ragil bii illy fi gibuh wi bi felusuh*). Marriage is a deal. He provides for me and I take care of him, his dirty requests, and his children. What do they think that we are, their slaves, workers and whores for free?

The concept of a useless husband emerged repeatedly during my fieldwork. What was striking was that the more a woman considered her husband to be 'useless', the more she was physically abused by him. Both Intisar and

Hanan were beaten continuously and heavily by their spouses. During my fieldwork, both had to go for medical help twice. However, neither reported their husbands to the police because this was unheard of. In addition, as the income these women brought to the household increased, the resentment between both sides grew deeper. Men's frustration at their inability to fulfil their traditional roles led them to compensate for such social impotence by increasing their grip and their exploitative and abusive behaviour towards their women. Women, on the other hand, might lose their respect towards their men by calling them useless. So the concept of 'useless husbands' developed. Within such a context, a new type of patriarchy has been emerging where women have become the major breadwinners although they continue to endure domestic violence and sexual abuse.

Oppressed Women: Daughters of a Lesser God
Shadia

> My name is Shadia. I have eight brothers and sisters, three boys and five girls. One of the five girls in addition to myself worked as maids in private homes. However, she worked in a house in our town, but I came all the way to Cairo and worked for an upper-class family in Masr El Gadida. I went to work for them when I was six years old.

Oppressed and marginalised all her life, Shadia found in me a chance to dream. She told me tales about herself that were untrue. She disclosed her daydreams as stories but also recounted facts. She placed herself in the central role of her story, thus overcoming her life-long marginalisation. Through the use of fantasy, she constructed an identity that enabled her to subvert the traditional, imposed limitations she felt due to her gender, poverty and frustrations. All this allowed her a more egalitarian, just and central social role in her stories.

Armed with the freedom to say what she pleased, as I was non-judgmental and did not contradict her lies, she revealed to me not only her ambitions and aspirations but a great deal about the social and emotional dynamics of being a woman in a low-income urban area. Through her fantasies and real life stories, I learned many things about Shadia that I would not have learned if our relationship had been limited to the 'professional' aspects of research and had not touched on the 'personal' and 'intimate' aspects of her life.

However, my relationship with Shadia was very complex. She confessed to me that she was miserable with her husband, that she was sexually unsatisfied and that she had been looking for love and warmth in other men. Right in front of my eyes, Shadia was transformed from a subservient

Women as Victims, Women as Survivors?

and oppressed woman who works as a poorly paid maid into a lover, and then, as I feared, into a whore. This transformation took place during the four months when I knew and interviewed her. We used to meet regularly three times every week in a room at the NGO's office and stay for hours talking – rather, she talking and I listening.

During that period Shadia took off the old scarf that covered her hair, dyed her hair blonde, put on make-up, and started wearing colourful Western dresses instead of her shabby *jalabia*. During this period, the skinny little woman was completely transformed and my sleepless nights began.

In the beginning, Shadia told me the story of her childhood and how her father threw her out to work as a servant when she was still a little girl:

> When I was six years old, I used to stand on a small chair in order to reach the sink and wash the dishes. My father used to come every month to collect my wage from the mistress. He never bothered to check on me or speak a kind word to me. I continued to be a major source of income for my family and continued to suffer neglect. My father cared more about money than about me.

Shadia felt that her father had abandoned her and that he did not love her, but only wanted to use her.

> *A'buuya dah ragil a'si malush a'lb* (My father is a cruel man who has no heart). He cared much more for the money that I brought him than about my health and well-being.

When she was 19 years old, her father tried to marry her off to a 60-year-old man who owned land and a store. But Shadia refused and ran away.

> My parents called me back to live with them, but in reality they wanted to marry me off to a rich old man who was 60 years old. After I refused him, my family started treating me badly, insulting and beating me for the slightest reason. So I ran away.

She ran away and stayed away for a couple of months when she worked in coffee shops and got to know a man. He took her to Upper Egypt with him and promised to marry her, but let her down. She went back to her parents, who nearly killed her. They brought the local midwife to check whether she was still a virgin.

> They got the *daya*, who proved that I was still a virgin and she shouted at them for ruining my reputation like this. However, they all continued to be mean to me and insult me. For two months they watched me, expecting my stomach to grow, not believing the *daya*.

Finally, she could not bear this treatment any more and ran away again.

She married the first man she found in the streets, Fawzi, whom she sought for protection. But he also let her down, she sadly said:

> I found Fawzi. I thought he would be my protector and my haven. He was a mechanic and promised to take care of me. But like all men, like my father before him, he let me down. He turned out to be a gambler who forced me to borrow money for him from all the neighbours and the people in the community. He even beat me up when I could not get him the money he wanted. All I wanted was love and tenderness, something I never found except in my dreams.

After giving birth to her son, Shadia went back to work, as a part-time maid and a worker in a local clinic. She was forced back to work because no one wanted to lend her money any more. Her husband had left his job and used to beat her if he had no money to gamble with.

> All he does everyday is to ask me for 10 or 20 pounds and he never asks me about the source of this money. Now that I work, he expects his pocket-money every day. I married him to feel like a lady and not to be forced to be a servant and to be humiliated. I now earn the money, so I must be the man of the house and not him.

The original reason that Shadia had married ceased to exist because her husband no longer provided for her. She described him as someone who had become useless.

> A man becomes useless if he doesn't perform his main job, which is to provide for his wife and children. What is his use if he depends on his woman to work and bring the food to his home? Men cannot be in control of their homes and families if they no longer provide for them; they are no longer men. They really become useless.

By the time we reached this part of her story, our relationship had strengthened. She started telling me that her husband was inhuman to her, that she did not enjoy his sexual advances, and tried to avoid them as much as possible. She then told me about the two men in her life: the man who had been nice and kind and warm to her at work, and whom she thought was in love with her, and his friend. The first man was a physician at the mosque's health clinic, where she worked as a janitor. The second was also a physician who worked in another clinic. When she found me to be a good listener who voiced no objections, she started telling me about her sexual fantasies and desires for this man.

Over time, an affair began and Shadia was transformed, as I mentioned earlier. I began to worry, and spent sleepless nights fearing that my silence had encouraged her. I learned later – after she disappeared

Women as Victims, Women as Survivors?

and stopped coming to our weekly meetings – that she had taken her son and left her husband.

Using me as a sounding-board, Shadia got her dreams off her chest and gained the courage to act upon them. She rebelled and tried to oppose the restrictions put on her. By leaving her husband, Shadia might have taken the first step towards empowerment. However, in her recurrent attempts to seek freedom through men, she might be repeating a cycle of oppression rather than escaping it.

U'lfat U'lfat's story demonstrates how a young woman was forced to maintain her family without any recognition, appreciation or respect for her role. It is the story of one type of female headship, where a daughter is forced by her parents into the role of provider but is oppressed precisely for playing that role. It is a situation in which traditional norms are enforced only when they serve to silence the woman and eliminate her voice. When her father or brothers needed money, she was sent out to work. When they chose another path to exploit her, such as marrying her off to a wealthy man, she was beaten and forced to stop work, which was then considered a disgrace to the family honour.

I will narrate U'lfat's story as she recounted it to me. Her case is an excellent representation of what I call the new form of patriarchy within families in low-income urban Egypt.

She has been the main, if not the sole, economic contributor to her family for the last twelve years. Her father has not stopped abusing and exploiting her or shown any acknowledgement of or appreciation for her support or contribution.

> My name is U'lfat. I will be 30 years old next month, November 1997. I was born in 1967. When I was born, my father used to work as an employee at a big public sector company. My mother was, and still is, a housewife. I have two sisters, one older and the other younger and two older brothers. When I was three years old, my mother gave birth to two more children. Thus we became seven children. During that time, we were very poor but we were a loving family and we respected each other. My father used to care for us then.

Girls are circumcised when they reach the age of seven. It is a rite of passage that all girls must pass through. Although Egyptian circumcision is mild in comparison to the Sudanese practice, it is nevertheless a very traumatic experience:

> Circumcision, in classical Arabic, is known as *khafed* and in colloquial Egyptian as *tahara*, i.e. purification. It can vary from partial or complete removal

of the external genitalia to removal of the prepuce of the clitoris only. There are three types of circumcision: the removal of the foreskin of the clitoris (the mildest form known as sunna, or orthodox method); excision, which involves the removal of the clitoris and part of the labia minora, and infibulation, which involves removal of the clitoris, the labia minora and the labia majora (known as the Pharonic circumcision). The practice dates back to centuries ago, however reasons given at present in Egypt range from controlling women's sexuality to hygiene. (Hijab 1988: 156)

The most common practice in Egypt is the first degree of circumcision, in which the labia minora and sometimes the tip of the clitoris are removed. Among the older generations, the second degree of circumcision was practised. In this type the labia minora and a part of the clitoris are removed (Khattab 1996: 16).

In all seven areas of research, all the women and young girls I met from the age of 16 to 50 were circumcised, and all young mothers were intending to circumcise their young daughters. Education, age, class and profession did not change the picture. All were advocates of female circumcision. When they were asked about the reason, religion was cited as the first excuse. But when I probed more deeply, other factors became more significant than religion.

Female circumcision is related to sexuality and gender. Most women reported that this tradition is practised to beautify girls, to please their husbands, or to restrain sexual desire. Although it is commonly believed that men originally established such a ritual, it is women who are its keepers. It was almost always the mother or mother-in-law who insisted on the circumcision of young girls. Women are used to transmit social messages and to perpetuate the images embedded in the culture (Hijab 1988; Khattab 1996).

U'lfat's experience was also traumatic:

> I was circumcised when I was eight years old. They took my sister first, and they took me to stay at the neighbours. When I heard her screams I fled their flat and started banging at our door and so they took me inside. I remember that the woman was ugly and very dark. My aunt took me on her lap and pushed my legs apart and there were scissors and a knife. All I remember was the pain. It hurt so much for a whole week. I still suffer until now for the cut was not done properly and this part is deformed now.
>
> We were told that girls who are not circumcised grow penises and will be rejected by their husbands. My cousin was returned to her family after the wedding night because her circumcision was not good enough and her clitoris was too long for her husband's taste.
>
> It is also believed that circumcision curbs the sexual desires that the

Women as Victims, Women as Survivors?

devil has put in young girls. It will also curb their desire during marriage and they will thus be faithful to their husbands even if he is unable to satisfy them sexually.

Another common form of oppression and discrimination against girls is to deprive them of their right to a better life through education. As in the case of Hedeya, U'lfat was a clever student who was discouraged from seeking better and higher education on the pretext that she was a woman and would end up as a wife and mother. Her family, and certainly her brothers, played a major role in limiting her prospects for a better education. She sadly recounted:

> I went to school and I was very clever. When I reached the fourth grade, I replaced my sister in assisting mother in housework ... I was doing very well at school but it was my turn as the elder sisters left.
>
> I used to go home after school and stay up until midnight, cleaning, washing and preparing meals for my older and younger brothers. I had to be available to heat water for any of my brothers if they wanted to wash. Finally, my parents told me that since I could not handle school work and my duties towards them I should stop going to school. So I left school and stayed at home, and I took my turn as the maid of the men in the house.
>
> Four months later, and before the beginning of the next academic year, my sister got a divorce and returned to live with us. She took back her place and started helping my mother with house chores. After begging my parents, I returned to school and passed that year with excellent grades. With such good grades I could have entered the best public schools. However, my brother insisted that I must go to the nearby school. But the nearby school was very bad and its educational standard and capacity was very low. As a girl, I could not say anything and had to oblige.
>
> After passing preparatory school with high marks, I could have entered the more respectable secondary school, but again my elder brother refused and said that it was enough for a girl to get intermediate education So I joined the technical secondary school of commerce.
>
> I finished the commercial technical school with excellent marks and could have applied to the University of Commerce, but my brother and mother refused.
>
> My mother was against continuing my education because of the expense involved and because she wanted me to help at home. My brother was already at university and said that universities are night-clubs where the girls are loose and hookers. My father, on the other hand, said that I could easily get a job and help maintain the household. Thus, my two sisters were married and my two brothers were studying and I went out to work.

Victims and Heroines

The beginning of U'lfat's working career marked a turning point in her life. Her role in the family changed, but not her obligations or place or status. She was transformed into the major breadwinner but not the main decision-maker. In fact, she was completely excluded from the decision-making process within her immediate family. To ensure that she did not transcend the limits they put on her, the abuse she received from her father, mother and brother increased as her role as the sole provider for the family grew.

Not only do women have a hard time carrying dual responsibilities and dual workloads inside and outside their homes, not only do they endure their parents' control over their lives, but in going out to work women are paid less than men and are exposed to sexual harassment and sexual advances.

> I started working in a clothes shop for two years. I worked hard from 9 a.m. till 9 p.m., and I had to do all the housework when I returned home. I used to sleep after midnight every day and wake up by dawn. I made 25 pounds every week. However, the men in the shop who did similar tasks made 40 pounds a week. I had to give my salary to my father and he gave me 50 piasters per day as my allowance. He had no regular source of income and worked whenever he found a person who wanted to forge a document. At that time, my salary was the main source of income and every two or three months my father was able to make about 300 or 400 pounds. However, even when he had money he still took all of my salary.
>
> When my mother suspected that I liked a colleague at work, all hell broke loose and my brother engaged me to his friend, Aly, who was a very conservative man. He and my family forced me to stop working and stay at home. I had to obey for I had no other way out.
>
> My father started sending me to Aly to ask him for money. It was very embarrassing. My father also took my golden bracelets and promised to get me better ones and told me not to tell Aly. This withdrawing of money became too much for my fiancé, who stopped coming to our house. The tension between my father and him increased. Then when the time came to determine the wedding day, my father created all kinds of obstacles and ruined the plans. Not only that but he refused to give him back his gold, gifts and what he bought for our future home with his money. And of course he refused to give back the money he borrowed from him.
>
> After Aly, I stayed at home to serve everyone, but my father wanted me to work for he was broke. However, my cousin proposed at that time, and my father agreed. My cousin had money with him, and so my father saw a new source of income in front of him. Whenever Hakim came to our house, my father used to ask him for money and Hakim would give him what he

Women as Victims, Women as Survivors?

had. Eight months later, Hakim's money was finished. This was his savings after working for several years in the Gulf countries. Then my father said that he was not a suitable husband and forced me to leave him.

After this I did not want to get married or engaged ever. I started working at my current job in the morning and at a clinic in the evening. As usual, my father took my money and my mother expected me to serve them all at night.

Every day my father used to call me at the office where I worked to tell me that he was starving and that he needed me to get lunch and food for the house. So I used to borrow from my colleagues and others every day. Whenever my father found me with a new thing, he would beat me and accuse me of very bad things. He told me that a girl should not decide for herself, and that he took all my money to curb the devil in me so that I would not think I am too big and too independent for him.

U'lfat's story is a good example of how the structure of classical patriarchy, where the family was maintained by the adult male, has changed because the material and social bases of men's power have eroded. The 'typical household' has given way to new structures where women not only share in the responsibilities but, in many cases, carry the whole financial, social and legal responsibility of the family. However, although women's roles in the family have changed and their burden has increased, their obligations and society's expectations have not changed, thus increasing the load on and oppression of women. A new type of patriarchy has emerged where some women are the chief economic contributors, but not necessarily the main or the only decision-makers, nor are they equally empowered as men. In addition, state programmes appear to reinforce this curious blend of old and new patriarchy because they still function on the assumption that husbands and fathers support women and do not recognise that it is almost the other way around in many families.

What do these Stories Tell us?

The stories of these eight women are the most representative and comprehensive of all the cases I studied during my fieldwork. They show how far removed is the government's interpretation of women's needs from reality. In addition these stories bring to life the different findings of this study such as women's opposition techniques, the control of their sexuality and their reduced citizenship, among other things.

Women do oppose We can begin by stating that women are oppressed, although they have learned through experience to subvert the different types of oppression in different ways. The strongest act of rebellion was, in my opinion, that of regaining control over their bodies and sexuality. In order to achieve full social participation and complete citizenship, it is essential that a woman has control over her body and sexuality. Men take this right for granted, but, as has been shown throughout my study, it remains highly contested for women (Shaver 1990; Orloff 1993). However, women are not entirely powerless, for they undermine men's decision-making power in different ways. Although they may appear to perpetuate some aspects of patriarchy such as female circumcision and the deflowering rituals, they manipulate such rituals to their own favour in order to assert their power and subvert men's dominance over their sexuality and freedom.

Other means of defiance include what U'm Nagah chose to do: to break the law. She opted to reject the system that had failed her by abandoning it and breaking its rules. The rest of the women used other mechanisms in order to access government services. U'm Saber used a combination of tactics and mechanisms to gain access to the state's welfare programmes and help her family. She created networks with the different government and NGO bureaucrats that worked better than the usual system because she provided these bureaucrats with an image of the deserving poor that satisfied their stereotyped ideas.

Intisar also used the weapon of conforming to the stereotype of the helpless and needy woman. Women like Intisar played on society's expectations of them. Since women are denied personhood (see Orloff 1993) because of their reduced citizenship, they play, in defiance, the role of the helpless and subordinate to get what they want from the system and society. Among the women I interviewed, one piece of common advice given to the younger girls and, sometimes, to myself was *I'tmaskin lyhad ma titmakin*, meaning act weak until you are in control. Another common piece of popular wisdom was *lau kanlak 'und il kalb haga u'luh ya sidi*, which means 'if you need a service from a dog call him your master'. This was the policy and philosophy of women who were almost always placed in a weaker position than men by their families, traditions and society.

A new patriarchy is emerging Another very important discovery that resulted from my research in general and is highlighted by these stories is that a new patriarchal structure is evolving. In this new patriarchy, men are no longer delivering on their obligations, although women continue to allow them to maintain a front of power. This new situation – where women work and are becoming the major contributors to the household but are not necessarily its most powerful members – has been emerging during the last several years. While women's work might, in theory, give them more economic resources and thus greater bargaining power within the household compared to the past, their access to these new gains is embedded within familial and domestic responsibilities. Women's relative autonomy over material resources may not necessarily translate into better levels of well-being and status within the family. In other words, women's visible contribution to household income and labour does not necessarily lead to greater bargaining power. On the contrary, the harmful aspects of patriarchy have worsened, and, for example, violence against women has increased or at least has not been reduced. As men become frustrated and are unable to fulfil their expected social obligations, they tend to resent and abuse their women.

What these stories tell us is that 'classical patriarchy' as we have come to know it is being replaced by a new structure and type of patriarchy. Classical patriarchy was based on a particular kind of exchange between men and women. Marriage, to the traditional woman, meant a host of reciprocal commitments: money for food, furniture and clothing to be provided by the husband in return for care, protection of honour, obedience and, above all, sexual favours from the wife (Rugh 1984: 74). The woman's role was confined to the private realm, though within these boundaries she established her own power zone.

The main findings of my fieldwork show that although women and men still theoretically perceive the rigid roles as the ideal, in reality, the roles have changed, and are affecting and disturbing the status quo. The family, in its traditional form and as the basic social unit of Egyptian society, is undergoing sweeping changes. Challenges to the traditional type of family have emerged, and with them, new family structures headed and maintained by women. In these new structures women are the major income-earners and economic contributors to the household.

Given such conditions, it is to be expected that the patriarchal structure of the household will change. Men are no longer fulfilling their traditional roles, which warranted women's submission and gave men the right to control the power within the household and demand obedience from all its members. However, the situation in real life is now different. Ninety-six per cent of all the women I interviewed were battered wives who endured humiliation whether or not they were the main economic contributors to the household.

Resistance to being the head of the household: work as a source of stigma Men are seen as the providers and women as the receivers and carers in return for men's toil. It has thus been logical for many feminists to argue that women's empowerment lies in their ability to earn income through work, substituting themselves as the providers instead of men (Folbre 1983; Macleod 1991; Kabeer 1991; Moghadam 1992a). It has been argued that the economic independence of women through work would lead to their empowerment and to the alleviation of all forms of gender inequality within the family. Women's work has been seen by some feminists as the only way out of disguised serfdom and the means to free themselves from sexual and gender inequalities.

In spite of their work and economic independence, women in this study have neither been offered nor developed an institutional alternative to the male provider. Work was not a welcome alternative to these women, largely due to their lack of skills and education. This situation usually forced them to accept manual and demeaning jobs. Most of these women entered the labour force as a hard fact of life, due to economic need, from the necessity of feeding their children, and not as a choice for reasons of self-development. Thus their burden has increased. Women still have to do all the housework, and they still have to obtain their husbands' permission to leave the house (Macleod 1991: 69–71). The people in the different research areas, which are typical of many low-income urban areas, stigmatise women who work whether they are educated or not. Although some of these working women did gain more power over some decisions in the household, men continued to abuse and exploit them. Furthermore, the restrictive rituals on women's behaviour continued and, in some cases, increased.

To many of these women the demeaning jobs they end up in were not worth the sacrifice they felt they entailed. Many of them did not want to be responsible for their families because they believed this was their husbands' role. In that sense referring to their spouses as 'useless' was their way of getting back at them.

Citizenship and sexuality These stories also highlight the role and importance of sexuality in defining the identity and rights of women. Women's citizenship is defined through their sexuality. Their acceptance in society and by the state is heavily dependent on their conformity to the sexual limitations and control put on them. As mentioned earlier, an unmarried woman reaching 48 years of age is not eligible for the spinster's pension unless she provides a medical or administrative certificate that she is still a virgin and has not been married.

A woman's sexuality also determined her status. A young divorcee was seen as a threat to others and was encouraged by some MOSA officials to remarry. Although the state claims that all clients of welfare programmes are treated objectively, the sexuality and sexual status of women determine their access to services and the way they are treated. In that sense, these women are not equal to men or even to other married women.

Women as Victims, Women as Survivors?

The issue of the identity card and how it affects women's access to services was flagged in several of the accounts cited here. As shown earlier, without an ID women do not exist legally as far as the state is concerned. More relevant to this study is that women without an ID cannot join the formal labour market and are therefore pushed into the more exploitative informal market. The informal market provides neither protection nor an institutional alternative to women's dependency on men. In addition, as mentioned earlier, lack of an ID prevents women from accessing the welfare system.

Relationship with the state and the government bureaucrats As illustrated by these cases, the relationship with the government differed from one woman to the other based on her personal relationship with the bureaucrats who represent the state in the eyes of these women. Although it became evident that there are tensions of different types, the tie to the state was personalised. U'm Saber, for example, was able to get around any obstacle and developed strong ties with specific individuals who facilitated matters for her. On the other hand, Hedeya and especially U'm Nagah had very unpleasant experiences that affected their lives. In all the cases, the state was seen as an 'alien' rather than a representative body, and the women did not feel they had either rights or obligations towards the state. As Hedeya put it, 'The more one could avoid dealing with the state the merrier.' What was established in the relationship with the state was a quasi-formal ritual of the ordeal. The provision of public services and its rules were an important tool used by officials of the state to punish women for being single. There was a deliberate ritual for screening out non-desperate people, and state officials embellished this process by making it more humiliating.

This chapter presented the voices of the women and highlighted my major findings. In the next chapter only one of the above findings will be addressed more deeply: women's ability to oppose or contest patriarchal controls. Although the other findings are important and relevant, each could serve as a theme for an independent study and I highlighted their importance only in the hope that other researchers might be interested in them.

Notes

1. 'U'm means "mother of" and is used as a term of respect. U'm shows that a woman has fulfilled her calling, that of becoming a mother' (Atiya 1980).

2. And urbanites as well.

3. See al-Khayyat (1990) on honour and shame in Iraq and Peristiany (1966) on honour and shame in Mediterranean societies.

4. The woman who combs and prepares the bride.

5. They had originally run away from a feud in their village.

6. The *shabka* is usually the golden bracelets and earrings that are a gift from the groom to his bride. Its value determines how much he values her.

7. Heba el-Kholy in her D.Phil. devotes an entire chapter to the *ayma* or inventory of furniture, its implications and meaning for women in low-income Cairo. See Heba el-Kholy, 'Defiance and compliance: negotiating gender in low-income Cairo', Department of Sociology and Anthropology, SOAS, University of London, unpublished, 1998.

8. A mixture of abandonment and betrayal.

8

Conclusion: Do Women Resist?

In this study, I have explored the nature of the welfare bureaucracy and how it interprets the needs of women – especially FHHs – and how the state's resources and policies constrain women's social and economic prospects. I also examined the ways in which these women responded to state social welfare policies and negotiated for their needs with the state.

Throughout this study the objective has been to evaluate the impact of social and welfare programmes on the status and autonomy of FHHs. One clear conclusion is that social policies and the non-contributory welfare programmes do indeed treat women as secondary and dependent. They also apply procedures that have the effect of imposing controls on women's sexuality. In addition to state policies, the daily practice of officials also signals to these women that they are backward, unproductive dependants and helpless without a male and a protector. These programmes discriminate against women who are single mothers, especially those who are divorcees and deserted women.

The spinster's or 'chastity' pension, administered by MOSA, for example, is a tool used by the state to impose male norms and values on women.[1] As Mernissi argues, virginity is a manifestation of a male preoccupation in societies plagued with inequality and scarcity: 'The concept of honour and virginity locate the prestige of a man between the legs of a woman' (Mernissi 1985: 183). Women are punished if they defile men's honour by losing their virginity outside the institution of marriage. The state therefore enforces eligibility conditions on poor women seeking its services to ensure the protection of men's honour at the cost of women's freedom and control over their sexuality.

I also studied different religious welfare programmes, Islamic and Coptic, with the aim of examining the impact of and comparing these systems parallel to the state, and assessing how they address and treat women and especially FHHs. Although women felt more welcomed by the Islamic programmes, this was contingent on whether they followed the rules. Only widows with children were eligible for the Kafalet al-Yateem programme of the Shari'iyya NGO. The only permissible forms of sexuality and social role for women, according to these Islamic programmes, are those centred around childbearing and childcare.

When comparing the approaches, attitudes and assumptions of the different religious welfare programmes towards women, one is astonished by their similarity. The Islamic and Coptic systems hold the same underlying assumptions and beliefs regarding women's role and status within their families. As shown earlier, these religious NGOs perceive women's domestic and reproductive functions as their primary roles in life. Different types of female headship are neither recognised nor appreciated. In the religious programmes studied, there was no tolerance for divorcees or women on their own. Subtle messages delivered to society at large and to the family unit in particular through these religious programmes continue to marginalise women and FHHs.

This study also found that the state's welfare system in Egypt is not woman-friendly. However, it is important to note that the state's attitude towards the poor in general is condescending, and that the poor in Egypt find it difficult to access the state's public services. The situation of women, and especially FHHs, is worse because they tend to be at the lowest rung of the ladder with regards to rights and opportunities. Within this context the danger of the religious alternative, especially the Islamic alternative, becomes more serious. When the poor find no avenue for expressing their needs and no effective or humane system responding to such needs except the new Islamic groups, then it becomes more logical to join them. This poses a serious threat to the legitimacy and credibility of the state. The Egyptian state must revise its targeting system and procedures for eligibility. The continuous sacrificing of women's issues and the woman question to appease and accommodate the Islamic groups will, in the end, compromise the state and the current regime as the Islamic groups gain more ground with the poor, be they men or women.

On the other hand, this study also learned that in spite of the different restrictions on women, they have found ways to negotiate for the satisfaction of their needs. The evidence presented in Chapter 7 of how oppressed women have learned to manipulate the situation through deception (Intisar and the fake deflowering) or by escaping to a world of fantasy[2] is proof of women's ability to protest and oppose different restrictions and conditions. The three coping mechanisms identified by this study in Chapter 5 – confirming the stereotype, networking, and exchange of favours – are tactics for opposition. These are techniques used by subordinate groups in their relationship with the dominant group.

James C. Scott, studying Malaysian peasants in *Weapons of the Weak* (1985) and general systems of oppression in *Domination and the Arts of*

Conclusion

Resistance: Hidden Transcripts (1990), examines the wide range of low-profile and subtle forms of 'resistance' that constitute the political discourse between the weaker group and the more powerful group and identifies four types of political discourse. The first is the flattering self-image of the elite. The second is the concept of 'hidden transcripts', which is limited to criticisms by the weaker group (slaves) about the more powerful group behind their backs. The third is the politics of disguise and anonymity that takes place in public view but is camouflaged under other forms such as rumours, jokes, folk-tales or gossip. Scott labels this third type the infra-politics of subordinate groups. The fourth is the political outburst, which in most cases is momentary but is a reproduction of what has been stated in the hidden transcripts of a particular group (Scott 1990: 18-19).

In my fieldwork I identified three specific coping mechanisms. The first is negative self-representation, whereby women conformed to the image expected of them. They lived up to the stereotype of low-income illiterate women as poor, ignorant, helpless and unhealthy. By appealing to the egos of the officials and living up to their expectations, these women ensured access to the state's services. This performance by the weaker party is described aptly by Scott: 'What is seen from above by the dominant group as the interaction of a required performance can look from below like the artful manipulation of deference and flattery to achieve its own ends' (1990: 34). Informal networking, in which women use personal, kinship and family ties, is the second coping mechanism. Women form informal networks of assistance that help them learn about the procedures for application and the papers needed for each programme. Several women I met had cultivated relationships with key people who facilitated their access to basic services. Finally, log-rolling or the exchange of favours is the third coping mechanism of the women identified in this study. In this instance, applicants provide favours to the employee in return for enrolment in the welfare programme. These three mechanisms subverted some of the bureaucratic obstacles faced by women applicants, and helped them gain access to the state's services.

I also demonstrated through the case-studies how different women learned to adapt to situations of oppression, whether public or private. Intisar, in her opposition to society's control over her body and sexuality, faked the deflowering process and blamed others for her problems. She acted as the irresponsible minor that everyone expected her, a female, to be. U'm Nagah broke out of the legal system that refused to recognise her needs and to show her respect. Shadia's rebellion and opposition took the form of running away from her parents and then from her husband, and also by running away into a world of dreams and fantasies.

In this final chapter, I argue that although the women I studied have managed to subvert some aspects of their oppression, whether the source is the state, society or the men in their lives, the fact remains that these women continue to be oppressed and unable to change their situation. To say this is to challenge some currently popular notions about women's resistance and, by doing that, I am putting myself in a very difficult position. I argue that these women oppose their oppressive conditions but do not resist them. They manipulate an oppressive system, but a system manipulated is a system reinforced (Burton 1997: 6–8). I also argue, based on my findings in the fieldwork and on my 20 years of experience working in development in Egypt, that these women are oppressed by their families, the men in their lives, society and traditions, and that their means of opposing this oppression do not add up to sustainable strategies for changing their subordination to men. Finally. I argue that women's survival strategies are not struggles for resistance but are just coping strategies.

Taking this academic position means that I could be accused of treason, that I have betrayed my own people and that I am a 'Westernised' middle-class woman who is applying Western standards to non-Western Egyptian women. I could easily be accused of calling these women 'passive', which would add up to being a white Western woman seeing black women as victimised and as passive (Amos and Parmar 1984). I could also be grouped with colonial researchers and colonial feminists who consider the West to be the normative model and who apply universal Western standards to evaluate all peoples of the world. (Mohanty 1991: 52–4). Mohanty argues that cultural colonisation is not monopolised by Western feminists but that Third World women who apply the same universal ethnocentric principles and believe in Western superiority are also implementing a form of cultural colonisation. Such middle-class Third World women are Western-educated and theorise about rural or lower-income women in their countries in the same way that Western women address 'the other' (1991: 52–5). I fear that Mohanty would include me in this category.

Recent feminist thought has been promoting the idea that women resist their oppression and have developed mechanisms to subvert any social, legal or economic male-dominated systems. Women's bargaining power within the household (Kabeer 1991, 1992; Hansen 1991; Kandyoti 1991b; Zinn 1991), their coping mechanisms (Macleod 1991; White 1992), and their ability to subvert autocratic systems 'in their own way' are arguments used to prove that women, especially Third World women, are not as helpless or weak as they have been portrayed to be by western researchers. These women are 'resisting' in their own cultural way (White 1992; Macleod 1991). Feminist historians argue that, for example, historically, women resisted the imposition of state power by seeking autonomy in strategies of refusal and withdrawal. These strategies might, to the un-

Conclusion

trained observer, be equated with victimisation or passivity, but instead they are being reinterpreted as conscious strategies to counter patriarchy (Charlton et al. 1989: 188; Staudt 1990; Goetz 1991b).

Some feminists argue that the images of 'helpless' and 'victimised' Third World women were held up as rationalisations for colonisation. Sarah White argues that the discourse in contemporary development literature on women in Bangladesh chose to present a particular image of them and thus reflects a colonial set of values and interests (1992: 3). She claims that concern with the status of women (in her case in India) was used to assert British superiority and justify colonialism. She adds that there is a gap between the researcher who is 'the Westerner' and the researched who is 'the victimised Indian' woman. This school of thought follows that of Said's *Orientalism*, which argues that the production of Western knowledge about Arabs was closely tied to the will and aim of establishing an empire. In other words, the Western discourse describing Muslim Arabs as backward and barbaric was driven by a logic of domination in which Western white superiority had to create an 'inferior Eastern' opposite to itself to justify colonisation and deprive these people of their rights (Said 1985: 3). Following the same logic, it is argued that 'labelling' is used to justify interventions by richer countries in the politics of developing countries. The labelling of Third World countries as poor and in need of assistance justified colonialism in the past (Wood 1985; White 1992), just as it is now held to justify the intrusions of contemporary development agencies.

By arguing that the women I have studied are oppressed I could be accused of saying that these women are passive, that they are victims. However, this is not my claim: I am saying only that the ways in which these women oppose the dominant patriarchal system do not contribute to challenging its basic premises. At the very best, they give them a stronger position as women within a male-dominated world, conforming to male expectations, and getting rewards for being the kind of women men expect them to be. They do not challenge male dominance itself, and in fact they do not really fundamentally subvert it. In saying this I go against the current trend of celebrating women's coping strategies as more than just coping, as resistance, as ways of carving out a special space for women's worlds. I argue that this current trend goes too far.

I thus find myself in an ideological, cultural and religious dilemma. I am writing in English for a Western readership and any criticism of my own culture and religion could be held against me. Readers could use this study to prove that Islam is a repressive religion at a time when Islam has replaced communism as the 'new enemy' of the Western world, at a historical period when the economic conditions and political positions of the Arab countries are deteriorating. By arguing that these Egyptian women are oppressed due to cultural, legal and structural conditions, I would be confirming the Orientalist's image of the victimised Muslim woman who is repressed by Islam. At this point in time, it would add to the subtle attack on Islam and Muslims who are being portrayed by the Western media as terrorists and barbarians. Under all these circumstances, should I then give the West another weapon and confirm their image of 'the victimised Muslim' woman? Or should I be politically correct and nationally aware and follow the current feminist trend to show that in spite of all oppression these women are heroines and resist their oppressors, even if I do not believe that? The dilemma we experience as non-Western feminists – in our desire to be critical of how some of our traditions oppress women – conflicts with our desire as members of once colonised cultures to affirm the value of these same traditions.

Nevertheless, the feminist activist in me decided that I could not conform to such ideological oppression. I decided to stick to my ideas and prepare to defend them. I would like to begin by saying that I am not juxtaposing Egyptian women against Western women and that there is no place for any comparison. In this study I am talking about oppressed and battered women in Egypt, but I believe that they are found in the USA and Europe as much as in Egypt. All over the world, women are oppressed, because, Western or not, we all live in a male-dominated world. I also believe that all religions have elements of patriarchy that render women dependent and place them in a secondary position. Having said all that, I can now go back to the specificity of my research and the women I studied.

Opposition versus Resistance: A Definition

The three mechanisms mentioned above are techniques by which oppressed and marginalised women have coped with the different cultural, social and legal restrictions put on them. It is important to note that although these women coped with and opposed oppression, they did not resist it. One must distinguish between continuous resistance or complete rebellion and opposition or objection through moments of subversion (Burton 1997; de Certeau 1980). Indeed, women do oppose and have developed coping mechanisms, but the issue I would like to emphasise is that manipulation and deception do not add up to a form of resistance or a resistance strategy. In this chapter I am making a distinction between resistance, which I see as an act of 'challenging oppressive structures', and opposition, which is 'coping within constraints'.

In other words, this research forced me to rethink the whole notion of resistance. I draw on Burton (1997), de Certeau (1980) and Scott (1985, 1990) in thinking through the difference between resistance and opposition.

Conclusion

This distinction is developed further in Burton's work on the Caribbean. In his (1997) book *Afro-Creole: Power, Opposition and Play in the Caribbean*, Burton traces the history, origin and development of Afro-Caribbean culture and studies the different means of cultural resistance of its people. He focuses on the cultural resistance of the natives and the slaves in Jamaica, Trinidad and Haiti. He draws on the distinction, first developed by Michel de Certeau (1980), between resistance and opposition. It is this distinction that I also adopt in this study. Resistance, according to de Certeau, is a form of contestation and rebellion from outside any system using concepts and means that are derived from sources other than those of the system in question with the aim of overthrowing that system.[3] Opposition is an act of contestation that is constructed from within the system and uses concepts of and from the system itself. Thus the process of opposition reinforces the system. In other words, for women to resist their husbands and the oppressive men in their lives, they have to be able to step out of the system of oppression, not only that of marriage, but the broader relationship where men are the dominant power and women are the dominated weaker group. However, to resist these conditions (system) by elements from the 'outside' does not necessarily mean borrowing Western standards or values, because outside does not always mean the West. Women – both Muslim and Christian – need to go back to the humanitarian elements of their religions and use them in trying to change their oppressive situations. For example, female circumcision is not condoned in Islam or even called for, and women activists are using this argument to ban FGM and change people's attitudes. Manipulation and deception as a means of coping with or subverting the oppressive conditions under which they live are only instances of subversion whereby women use concepts from within the system to express their frustration. These actions do not help them break free from the relationship. Their oppressed situation does not change. In that sense, by objecting to and challenging the unequal gender relationships without overtly rebelling against them, women unconsciously tend to reproduce these basic oppressive structures of hegemony and dominance, although consciously they are attempting to challenge the very same structures (Burton 1997: 8).[4] It is this problem of the relation between opposition and resistance (using de Certeau's definition) and the subtle distinctions between the two that will be discussed here with regard to women's, and especially FHHs', relationship to their men and the state.

To me, women might be bargaining or strategising within a set of rules of the game and the 'parameters' of a given culture. That is what Kandiyoti called a 'patriarchal bargain' and, as she notes, it is not a bargain between equals, for women bargain from a weaker position (1991d: 104). I believe that the issue here is what I would call not actions, such as coping or bargaining, or even covert resistance, but survival mechanisms. Resistance is what the women in Kenya did when they were deprived of their own plots in the Mwea irrigated rice settlements: they deserted their husbands (Hanger and Moris 1973 in Kandiyoti 1991a: 105). Gambian women, on the other hand, resisted by making their husbands pay them wages for their labour (Dey 1981 in Kandiyoti 1991a: 105–6). Kandiyoti has recently defined resistance as 'the capacity of disadvantaged groups to achieve a degree of articulation of their interests and to acquire means to act in their furtherance' (forthcoming: 4). In other words, it is the ability to express and interpret one's needs and to act on those needs.

Had Intisar refused the ritual of *dukhla baladi* instead of faking it, that would have been resistance and not manipulation and deception. If battered women took legal action against the violence of their husbands that would be resistance, because they could consequently stop such abuse. However, women cannot do that because they have no institutional survival alternative to the husband, marriage and family. They stand to lose the 'fragile shelters' of marriage in which they live. The only thing they can do is to bargain and negotiate on a limited scale to make their lives more bearable. In that sense their actions are not those of resistance.

Under these constraints women object to and complain about injustices. They may even manipulate their men or their families, but such acts do not constitute an act of resistance. My point is that they are highly constrained in their capacity to change their status because neither the state nor the community has provided them with an institutional alternative to the male provider. As shown earlier in this study, the welfare benefits given to women through state non-contributory programmes are low and insufficient for maintaining their families. In addition, public officials and the community perceive women and especially FHHs as dependants who cannot survive on their own and need a man to protect and also to control them. The women I studied were not passive: they were able to cope with, challenge and subvert the different systems of oppression imposed on them. However, these forms of objections did not get them out of their 'oppressive' environment, nor did these actions change their marginalised positions. In other words, their manipulative actions were not 'forms of resistance'.

If women's so-called 'resistance' is limited and constrained by 'external factors' (Agarwal 1994) or by the 'boundaries of the dominant group and its ideology' (Kandiyoti, forthcoming) then in reality we are exaggerating the impact of these acts on women's status within the household and we might be legitimising the status quo. The recognition of some acts of subversion as resistance may blind women to their powerlessness as they are given the space to 'let off steam' without gaining real power in their

Conclusion

relationship with the dominant group. Such action does not lead to a significant renegotiation of roles and power status within the marriage relation. It could be a form of resistance but only leads to a release of tension, which is a form of accommodation (Kandiyoti, forthcoming: 8). It is in that sense that I call these actions 'opposition', because I believe that the term 'resistance' – despite all efforts to expand its meaning and connotations – carries within it elements of overt defiance and challenge, leading to action and change. I am not challenging the fact that women are able to bargain and negotiate some benefits for themselves, but I prefer to call this 'opposition'. As mentioned earlier, one is 'coping within constraints' and the other is 'challenging the status quo for change', and the difference is not just a difference in semantics.

In Kandiyoti's article 'Gender, power and contestation', she states that when she originally argued in 'Bargaining with patriarchy' (1991d) that resistance is possible but constrained by the predominant culture, she thus concealed evidence of hegemony by giving its impact and effects another name, that of ' resistance', although it was in reality only bargaining techniques or coping within constraints. Mitchell makes the same critique of James C. Scott, arguing that, in reality, Scott's peasants conformed because they had no alternative. That means that Scott 'hid' evidence of hegemony by not analysing the limits to peasants' resistance and thus disguising the effects of such hegemony (Mitchell 1990 in Kandiyoti, forthcoming: 8). This is precisely my point. By selecting moments of subversion from the lives of oppressed women and by describing these moments as resistance we are ignoring the external patriarchal environment within which these women live and concealing the oppressive impact of the hegemonic relationship between women and men.

Feminism, Post-modernism and Cultural Relativism

Challenges to misogynist claims to know the nature of women and the nature of the world have been the basis of feminist analysis since its inception. Early work criticising the traditional male epistemology (Wollstonecraft 1967; J. S. Mill 1970) established the model for subsequent female analysis (Hawkesworth 1987: 115–16). In fact the basis of feminist assaults on the works of male social research was a challenge to the authoritativeness of their claim to knowledge about the world and the nature, interests and needs of women (Jones 1993: 193–6). Feminists started correcting this bias by placing women's experiences at the core of their analysis. However, the pioneer feminists of the West began adopting an authoritative position regarding knowledge about the universal oppression of women. With the advent of post–modernism this claim to knowledge, authority and the ability of anyone to tell the true story was challenged. Consequently, authority became a taboo and a feminist making definitive statements or giving herself the right to speak in sure terms about someone apart from herself was viewed with suspicion (Jones 1993: 189).

Post-modern feminists argue that we must be culturally sensitive, avoid cultural colonialism and recognise that women's situations differ due to difference in class, rank, race and culture. In other words, women are not a homogeneous group universally subject to the same pattern of patriarchal or class or race oppression (Scott 1988; Amos and Parmar 1984).

The post-modern approach has its strong and weak points. Its strength lies in its critique of the Western model as the superior model to be followed. However, the culturally specific argument may be taken too far: one could argue, for example, that practices such as female circumcision should not be assessed as acts of oppression, as this would be a form of applying Western standards. Instead, female circumcision should be assessed within its proper contexts. Such attention and deference to tradition means that if something exists in a traditional society, then it must be of use or serves an important function in that society. In other words, post-modern feminists would argue that it is mistaken to condemn FGM universally without an understanding of the function it serves within its own society. Actually that is a form of functionalism, which post-modernists are assumed to have rejected. To outlaw FGM, according to post-modernists, would be ineffectual if other aspects of gender relations were not changed in a particular culture. People will carry on with it if it is still important to the way in which families and societies function. Yet by not reporting on or analysing these rituals we would be implicitly condoning them. To expose and analyse them would, in my opinion, be the first step towards changing and deconstructing such actions.

Habermas (1987), Dews (1987) and Norris (1990) argue that relativism, if taken to extremes, is self-contradictory. The claim that there are no criteria to assess the different discourses and situation is in itself an 'absolute claim to validity' and is therefore what the relativists argue is impossible to have (see McLennan 1992: 339 in Kiely 1995: 155). Another problem with the post-modernist argument is that it too classifies women into categories: Third World women and 'the others', be they Western or Third World middle-class Westernised women. This argument also labels those who describe Third World women as victims or as oppressed by a patriarchal order as 'ethnocentric', 'culturally insensitive' or 'imperialist feminists'. The fear of being labelled as such prompts many Western and other feminists to select moments of subversion and call them resistance. It persuades them to ignore aspects of oppression in order to be able to describe their subjects as resourceful and empowered. There is an under-

Conclusion

lying assumption that any work about Third World women puts them in an immediate comparison with the better-off First World and Western women. There is a reluctance by feminists (Western and non-Western) to use words such as subordination because they can suggest victimisation and can fail to understand ways in which women actively bargain with patriarchy in order to make their lives more bearable.

However, without some acceptance of universalism, how can different forms of oppression be criticised? There is a need to agree on a shared level of basic human rights against which we can assess whether injustices have occurred. Female circumcision and marital rape are acts of violence against women, regardless of the age, race and class of the women. They are an invasion of women's right to control their bodies and their sexuality. Women suffer physically and mentally as a result of these acts, even if their societies and cultures condone such behaviour. And even if these women find ways to manipulate and subvert these rituals (as in the case of Intisar), the fact remains that these oppressive rituals continue to exist.

This brings me to the concept of culture: it is not static and it changes, develops and has different interpretations. In many of the post-modernist concerns for cultural relativism I detect a romantic and static view of culture. There is a romantic view about Egyptian culture, for example, in ideas such as the belief that the role of mother and wife is highly praised and that women are the corner-stones of the well-being of their husbands and children. Society values the woman's place as long as she keeps to that place prescribed for her (Macleod 1991). It is true that society might respect a married woman more than a single unmarried or a divorced one. However, this high regard and respect does not prevent this wife and mother from being battered by the husband or raped within marriage, because she has no right to refuse her spouse's sexual advances. In addition, neither society nor the state, as we have seen throughout this study, recognises that this sacred mother has any independent or individual needs or interests: men's interests are taken as representative of the whole family. When ADEW[5] started a project to provide poor women with credit and legal aid in 1987 and identified FHHs as the target group, we were accused of being 'Westernised' and of not understanding the Egyptian culture. Officials, public figures and other national development agents told us that women were never left to fend for themselves and that male relatives would always 'take care of their women'. We conducted research because we believed that, traditionally, this might have been the case, but that the situation and therefore traditional cultural behaviour had changed. We discovered that in the slum area where we worked, FHHs constituted 30% of the population and that women were left to fend for themselves even when their husbands were physically present. Had we succumbed to the static and romantic view of culture, we would not have helped the thousands of FHHs in that slum area.

As mentioned earlier, I could be accused of applying my Westernised middle-class biases in assessing, interpreting and analysing the stories of the women interviewed in this study. Yet when U'lfat talked about female circumcision, it was she who described it as an act that harmed her physically and psychologically. Although Hedeya stated that she would continue this ritual with her daughter, she also described it as an act of cruelty but one that had to be done: 'dah sharr la bud minuh' (this is a necessary evil).

Wife-battering is a violent and humiliating experience, as stated by the women themselves in their own words, without any interpretation or analysis on my part. Here is what Halla said:

> I felt like dying. I hated him and hated my life. I even hated this world, which has no justice. He beat me with an electric cable and it hurt, but what really hurt most is when he slapped me on my face in front of my children. How can they respect me after that. I have no personality in their eyes. (Halla, 29, married to an *u'rzu'i*, 'The Shelters')

Shadia had a similar story to tell:

> My father used to beat me, and he allowed my younger brother to beat me too. He said that girls need to be disciplined and that men are in charge of the women in their families regardless of age. So when Fawzi, my husband, began beating me too, I realised that as a woman I have no way out. This is our destiny, to be treated like trash by all the men of our lives. We have no alternative. This is the destiny of our mothers before us and our daughters after us. We are made to serve the men even if we do not like it. (Shadia, 28, married to an unemployed man, 'The Shelters')

The cases of U'lfat, Shadia and Halla are similar to many stories I heard from women in the different research sites. When I described wife-battering as a tool for patriarchal oppression I was not using Western standards, but was conveying the messages of these women with as much integrity as possible. Similarly, some of the women interviewed expressed anger and frustration about their lack of opportunities and their denial of better education. The stories of Hedeya and U'lfat are only examples of how, because they were women, they were denied better and higher education although they had the potential to succeed and progress. Both women saw this as a form of injustice and oppression and both women 'accommodated' because they had no alternative. Both women claimed that they would fight for a better future for their female children. The issue is whether they will succeed, given that we are living in a patriarchal society that gives women few choices and alternatives. Should feminists, human rights groups and activists campaign to help these women or should we, because we cannot claim to know what is really good for other women, do nothing? How can their lives be improved, and whose responsibility is it?

Women, Society and the State: A Relationship of Opposition or Resistance

The argument of post-modern feminists continues by claiming that the absence of uprisings and violent resistance does not mean that the dominated group has accepted its situation. There are other forms of resistance, such as inward, non-violent and cultural resistance. According to this argument one must distinguish between overt resistance, which is open and confrontational, and the different degrees or levels of covert resistance. In some cases, it is argued that the accommodation to oppression is, in itself, an act of covert resistance. Patterson (1967) argues that by producing the image of the smiling and 'fawning dullard' that his master expects of him, the slave is preserving his inner freedom (in Burton 1997: 49). This is similar to what I discovered when impoverished illiterate women presented themselves as helpless, ignorant and poor to the state's welfare officials in order to live up to their expectations and, by doing so, gain access to the state's services. They too might be preserving their inner freedom and might be using ridicule or jokes behind the officials' backs as to how they deceived them and got what they wanted.[6]

However, I do not consider this an act of resistance: they are not resisting, but merely coping with an unjust and humiliating situation. By confirming the stereotype, they are reinforcing the structures and underlying assumptions of this oppressive relationship and, more importantly, they are confirming their demeaning image in their own minds and the minds of the officials. By adopting these coping mechanisms, such women are not changing the status quo and are not challenging imposed images and values that are embedded with male norms.

Talking to the different women, observing their daily lives and listening to their stories made me realise that we have taken women's oppression for granted. The belief in women's ability to resist their oppressors came as a relief not only to the oppressors but, I believe, to the feminist researchers and activists as well. The currently popular discourse of women's resistance distracts attention from the pain of subordination. It lets oppressors off the hook because if women can resist, the oppression must not be so absolute or tyrannical. And for feminist researchers, it gives us positive stories to tell, which is easier on our conscience than negative ones.

The following stories are direct citations from the fieldwork and could better explain the difference between resistance and opposition or manipulation in women's relationship with the state officials and their husbands. They are moments of subversion that I call acts of opposition, and not resistance.

This is the story of Sedika:

> Mr M., the social worker at the school, asked me to clean his house and help his wife and said that, in return, he would help me get the divorcee's pension from the state and exempt my children from the school fee. I work there four days a week from six in the morning till six in the evening. He pays me five pounds a day although the market rate is ten pounds. His wife is kind but he is very mean and he slapped me once because I broke a glass. I cannot leave them, for he threatened to cancel the pension and kick my children out of school. I have no one.

Sedika found several ways to get back at him. She gossips about him and his family to his colleagues all the time, and tells stories about his family disputes and problems. Since she began working there, Mr M. has had to buy four dozen glasses. Sedika slips into a sly smile every time she talks about how she sometimes loses control and 'unintentionally' glasses fall and break. In her own way, Sedika opposes the government bureaucrat who is abusing his power. However, she still works at his house for less than the market wage and she still endures his humiliation.

Affaf is married to Antaar, a 55-year-old drunkard who sends her to work in a shoe factory in the morning and with a seamstress in the late evenings. She returns home at 10p.m. every night and leaves to work at 5a.m. They have no children because she is barren. As a barren woman, she has no chance to remarry and her family is too poor to take her back if she gets divorced. Antaar beats Affaf nearly every day with an electric cable. I had to take her to the clinic twice. She refuses to file a complaint lest he divorces her.

Initially, Affaf denied that she felt any humiliation or insult. As we came to know each other, she told me how she dreams every night that she has poisoned him. But short of actually killing him, she gives him 'cheated alcohol'[7] every night. She also explained that on many occasions she burned his clothes while ironing them, especially the shirts he likes. She added that she would then endure the beating as long as she saw 'anger' and irritation in his eyes.

Affaf's story demonstrates how she is trying to find ways to get back at her husband and challenge his authority. She gives him cheated alcohol, burns his clothes, and causes him discomfort. But her situation is not changed. She still works to feed him, buys his drink for him, and is battered in the most violent way.

Conclusion

Howayda's story is yet another example of how women use deception to subvert the different oppressive systems and rituals:

> I am not ashamed to tell, for you will understand. You are different and I have grown to trust you. I was in love with this man who was tall and blonde and he looked like a movie star. He promised to marry me and I believed him, so I gave him the most valuable thing I own, my virginity. We had a wonderful time together, but when he proposed my father refused and insisted that I must marry my cousin and that no girl of his would marry outside the family.
>
> I cried for many nights, but my father insisted and even arranged with the priest all the wedding details. I was so scared that they would find out that I was no longer a girl.[8] They would kill me and my father would die of shame. I told my friend and we both went with her aunt to a doctor who made me a virgin again. I saved my family's honour and my husband thinks very highly of me. I am telling you this story because I want to share my victory with someone. They forced me into a marriage that I did not want but I was able to deceive them. Sometimes I am afraid my daughter will do the same. Therefore I will not force her to marry some one she does not love.

In the three cases cited above, as in all the cases mentioned throughout this study, women opposed and subverted male authority, but in the end the material, cultural and psychological aspects of their subordination had not changed.

The Veil: A Political Act or an Act of Surrender?

Macleod's (1991) defence of the 'new veiling' of lower middle-class (LMC) Egyptian women is a relevant contemporary example of the way in which a culturally relativist approach can select moments of subversion and translate them into social acts of 'political protest'.

Macleod argues that LMC women in Egypt wear the hegab (veil) as a mechanism of protest and resistance to ensure that they have freedom of movement and are not secluded in their homes. She argues that these women choose their own brand of Islamic dress that does not necessarily represent a political symbol. Macleod sees the new veiling of these women as an active revival of a traditional symbol for new purposes. This veiling is not an act that reasserts traditional ways, but a new social action (ibid.: 14).

In her book, Macleod criticises the westerners who have described Middle Eastern women as victims of an oppressive culture – that of Islam – as exemplified by the wearing of the veil. She argues that this is an incorrect and inaccurate image of women who are household managers and who play important social and economic roles (ibid.: 17). The issue of the veil is not only controversial but complex and sensitive, especially to women in my position. The 'veil' has been used historically by the West and by Western colonialists as a symbol of Islam's backwardness and oppressive treatment of women. Islamic countries are then compared to the Christian West, which shows their women more respect and deference. In that sense, colonialism was justified as a Western mission to civilise the backward Muslims (Ahmed 1992: 151–3). Since then the veil has become a target for all Western and Westernised attacks on Islam and Islamic societies, a symbol of the oppressive nature of Islam and its backwardness (ibid.: 152).

In response, the veil has been used by Islamic countries such as Iran as a form of resistance to Western domination and hegemony. Women in Iran wore the veil as a national symbol of identity in opposition to the Shah and his corrupt Western allies. So the veil for some became a symbol of political protest against the West. Following this argument, Macleod tries to see the veiling of LMC women in Egypt as a political protest. She critiques the traditional Western definition of political protest and claims that it should not always mean organised, systematic and public dissidence. According to Macleod, this definition is inappropriate for explaining the protest of many subordinate groups, especially non-Western women (1991: 128). By criticising the Western thought that relegates Middle Eastern and Muslim women to the category of helpless victims, and by redefining political protest, Macleod is trying to justify an apparently public act of submission such as wearing the veil as a hidden act of rebellion.

Macleod studied LMC Egyptian women with intermediate education, to whom work meant upward social mobility. These women were the direct beneficiaries of Nasser's revolution. They benefited from the free universal education and guaranteed government employment provided under his regime. Yet instead of gaining freedom and independence because of education and a guaranteed job, these women succumbed to wearing a veil that even their uneducated mothers did not wear.

It might be true that these women manipulated the traditional symbol of veiling to be able to gain more freedom of movement or respect on the streets. But what they have actually done is to play by the rules of the dominant group; they have not tried to change the situation. They did not challenge the status quo, did not challenge their right to go to work without wearing the veil, did not challenge their right to choose the attire that is appropriate for themselves. They admitted to Macleod that they wore the veil in order to be granted freedom of movement outside the home, to avoid harassment on the streets, and to be accepted in the workplace. In

Conclusion

other words, these women had to compromise in order to be accepted by men in the public realm. The veil in this instance is a symbol not of protest but of surrender.

If wearing the veil is an act of rebellion, then one should not worry about this growing phenomenon among young intermediately educated LMC women, for they have developed their own mechanisms for subverting their own system. Instead of arguing that women have gained nothing by joining the workforce because it is still a man's world, and instead of fighting the restrictive attire that is imposed on women by a male-dominated society, under the pretence that this is done to ensure their freedom of movement, we have eased our troubled conscience by finding a way to explain and justify the veil in a positive sense. I am not arguing that it is not true that these women could be using the *hegab* as a means for guaranteeing their mobility. However, to me this is but a manipulative technique against a system imposed on them: it is neither resistance nor rebellion. Macleod's women did not blame the men for harassing them on the street or at work. Instead they took the responsibility for this harassment on themselves and wore the veil to be allowed a place in the world of men. But they did not gain any such place.

Lower middle-class women in Egypt thought that education and a guaranteed government job would provide them with an alternative to dependence on a male, and that they would gain the economic independence that will give them control over their lives. However, the education they get is sub-standard, and the jobs they get are poorly paid and have no boosting impact on their self-esteem. In fact, they achieve little moral or material gain from these jobs, although they can no longer afford not to work because of their economic conditions. Their education and work do not give them more power *vis-à-vis* the men in their lives or the cultural constraints imposed on them. Macleod argues that this new veiling is their own way of resisting the restrictions put on their movement in public. I believe that they are only accommodating their oppressors; therefore, they are not resisting nor is their act a form of political protest.[9]

In conclusion, cultural relativism is an important critique of liberal, Western, white feminists, and it is true that women are not a universal homogeneous group. It is also true that class, race, religion, culture and other factors differentiate and deconstruct the universal image of women and a universal form of oppression. Nevertheless, one should not ignore clear aspects of oppression for the sake of being culturally sensitive. This does not mean that women are as helpless, ignorant and weak as some Western studies or state officials see them to be.

However, they are not as actively rebellious and covertly challenging as some feminists would like us to believe. For although women oppose these constraints and demands of the state welfare system and of society in general, they have not put together a discourse that offers a contradictory interpretation of their needs.

In this process of justifying women's tolerance for discrimination, the de-humanising effects of women's oppression have been forgotten. We have ignored the impact of oppressive traditions, cultures, policies and development programmes on these women. I argue that although women find ways to subvert and manipulate the system, their situation is not changed. The suffering and oppression that they face from childhood on is not reduced or alleviated, even when they become the breadwinners and enter the male public domain.

I was reminded throughout this study that women are oppressed and that their oppression is physical, psychological and mental. Women's bodies are controlled by others, their sexuality is curbed and cast with a shade of disrespect, they have no freedom of choice, and their marginal position is determined for them. As mentioned throughout this book and in the case-studies, a young girl is circumcised in a cruel ceremony. She is scrutinised and controlled until she gets married. In several cases, intelligent young women were refused the opportunity for education. Furthermore, women's purity is publicly tested through the spectacle of the *dukhla baladi*.

As a single *de jure* FHH, a woman is stigmatised or controlled to ensure that she conforms to what is expected of her. As a *de facto* FHH, a woman who maintains her family and her husband is still oppressed and abused. I discovered that 96% of all the women I interviewed were battered in spite of the fact that most of them were the breadwinners. It seems that traditional patriarchy has been replaced by a new form of patriarchy that remains unrecognised by many scholars and, more importantly, by the state's policy-makers, although it certainly exists and is flourishing.

Ironically, many of the rituals of oppression that were established in the interests of men are maintained by women. Why is it that women are becoming the reproducers of oppression and violence against their own gender? Why is the mother, mother-in-law or grandmother the most militant advocate of girls' circumcision and *dukhla baladi*? James Scott, in his analysis of power relations between classes and the powerful and the weak, provides a very appropriate analysis for the unexpected behaviour mentioned above. To Scott, the dominant values and discourse are continuously reinforced by the weak. In the short term, it is in the interest of the weak to produce a credible performance, speaking the lines they think are expected of them. Scott explains that the public performance of the weak is shaped to appeal to the powerful. Although Scott was talking about the relationship between peasants and landlords, I found it very appropriate for the cases of the men and women I studied. In their attempt

Conclusion

to appease the dominant group, women act in the way expected of them and thus reinforce their own oppression (Scott 1990: 2–4). Scott aptly states:

> In any established structure of domination, it is plausible to imagine that subordinate groups are socialised by their parents in the rituals of homage to keep them from harm. A cruel paradox of slavery, for example, is that it is in the interest of slave mothers, whose overriding wish is to protect their children, to train them in the routines of conformity. Out of love, they undertake to socialise their children to please, or at least not anger, their masters and mistresses. (ibid.: 24)

Women might use the hidden transcript of subverting a system as in faking the whole process of *dukhla baladi*, but they still publicly condone it and therefore reinforce it. Scott states:

> Those obliged by domination to act a mask will eventually find that their faces have grown to fit that mask. The practice of subordination in this case produces, in time, its own legitimacy. (ibid.: 10)

Burton found in his work on Caribbean slaves that in their relationship with the dominant group they develop a culture of opposition and not of resistance, because they draw heavily on materials furnished by the dominant culture: stereotypes, discourse, rules and tradition in order to modify, subvert and negotiate their needs (1997: 7–8). And by using the discourse and material of the dominant group, they reassert and reinforce the dominant culture.

It is important to note that I am not describing the status of all women and I am not comparing Egyptian women and Western women or describing the former as worse off than the latter. I am not even generalising my findings to include all Egyptian women regardless of class and rank. I am not trying to portray an image of the 'victimised Muslim woman', for I have studied Christian women as well. I am limiting my observations and conclusions here to the women whom I have studied, low-income urban women heads of households. They are not victims who need rescuing by Western superiors, but they are also not rebels struggling to acquire their freedom. They are oppressed women who challenge their oppressors but they certainly do not resist these oppressors in any systematic sense, or in any way that might change the structure of oppression.

Arguing that poor illiterate Egyptian women do not resist but oppose does not mean that I condone many of the theoretical conceptualisations and descriptions of Third World and particularly of Muslim women that exist within Western white feminist literature. What I am arguing is that there is a growing limitation in the feminist movement across borders, especially with regard to the issues feminists are opting to organise around. The power of feminist demands stops at the point when critical and bold political decisions need to be made, political decisions that require bold actions and a strong stand. By relegating the right to challenge, oppose and change existing systems of oppression to the women themselves through their resisting mechanisms, feminists are abdicating their role of helping to empower their sisters. The 'struggle' then is also diluted and loses its momentum. Women themselves will not feel the need or maybe the likelihood of changing their situations. If women, as is currently being claimed, do resist and if we, as feminists, are told to sit still under the pretence of cultural sensitivity, then my question is: how will change occur?

Notes

1. As mentioned earlier, there are other ways in which the state imposes certain values on women, such as the condition that divorcees must not be the initiators of divorce.

2. According to Scott (1990), the weak and subordinate are usually insulted and humiliated in their relationships with those in power and control. Women who are abused, battered and insulted and who cannot return the insult or vindicate their moral and physical abuse usually resort to one form of 'hidden transcript', that of fantasy (1990: 37–8).

3. De Certeau's definition is mentioned in Burton 1997: 5–6.

4. De Certeau (1980), Burton (1997) and Scott (1990) were not addressing women's oppression.

5. In the mid-1980s I and some Egyptian women activists established the first feminist NGO that provides credit and legal aid to FHHs in one huge urban slum area in Egypt. I am currently the chairwoman of that NGO.

6. As mentioned earlier, women stated that it is easier to deal with the male MOSA officials because they are easier to fool. See Chapters 4 and 6.

7. Cheated alcohol is methanol added to ethanol.

8. A girl, *bint*, is a virgin by default. A woman is a married female and is therefore no longer a virgin.

9. Macleod does admit that these women are accommodating their oppressors. However, it is her insistence that the new veiling is a political protest that I am critiquing.

Bibliography

Abdalla, Ahmed (1993) 'Egypt's Islamists and the state', *Political Islam*, 23 (4): 28–38, Middle East Research and Information Project (MERIP), Washington, DC.

Abdel Latif, Abla and Amina Kamel (1993) 'Application of targeting options to Egypt, background study for the Egyptian social welfare programme', research supported by the Social Fund for Development, Centre for Economic and Financial Research and Studies, Faculty of Economics and Political Science, Cairo University.

Abramovitz, Mimi (1988) *Regulating the Lives of Women: Social Welfare Policy from Colonial Times to the Present*, Boston, MA: South End Press.

Academy for Scientific Research (1979–80) 'Study of the productive family project and its impact on improving the income and economic standard of its clients and the problems that impede its progress', Wekalat el-Wezara Liltanmia at MOISA.

Ackerly, Brooke A. (1997) 'Measuring empowerment', draft prepared for submission to *World Development*, September.

Afshar, Haleh (1984) 'Muslim women and the burden of ideology', *Women's Studies International Forum*, 7 (4): 247–50.

— (ed.) (1987) *Women, State and Ideology: Studies from Africa and Asia*, London: Macmillan.

— (ed.) (1993) *Women in the Middle East: Perceptions, Realities and Struggles for Liberation*, London: Macmillan.

Agarwal, Bina (ed.) (1988) *Structures of Patriarchy: State, Community and Household in Modernising Asia*, London: Zed Books.

— (1994) *A Field of One's Own: Gender and Land Rights in South Asia*, Cambridge: Cambridge University Press.

Ahmed, Leila (1992) *Women and Gender in Islam: Historical Roots of a Modern Debate*, Cairo: AUC Press.

Alderman, J. and J. Van Braun (1984) *The Effect of the Egyptian Food Ration and Subsidy System on Income Distribution and Consumption*, Research Report 45, Washington, DC: International Food Policy Research Institute.

Allen, Katherine R. (1989) *Single Women's Family Ties: Life Histories of Older Women*, London: Sage.

Altman, Israel (1979) 'Islamic movements in Egypt', *Jerusalem Quarterly*, 10: 87–105.

Altorki, Soraya and Camillia Fawzi el-Solh (eds) (1988) *Arab Women in the Field: Studying Your Own Society*, Syracuse, NY: Syracuse University Press.

Amin, Hussein A. (1994) 'The Islamic movement in Egypt', Mimeo 13, Cairo: New Civic Forum.

Amos, Valeri and Pratibha Parmar (1984) 'Challenging imperial feminism', *Feminist Review*, 17.

Amott, Teresa L. (1990) 'Black women and AFDC: making entitlement out of necessity', in Linda Gordon (ed.), *Women, the State, and Welfare*.

Ansari, Hamied (1986) *Egypt: The Stalled Society*, Albany: State University of New York Press.

Appleton, Simon (1995) 'Women-headed households and poverty: an empirical deconstruction for Uganda', Oxford: Centre for the Study of African Economics.

Assad, Ragui and Malak Rouchdy (1998) 'Poverty and poverty alleviation strategies in Egypt', Cairo: Ford Foundation.

Ashenden, Samantha (1997) 'Feminism, postmodernism and the sociology of gender', in David Owen (ed.), *Sociology after Postmodernism*.

Ashton, Frankie and Gill Whitting (eds) (1987) 'Feminist theory and practical policies: shifting the agenda in the 1980s', Bristol: University of Bristol School for Advanced Urban Studies.

Atiya, Nayra (1988) *Khul-Khaal: Five Egyptian Women Tell Their Stories*, London: Virago.

Attalah, Borham M. (1994) 'Structural and financial regulations of the social security system in Egypt and Germany', in Thomas Scheben (ed.), *Social Security: Egyptian and German Experiences*, Egypt: Wahba Press.

Auda, Gehad (1991) 'Egypt's uneasy party politics', *Journal of Democracy*, 2 (2): 70–8.

Aulas, Marie-Christine (1982) 'Sadat's Egypt: a balance sheet', *Middle East Report*, 107: 6–18.

Ayubi, Nazik (1980) 'The political revival of Islam: the case of Egypt', *International Journal of Middle East Studies*, 12: 481–99.

Azer, Adel (1995) 'Social security for the lower strata of the working population: a socio-legal assessment', in Thomas Scheben (ed.), *Social Security: Egyptian and German Experiences*, Egypt: Wahba Press, pp. 106–18.

Baden, Sally (1993) *The Impact of Recession and Structural Adjustment on Women's Work in Selected Developing Countries*, Sussex: Institute of Development Studies.

Baden, Sally and Bridget Byrne (1996) *Gender Profile of Egypt*, Sussex: Institute of Development Studies.

Baden, Sally and Anne-Marie Goetz (1996) 'Discourses on gender at Beijing: the depoliticisation of feminism', IDS seminar, AFRAS, University of Sussex, 20 February.

Baden, Sally with Kirsty Milward (1995) *Gender and Poverty*, Sussex: Institute of Development Studies.

Badran, Ahmed (1995) 'Health care of children in difficult circumstances', New York: UNICEF.

Badran, Hoda (1904) 'Women responsible for families: towards a national policy and specific programmes', paper presented to the Population Council Conference on Women Headed Households, Cairo, 20 March.

Badran, Margot (1991) 'Competing agendas: feminism, Islam and the state in 19th and 20th century Egypt, in Deniz Kandiyoti (ed.), *Women, Islam and the State*, London: Macmillan, pp. 201–36.

Bahie el-Din, Amira (1994a) 'A legal study on families supported by women', paper presented to the Population Council Conference on Women Headed Households, Cairo, 20 March.

Bibliography

— (1994b) 'Women in front of the law: the Egyptian penal code and women', background paper for the NGO forum 'Task Force on Women in Front of the Law' in preparation for the Fourth UN International Conference on Women, Beijing.

Bahro, Rudolf (1978) *The Alternative in Eastern Europe*, London: New Left Books.

el-Baradei, Mona (1995) 'Egyptian children's affordability to education', Cairo: UNICEF.

Barrett, Michele (1980) *Women's Oppression Today*, London: Verso.

Barrett, Michele and Mary McIntosh (1985) 'Ethnocentrism and socialist feminist theory', *Feminist Review*, 2, Summer: 23–48.

Barros, Ricardo, Louise Fox and Rosane Mendonca (1997) 'Female-headed housholds, poverty and the welfare of children in urban Brazil', *Economic Development and Cultural Change*, 45 (2): 231–57.

Bazoglu, Nefise (1997) *Assessment of the Urban Community Development Project in Cairo: Ein Helwan and Al-Nahda*, 4–12 August, Amman: MENA Regional Office.

de Beauvoir, Simone (1972) [1949] *The Second Sex*, Harmondsworth: Penguin.

Beck, Lois (1980) 'The religious lives of Muslim women', in Jane I. Smith (ed.), *Women in Contemporary Muslim Societies*, Lewisburg, PA: Bucknell University Press, pp. 27–57.

Becker, H. S. and B. Geer (1982) 'Participant observation: the analysis of qualitative field data', in R. G. Burgess (ed.), *Field Research: A Source Book and Field Manual*, London: Allen and Unwin.

Berger, Morroe (1970) *Islam in Egypt Today: Social and Political Aspects of Popular Religion*, Cambridge: Cambridge University Press.

Bernard, H. R. (1994) *Research Methods in Anthropology: Qualitative and Quantitative Approaches*, London: Sage.

Bibars, Iman, Diaa el-Din (1988) 'Womens political interest groups in Egypt: an analysis of women's political interest groups in Egypt and an evaluation of their effectiveness in the establishment of personal status law no. 100 of 1985', MA thesis, Economics and Political Science Department, Cairo: American University.

— (1998) 'Poverty alleviation mechanisms and community empowerment: do credit projects empower the marginalised and the destitute?', paper presented to the Inter-University Consortiun for International Social Development and the Social Fund for Development Egypt Tenth International Symposium 'Livelihoods, NGOS, and Development: Global Dimensions and New Directions', Cairo.

— (1998) 'The social security system in Egypt: a grassroots perspective', report presented to Egypt's social sector Review Mission, Washington, DC: World Bank.

Black, T. R. (1993) *Evaluating Social Science Research: An Introduction*, London: Sage.

Bock, Gisela and Susan James (eds) (1992) *Beyond Equality and Difference: Citizenship, Feminist Politics and Female Subjectivity*, London: Routledge.

Borchorst, Annette and Birte Siim (1987) 'Women and the advanced welfare state – a new kind of patriarchal power?', in Anne S. Hutchinson Sassoon (ed.), *Women and the State*, pp. 128–57.

Boserup, Ester (1970) *Women's Role in Economic Development*, London: George Allen and Unwin.

Bradshaw, Jonathan and Jane Millar (1991) *Lone-parent Families in the UK*, London: HMSO.

Bradshaw, Sarah (1995a) 'Female-headed households in Honduras: perspectives on rural–urban differences', *Third World Planning Review* (special issue on gender and development), 17 (2): 143–58.

Bradshaw, Sarah (1995b) 'Women's access to employment and the formation of women-headed households in rural and urban Honduras', *Bulletin of Latin American Research*, 14 (2): 143–58.

Brocas, Anne Marie, Anne-Marie Cailloux and Virginie Oget (1990) *Women and Social Security: Progress Towards Equality of Treatment*, Geneva: International Labour Organization.

Brown, Sarah G. (1991) 'New writing on women, politics and social change', *Middle East Report*, 173: 29–34.

Brown, Wendy (1992) 'Finding the man in the state', *Feminist Studies*, 18 (1), Spring.

Bruce, Judith and Cynthia Lloyd (1992) *Finding the Ties that Bind: Beyond Headship and the Household*, New York: Population Council and Washington, DC: International Center for Research on Women.

Brydon, Lynne and Sylvia Chant (1989) *Women in the Third World: Gender Issues in Rural and Urban Areas*, Aldershot: Edward Elgar.

Bryman, Alan (1988) *Quantity and Quality in Social Research*, London: Unwin Hyman.

Bryman, Alan and Robert G. Burgess (eds) (1994) *Analysing Qualitative Data*, London: Routledge.

Bulmer, M. and D. P. Warwick (1983) *Social Research in Developing Countries: Surveys and Census in the Third World*, Chichester: John Wiley.

Burgess, R. G. (1982) *Field Research: A Source Book and Field Manual*, London: George Allen and Unwin.

— (1984) *In the Field: An Introduction to Field Research*, London: George Allen and Unwin.

Burghes, Louie (1994) 'Lone parenthood and family disruption: the outcome for children', Occasional Paper 18, London: Family Policy Studies Centre.

Burton, Clare (1985) *Subordination: Feminism and Social Theory*, Sydney: George Allen and Unwin.

Burton, Richard O. E. (1997) *Afro-Creole: Power, Opposition, and Play in the Caribbean*, Ithaca, NY: Cornell University Press.

Buvinic, Mayra (1984) 'Projects for women in the Third World: explaining their misbehaviour', USAID, Washington, April: 1–29.

— (1993) 'The feminisation of poverty: research and policy needs', presented at symposium on Poverty: New Approaches to Analysis and Policy, Geneva: International Institute for Labour Studies.

Buvinic, Mayra, N. H. Youssef and B. Von Elm (1978) *Women Headed Households. The Ignored Factor in Development Planning*, Washington, DC: International Center for Research on Women (ICRW).

Buvinic, Mayra and Geeta Roa Gupta (1994) 'Targeting poor women headed households and woman maintained families in developing countries: views on a policy dilemma', paper presented to Population Council, New York International Center for Research on Women, Joint Programme on Female Headship and Poverty in Developing Countries, February: 1–58.

— (1997) 'Female-headed households and female-maintained families: are they worth targeting to reduce poverty in developing countries?', *Economic Development and Cultural Change*, 45 (2).

Cairo Regional Union for NGOs (1972) *The Impact of the PFP Project on the Families in Cairo*, Cairo: Regional Union for NGOs.

Bibliography

Caplan Pat (ed.) (1987) *The Cultural Construction of Sexuality*, London Routledge.

de Certau, Michel (1980) 'On the oppositional practices of everyday life', *Social Text*, 3: 3–43.

Chambers, Robert (1983) *Rural Development: Putting the Last First*, London: Longman.

Chandler, Joan (1991) *Women Without Husbands: An Exploration of the Margins of Marriage*, Basingstoke: Macmillan.

Chant, Sylvia (1997) *Women Headed Households: Diversity and Dynamics in the Developing World*, London: Macmillan.

Charlton, Sue Ellen, Jana Everett and Kathleen Staudt (eds) (1989) *Women, the State and Development*, New York: State University of New York Press.

Chen, Marty and Jean Dreze (1995) 'Recent research on widows in India: workshop and conference report, *Economic and Political Weekly*, 30 September.

Chester, Robert (1977) 'The one parent family: deviant or variant?', in Robert Chester and John Peel (eds), *Equalities and Inequalities in Family Life* (Proceedings of the Thirteenth Annual Symposium of the Eugenics Society, London, 1976), London: Academic Press.

Chhachhi, Amrita (1989) 'The state, religious fundamentalism and women', *Economic and Political Weekly*, 24 March: 18.

Chhachhi, Amrita and Renee Pittan (1995) 'Multiple identities, multiple strategies: confronting state, capital and patriarchy', working paper 192, Institute of Social Studies.

Clay, E. J. and B. B. Schaffer (eds) (1984) *Room for Manoeuvre: An Exploration of Public Policy in Agriculture and Rural Development*, London: Heinemann.

Clement, Priscilla Ferguson (1992) 'Nineteenth century welfare policy, programmes and poor women: Philadelphia as a case study', *Feminist Studies*, 18 (1).

Cocks, Joan (1989) *The Oppositional Imagination: Feminism, Critique and Political Theory*, New York: Routledge.

Coleman, Gillian (1993) 'Investigating organisations: a feminist approach', occasional paper 37, Bristol: University of Bristol School for Advanced Urban Studies.

Collins, Stephan (1991) 'The transition from lone-parent families to step family', in Michael Hardey and Graham Crow (eds), *Lone Parenthood*, pp. 156–75.

Cummings, Joan (1980) 'Sexism in social welfare: some thoughts on strategy for structural change', *Catalyst*, 8: 7–141.

Dahlerup, Drude (1987) 'Confusing concepts – confusing reality: a theoretical discussion of the patriarchal state', in Anne S. Showstack Sassoon (ed.), *Women and the State*, London: Unwin Hyman, pp. 93–127.

— (1994) 'Differences and commonalities: learning to live with the state: state, market and civil society: women's need for state intervention in East and West', *Women's Studies International Forum*, 17 (2/3): 117–27.

Dallos, Rudi (1995) 'Constructing family life: family belief systems', in John Muncie, Margaret Wetherell, Rudi Dallos and Allan Cochrane (eds), *Understanding the Family*, London: Sage, pp. 173–211.

Dallos, Rudi and Roger Spasford (1995) 'Patters of diversity and lived reality', in John Muncie, Margaret Wetherell, Rudi Dallos and Allan Cochrane (eds), *Understanding the Family*, London: Sage.

el-Damarani, Abeer (1997) 'The lost insurance' (in Arabic), *al-Ahram*, p. 3.

Dandvate, Pramila (1989) 'Social legislation and women', in Pramila Dandvate, Ranjana Kumari and Jamila Verghese (eds), *Widows, Abandoned and Destitute Women in India*, London: Sangam Books.

Dawood et al. (1991–93) *A Research Study on the Management and Organisation of PFP, 1991–1992*, Egypt: Egyptian Society for Social Research and Technology for Community Development and Academy for Scientific and Technological Research.

Dennis, Norman and George Erdos (1992) *Families Without Fatherhood*, London: Health and Welfare Unit, Institute of Economic Affairs.

Dessouki, Ali E. Hilal (1982) *Islamic Resurgence in the Arab World*, New York: Praeger.

Dews, Peter (1987) *Logics of Disintegration: Post-structuralist Thought and the Claims of Critical Theory*, London: Verso.

Diaey, Samir (1995) 'Health and causality insurance in Egypt', in Thomas Scheben (ed.), *Systems of Social Security: Egyptian and German Experiences*, , Egypt: Wahba Press, pp. 88–92.

Dixon, John (1987) *Social Welfare in the Middle East*, London: Croom Helm.

Dohaia, Sayed A. (1988) 'Egyptian government expenditures on basic social services and the 20/20 initiative', Egypt HDR UNDP–INP, 19–21 March.

Donzelot, J. (1979) *The Policing of Families*, New York: Pantheon.

Dreze, Jean (1990) *Widows in Rural India*, London: Suntory Toyota International Centre for Economics and Related Disciplines, London School of Economics, Development Economics Research Programme No. 26.

Duncan, Simon and Rosalind Edwards (1996) 'Lone mothers and paid work: neighbourhoods, local labour markets and welfare state regimes', *Social Politics: International Studies in Gender, State and Society*, 3 (4).

Early, Evelyn A. (1993) *Baladi Women in Egypt: Playing with an Egg and a Stone*, Cairo: AUC Press.

Eisenstein, Zillah (1979) *Capitalist Patriarchy and the Case for Socialist Feminism*, New York: Monthly Review Press.

— (1981) *The Radical Future of Liberal Feminism*, New York: Longman.

EQI (1987) *Porject Proposal for ADEW and FHHs Project*.

— (1988) *Progress Report: FHH Project in Zabaleen and Manshiet Nasser*.

Esim, Simel (1997) 'Can feminist methodology reduce power hierarchies in research settings?' *Feminist Economics*, 3 (2): 389–91.

Esping-Andersen, Gosta (1985) *Politics Against Markets*, Princeton, NJ: Princeton University Press.

— (1989) 'The three political economies of the welfare state', *Canadian Review of Sociology and Anthropology*, 26 (2): 10–36.

— (1990) *The Three Worlds of Welfare Capitalism*, Cambridge: Polity Press.

Esping-Andersen, Gosta and Walter Korpi (1987) 'From poor relief to institutional welfare states: the development of Scandinavian social policy', in R. Erikson, E. Hansen, S. Ringen and H. Uusitalo (eds), *The Scandinavian Model: Welfare States and Welfare Research*, New York: M.E. Sharpe.

Esposito, John (ed.) (1980) *Islam and Development*, Syracuse, NY: Syracuse University Press.

Evans, Peter, Dietrich Rueschemeyer and Theda Skocpol (eds) (1985) *Bringing the State Back In*, Cambridge: Cambridge University Press.

Bibliography

Falco, M. J. (ed.) (1987) *Feminism and Epistemology: Approaches to Research on Women and Politics*, New York: Haworth Press.

Farah, Nadia Ramsis (1994) 'Panel discussion on women-headed households', ICPD NGO Forum.

— (1997) *Poverty Alleviation with a Focus on Women-Headed Households and Micro-credit Programmes in Egypt*, New York: UNICEF.

Ferber, Marianne A. and Julie A. Wilson (eds) (1993) *Beyond Economic Man: Feminist Theory and Economics*, Chicago: University of Chicago Press.

Fergany, Nader (1993) *Research Notes: Characteristics of Women-Headed Households in Egypt*, Al-Mishkat Centre for Research and Training.

— (1994a) 'Panel discussion on women-headed households', ICPD NGO Forum.

— (1994b) ILO, UNDP and UNICEF Workshop on Preliminary Results of the Pilot Study on Urban Women, Work and Poverty Alleviation in Egypt, Cairo: Al-Mishkat.

Ferguson, Kathy E. (1984) *The Feminist Case Against Bureaucracy*, Philadelphia, PA: Temple University Press.

— (1990) 'Women, feminism and development', in Kathleen Staudt (ed.), *Women, International Development and Politics*.

Firestone, W. A. (1987) 'Meaning in method: the rhetoric of quantitative and qualitative research', *Educational Researcher*, 16 (7): 6–19.

Flores, Alexander (1988) 'Egypt: a new secularism?', *Middle East Report*, 153: 27–30.

— (1993) 'Secularism, integralism and political Islam: the Egyptian debate', *Middle East Report*, 183: 23–38.

Folbre, Nancy (1983) 'Of patriarchy born: the political economy of fertility decisions', *Feminist Studies*, 9 (2), Summer.

— (1991) 'Women on their own: global patterns of female headship', *Women and International Development*, 2, 89–126.

— (1994) *Who Pays for the Kids? Gender and the Structures of Constraint*, New York: Routledge.

Foucault, Michel (1972) *Power/Knowledge*, New York: Pantheon.

Fowlkes, Diane L. (1987) 'Feminist epistemology is political action', in M. J. Falco (ed.), *Feminism and Epistemology*.

Frankel, Boris (1983) *Beyond the State? Dominant Theories and Socialist Strategies*, London: Macmillan.

Franzway, Suzanne, Dianne Court and R. W. Connell (1989) *Staking a Claim: Feminism, Bureaucracy and the State*, Cambridge: Polity Press.

Fraser, Nancy (1989) *Unruly Practices: Power, Discourse and Gender in Contemporary Social Theory*, Cambridge: Polity Press.

— (1990) 'Struggle over needs: outline of a socialist-feminist critical theory of later capitalist political culture', in Linda Gordon (ed.), *Women, the State, and Welfare*.

Friedan, Betty (1981) *The Second Stage*, London: Michael Joseph.

Gardner, Katy (1995) *Global Migrants, Local Lives: Travel and Transformation in Rural Bangladesh*, Oxford: Clarendon Press.

Garfinkel, Irwin and Sara S. McLanahan (1986) *Single Mothers and their Children*, Washington, DC: Urban Institute Press.

Gellner, Ernest and John Waterbury (eds) (1977) *Patrons and Clients in Mediterranean Societies*, London: Duckworth and Hanover, NH: Center for Mediterranean Studies of the American Universities Field Staff.

Gimenez, Martha E. (1994) 'The feminisation of poverty: myth or reality?', in Elizabeth Fee and Nancy Krieger (eds), *Women's Health, Politics, and Power: Essays on Sex/Gender, Medicine, and Public Health*, Amityville, NY: Bayood.

Ginsburg, N. (1992) *Divisions of Welfare*, London: Sage.

Glewwe, Paul and Jacques Van Der Gaag (1990) 'Identifying the poor in developing countries: do different definitions matter?', *World Development*, 18 (6): 803–14.

Gluck, Sherna Berger and Daphne Patai (eds) (1991) *Women's Words: The Feminist Practice of Oral History*, London: Routledge.

Goddard, Victoria (1987) 'Honour and shame: the control of women's sexuality and group identity in Naples', in Pat Caplan (ed.), *The Cultural Construction of Sexuality*.

Goetz, Anne Marie (1991a) 'The institutional politics of gender in development policy for rural women in Bangladesh', Ph.D. thesis, Faculty of Social and Political Sciences, University of Cambridge.

— (1991b) 'Feminism and the claim to know: contradictions in feminist approaches to women in development', in Rebecca and Kathleen Newland (eds), *Gender and International Relations*, Milton Keynes: Open University Press.

— (1992) 'Gender and administration', *IDS Bulletin*, October: 7–13.

— (1995a) 'The politics of integrating gender into the state development process: trends, opportunities and constraints in Bangladesh, Chile, Jamaica, Mali, Morocco and Uganda', paper presented to Fourth UN World Conference on Women, Beijing.

— (1995b) 'Institutionalising women's interest and accountability to women in development', *IDS Bulletin*, 26 (3).

— (1996) 'Local heroes: patterns of field worker descretion in implementing GAD policy in Bangladesh', IDS Discussion Paper 358.

— (ed.) (1997) *Getting Institutions Right for Women in Development*, London: Zed Books.

Goetz, A. M. and R. Sen Gupta (1996) 'Who takes the credit? Gender, power and control over loan use in rural credit programmes in Bangladesh', *World Development*, January.

Gordon, Linda (1988) 'What does welfare regulate?', *Social Research*, 55 (4), Winter.

— (ed.) (1990) *Women, the State, and Welfare*, Madison: University of Wisconsin Press.

— (1993) 'Destruction, adjustment, and innovation: social policy transformation in East Central Europe', paper presented to conference 'Constitution Politics and Economic Transformation in Post Communist Societies', Collegium Budapest, 17–19 December.

Graham, Carol (1995) 'The politics of safety nets', *Journal of Democracy*, 6 (2): 142–56.

Graham, Hilary (1987) 'Being poor: perceptions and coping strategies of lone mothers', in Julia Brannen and Gail Wilson (eds), *Give and Take in Families: Studies in Resource Distribution*, London: George Allen and Unwin, pp. 56–74.

Graham-Brown, Sarah (1988) *Images of Women*, New York: Columbia University Press.

Grant, Judith (1987) 'I feel therefore I am: a critique of female experience as the basis for a feminist epistemology', in M. J. Falco (ed.), *Feminism and Epistemology*.

Greeley, Martin (1996) 'Poverty and well being: policies for poverty reduction and the role of credit', in Geoffrey D. Wood and Sharif (eds), *Who Needs Credit: Poverty and Finance in Bangladesh*, UK: University Press.

Grella, Christino E. (1990) 'Irreconcilable differences: women defining class after divorce and downward mobility', *Gender and Society*, 4 (1): 41–55.

Guba, E. G. and Y. S. Lincoln (1988) 'Do inquiry paradigms imply inquiry methodologies?', in D. M. Fetterman (ed.), *Qualitative Approaches to Evaluation in Education*, London: Praeger.

Gunderson, Morley, Leon Muszynski and Jennifer Keck (1990) *Women and Labour Market Poverty*, Ottawa: Canadian Advisory Council on the Status of Women.

Habermas, Jurgen (1987) *The Political Discourse of Modernity*, Cambridge: Polity Press.

— (1992 'Citizenship and national identity: some reflections on the future of Europe', *Praxis International*, 12 (1).

Habib, Rafik (1990a) *Religious Protest and Class Struggle in Egypt*, Egypt: Dar Sinai.

— (1990b) *Political Christianity in Egypt: A Glimpse (an entry) into the Political Trends of the Copts* (in Arabic), Egypt: Yafa.

— (1991) *The Religious Revival: A Social Profile of Christian and Islamic Movements in Egypt* (in Arabic), Egypt: Al-Dar Al-Arabia.

Habib, Rafik and M. Afifi (1994) *The History of the Egyptian Church*, Egypt: Al-Dar Al-Arabia.

Hakam, Nabil (1995) 'The social security system in Egypt', in Thomas Scheben (ed.), *Systems of Social Security: Egyptian and German Experiences*, Egypt: Wahba Press, pp. 130–8.

Handoussa, Heba (1994) 'The economic dimension to policies affecting women-headed households in Egypt', paper presented at conference 'Women-Headed Households', Cairo: Central Agency for Public Mobilisation, 20 March.

Hansen, Karen V. (1991) 'Helped put in a quilt: men's work and male intimacy in 19th century New England', in J. Lorber and S. A. Farrell (eds), *The Social Construction of Gender*, London: Sage.

Hardey, Michael and Graham Crow (eds) (1991) *Lone Parenthood: Coping with Constraints and Making Opportunities*, Hemel Hempstead: Harvester Wheatsheaf.

Harding, Sandra (ed.) (1987) *Feminism and Methodology: Social Science Issues*, Milton Keynes: Open University Press.

Harlow, Barbara (1991) Book review of Fatma Mernissi, *The Veil and the Male Elite: A Feminist Interpretation of Women's Rights in Islam*, trans. Mary Jo Lakeland, *Middle East Report*, 183: 43–5.

Harris, Kathleen M. (1993) 'Work and welfare among single mothers in poverty', *American Journal of Sociology*, 99 (2): 317–52.

Harris, Olivia (1981) 'Households as national units', in Kate Young, Carol Workowtiz and Roslyn McClullagh (eds), *Of Marriage and the Market*, London: CSE Books, pp. 48–67.

Hartung, B., J. C. Ollenburger, H. A. Moore and M. J. Deegan (1988) 'Empowering a feminist ethic for social science research: Nebraska Sociological Feminist Collective', in Nebraska Sociological Feminist Collective, *Feminist Ethic for Social Science Research*, Lewiston, NY: Edwin Mellen Press.

Hashemi, S., S. Schuler and A. Riley (1996) 'Rural credit programmes and women's empowerment in Bangladesh', *World Development*, 24 (4): 635–96.

Hatem, Mervat F. (1986a) 'The politics of sexuality and gender in segregated patriarchal systems: the case of eighteenth- and nineteenth-century Egypt', *Feminist Studies*, 12 (2): 251–74.

— (1986b) 'The alliance between nationalism and patriarchy in Muslim personal status laws: the case of modern Egypt', *Feminist Issues*, 6 (1): 19–43.

— (1988) 'Egypt's middle class in crisis: the sexual division of labour', *Middle East Journal*, 4'2 (3): 407–22.

Hatem, Mervat F. (1992) 'Economic and political liberalisation in Egypt and the demise of state feminism', *International Journal of Middle East Studies*, 24 (2): 232–51.
— (1993) 'Towards the development of post-Islamists and post-nationalist feminist discourse in the Middle East', in J. Tucker (ed.), *Arab Women: Old Boundaries, New Frontiers*, Bloomington: Indiana University Press.
Hawkesworth, Mary E. (1987) 'Feminist epistemology: a survey of the field', in M. J. Falco (ed.), *Feminism and Epistemology*.
Hejaiei, Monia (1996) *Behind Closed Doors: Women's Oral Narratives in Tunis*, London: Quartet.
Hernes, Helga Maria (1987) 'Women and the welfare state: the transition from private to public dependence', in A. S. Sassoon (ed.), *Women and the State*.
Hetler, Carol (1990) 'Survival strategies and household headship (Java)', in Leela Dube and Rajni Palriwala (eds), *Structures and Strategies: Women, Work and Family*, New Delhi: Sage, pp. 175–99.
Hijab, Nadia (1988) *Woman-power: The Arab Debate on Women at Work*, New York: Cambridge University Press.
Himmelstrand, Karin (1990) 'Can aid bureaucracy empower women?', in Kathleen Staudt (ed.), *Women, International Development and Politics*, pp. 101–13.
Hinnebusch, Raymond (1985) *Egyptian Politics Under Sadat*, New York: Cambridge University Press.
Hobson, Barbara (1994) 'Solo mothers, social policy regimes and the logics of gender', in Diane Sainsbury (ed.), *Gendering Welfare States*, London: Sage, pp. 170–88.
Hoodfar, Homa (1988) 'Patterns of household budgeting and financial management in a lower-income Cairo neighbourhood', in Daisy Dwyer and Judith Bruce (eds), *A Home Divided*, Stanford, CA: Stanford University Press.
— (1989) 'Return to the veil: personal strategy to "public" participation in Egypt', unpublished paper.
Huber, Evelyne (1995) 'Options for social policy in Latin America: neo-liberal versus social democratic models', Discussion Paper 66, Geneva: United Nations Research Institute for Social Development.
Hussain, Freda (ed.) (1984) *Muslim Women*, New York: St. Martin's Press.
Ibrahim, Saad Eddin (1980) 'Anatomy of Egypt's militant Islamic groups: methodological notes and preliminary findings', *International Journal of Middle East Studies*, 121: 423–53.
— (1988a) 'Egypt's Islamic activism in the 1980s', *Third World Quarterly*, 10 (2): 632–57.
— (1988b) 'An Islamic alternative in Egypt: the Muslim Brotherhood and Sadat', *Arab Studies Quarterly*, 4 (1, 2): 75–93.
— (1988c) 'Arab social change: six profiles', *Jerusalem Quarterly*, 23: 13–24.
— (1993) 'An assessment of grass-roots participation in Egypt's development', Cairo: Ibn Khaldoun Centre for Development Studies.
— (1994) 'Egyptian law 32 of 1964 in Egypt's PVOs and PFs: a critical assessment', Cairo: UNICEF.
— (1996) 'Egypt's NGOs: volunteerism, autonomy, and trust', Cairo: Ibn Khaldoun Centre for Development Studies.
Ibrahim, Saad Eddin and Nicholas Hopkins (eds) (1977) *Arab Society in Transition*, Cairo: American University in Cairo Press.

Itzin, Catherine and Janet Newman (1995) *Gender, Culture and Organisation Change*, London: Routledge.

INP (Institute of National Planning) (1994) *Egypt: Human Devlopment Report*, Cairo: Ministry of Planning and UNDP.

— (1996) *Egypt: Human Devlopment Report*, Cairo: Ministry of Planning and UNDP.

Jackson, Cecile (1995) 'Rescuing gender from the poverty trap', unpublished paper, School of Development Studies, University of East Anglia.

Al-Jam'iyya al-Shari'iyya li aíl a'Milin bi al-Kitab wa aíl Sunna aíl Muhammadyya-Saríiyyaî (1996) *Annual Report*, Cairo.

Jaquette, J. S. and K. Staudt (1988) 'Politics, population and gender: a feminist analysis of US population policy in the Third World', in K. Jones and A. Jonasdottir (eds), *The Political Interests of Gender: Developing Theory and Research with a Feminist Face*, London: Sage.

Jasay, Anthony De (1955) *The State*, Oxford: Blackwell.

Jennings, Ann L. (1993) 'Public or private? Institutional economics and feminism', in Marianne A. Ferber and Julie A. Nelson (eds), *Beyond Economic Man: Feminist Theory and Economics*, Chicago: University of Chicago Press, pp. 111–30.

Johnson, Chris (1992) *Women on the Frontline: Voices from Southern Africa*, Basingstoke: Macmillan.

Jones, Kathleen B. (1993) *Compassionate Authority: Democracy and the Representation of Women*, London: Routledge.

Joseph, Suad (1986) 'Women and politics in the Middle East', *Middle East Report*, 138: 3–9.

— (1996) 'Patriarchy and development in the Arab World', 4 (2): 14–19.

Kabeer, Naila (1991) 'The quest for national identity: women, Islam and the state of Bangladesh', in Deniz Kaniyoti (ed.), *Women, Islam and the State*, London: Macmillan, pp. 115–43.

— (1992) 'Women in poverty: a review of concepts and findings', paper presented to seminar 'Women in Extreme Poverty: Integration of Women's Concerns in National Development Planning', Vienna, 9–12 November.

— (1998) 'Money can't buy me love? Re-evaluating gender, credit and empowerment in rural Bangladesh', IDS Discussion Paper 363.

Kabeer, Naila and Susan Joekes (1991) 'Editorial', special issue 'Researching the Household: Methodological and Empirical Issues', *IDS Bulletin*, 22 (1): 1–4.

Kagitcibasi, Cigdem (ed.) (1982) *Sex Roles, Family and Community in Turkey*, Bloomington: Indiana University Press.

Kahn, Alfred and Sheila Kamerman (eds) (1988) *Child Support: From Debt Collection to Social Policy*, Beverly Hills, CA: Sage.

Kamerman, Sheila B. (1986) 'Women, children and poverty: public policies and female-headed families in industrialised countries', in Barbara C. Gelpi, Nancy C. M. Harstock, Clare C. Novak and Myra H. Strober (eds),

Kamerman, Sheila and Alfred Kahn (1988) *Mothers Alone: Strategies for a Time of Change*, Dover, MA: Auburn House Publishing.

Kandil, Amany (1993) 'Defining the non-profit sector: Egypt', working papers of the Johns Hopkins Comparative Non-profit Sector Project.

— (1994) 'The civic society in the Arab World: a study of Arab NGOs', Cairo: International Press.

Kandil, Amany and Sarah Ben Nefise-Paris (1994) *Non Governmental Organisations in Egypt*, Cairo: Centre for Political and Strategic Studies.

Kandiyoti, Deniz (ed.) (1991a) *Women, Islam and the State*, London: Macmillan.

— (1991b) 'Women, Islam and the state', *Middle East Report*, 173: 9–13.

— (1991c) 'Islam and patriarchy: a comparative perspective', in Nikki R. Keddie and Beth Baron (eds), *Women in Middle Eastern History: Shifting Boundaries in Sex and Gender*, New Haven, CT and London: Yale University Press.

— (1991d) 'Bargaining with patriarchy', in Judith Lorber and Susan A. Farrel (eds), *The Social Construction of Gender*, London: Sage.

— (1996) 'Contemporary feminist scholarship and Middle East studies', in Deniz Kandiyoti (ed.), *Gendering the Middle East: Emerging Perspectives*, London: I.B.Tauris.

— (forthcoming) 'Gender, power and contestation: "bargaining with patriarchy" revisited' (draft).

— (forthcoming) in C. Jackson and R. Pearson (eds), *Divided we Stand: Gender Analysis and Development*, London: Routledge.

Karam, Azza M. (1998) *Women, Islamists and the State: Contemporary Feminism in Egypt*, London: Macmillan.

Kashef, A. S. M. (1987) 'Egypt', in John Dixon (ed.), *Social Welfare in the Middle East*.

Kelly, L., S. Burton and L. Regan (1994) 'Researching women's lives or studying women's oppression? Reflections on what constitutes feminist research', in M. Maynard and J. Purvis (eds), *Researching Women's Lives from a Feminist Perspective*.

Kelly, R. M., B. Ronan and M. E. Cawley (1987) 'Liberal positivistic epistemology and research on women and politics', in M. J. Falco (ed.), *Feminism and Epistemology*.

Kemp, Olda Van Der (1988) 'Planning for female-headed households: an overview of the issues and experience', background paper for ILO workshop 'Female-Headed Households and the Development of Guidelines for their Participation in Development', New Delhi, 26–28 April.

Khafagy, Fatma Aly (1984) 'Women and labour migration', *Middle East Report*, 124: 17–21.

— (1986) 'Impact of oil migration on Arab women's work patterns', paper presented to conference 'Women and Arab Society: Old Boundaries, New Frontiers', Center for Contemporary Arab Studies, Georgetown University, Washington, DC.

Khattab, H. (1996) 'Women's perception of sexuality in rural Giza', Monographs in Reproductive Health No. 1, Reproductive Health Working Group, Population Council Regional Office for West Asia and North Africa.

Khattab, H. and S. G. el-Daeif (1981) 'Impact of male labour migration on the structure of the family and the roles of women', Regional Papers, Cairo: Population Council.

al-Khayyat, Sana (1990) *Honour and Shame: Women in Modern Iraq*, London: Saqi Books.

el-Khawas, Mohamed A. (1996) 'Revolutionary Islam in North Africa: challenges and responses', *Africa Today*, 43 (4): 385–404.

el-Kholy, Heba (1994) 'Panel discussion on women-headed households', Cairo: ICPD.

— (1998) 'Defiance and compliance: negotiating gender in low-income Cairo', Ph.D. thesis, Department of Sociology and Anthropology, School of Oriental and African Studies, University of London.

Kiely, Ray (1995) 'The politics of the impasse II: challenging Third Worldism, in Ray Kiely, *Sociology and Development: The Impasse and Beyond*, London: UCL Press.

Kimenyi, M. and J. M. Mbaku (1995) 'Female headship, feminisation of poverty and welfare', *Southern Economic Journal*, 62: 1.

Kornbluh, Felicia A. (1996) 'The new literature on gender and the welfare state: the U.S. case', *Feminist Studies*, 22 (1): 171-98.
Korpi, Walter (1985) 'Power resources approach vs. action and conflict: on casual and intentional explanations in the study of power, *Sociological Theory*, 3: 31-45.
Kotb, Sayed (1970) *Social Justice in Islam*, trans. John B. Hardis, New York: Octagam Books.
Knauss, Peter (1987) *The Persistence of Patriarchy*, New York: Praeger.
Knuttila, Murray (1987) *State Theories: From Liberalisation to the Challenge of Feminism*, Toronto: Garamond Press.
Kramer, Gurdun (1993) 'Islamist notions of democracy', *Middle East Report*, 183, July-August.
Land, Hilary (1977) 'Inequalities in large families: more of the same or different', in R. Chester and John Peel (eds), *Equalities and Inequalities in Family Life*, Proceedings of the Thirteenth Annual Symposium of the Eugenics Society, London: Academic Press.
Lasswell, Harold D. (1950) *Politics: Who Gets What, When and Why?*, New York: Peter Smith.
Latowsky, Robert J. (1994) 'Financial profile of Egypt's PVO sector', draft working paper, Egypt PVO sector study, Washington, DC: World Bank.
— (1995) 'PVO social assistance: direct aid to the poor', draft working paper, Washington, DC: World Bank.
Latowsky, Robert J. and Alexander Rondos (1992) 'Egypt's non-profit NGO sector: observations and implications for World Bank action, World Bank seminar on non-governmental organisations.
Law, Sylvia (1983) 'Women, work, welfare, and the preservation of patriarchy', *University of Pennsylvania Law Review*, 131 (6), May: 1251-331.
Lazreg, Marnia (1988 'Feminism and difference: the perils of writing as a woman on women in Algeria', *Feminist Studies*, 14 (1): 80-101.
Lerner, Gerda (1986) *The Creation of Patriarchy*, Oxford: Oxford University Press.
Lewis, D. J. with M. Glasser, J. A. McGregor, S. C. White and G. D. Wood (1993) 'Going it alone: female-headed households, rights and resources in rural Bangladesh', Occasional Paper 01/93, March, Bath: Centre for Development Studies, University of Bath.
Lewis, Jane (1995) 'Lone parent families: politics and economics', *Journal of Social Policy*, 18 (4): 595-600.
Lewis, Jane and Gertrude Astrom (1992) 'Equality, difference, and state welfare: labour market and family policies in Sweden', *Feminist Studies*, 18 (1): 59-87.
Lindsey, Linda (1997) *Gender Roles: A Sociological Perspective*, New Jersey: Prentice Hall.
Lipsky, Michael (1980) *Street-Level Bureaucracy*, New York: Russell Sage.
Lloyd, Cynthia B. and Anastasia J. Brandon (1994) 'Women's roles in maintaining households: poverty and gender inequality in Ghana', paper presented to ICRW, Population Council and supported by the Ford Foundation and UNFPA.
Lloyd, Genevieve (1986) 'Selfhood, war and masculinity', in Carole Pateman and Elizabeth Gross (eds), *Feminist Challenges*, pp. 63-76.
McCarthy, Florence (1984) 'The target group: women in rural Bangladesh', in E. J. Clay and B. B. Schaffer (eds), *Room for Manoeuvre*.
MacDonald, Martha (1994) 'Social security policy and gender', presented to World Bank Gender Symposium, Washington, DC, 10 November.

Macleod, Arlene Elowe (1991) *Accommodating Protest: Working Women, the New Veiling and Change in Cairo*, New York: Columbia University Press.

Mackinnon, Catharine A. (1982) 'Feminism, Marxism, method, and the state: an agenda for theory', *Signs*, 7 (3): 515–44.

— (1989) *Toward a Feminist Theory of the State*, Cambridge, MA: Harvard University Press.

McLanahan, Sara S. (1988) 'Family structure and dependency: early transitions to female household headship', *Demography*, 25 (1): 1–16.

McIntosh, Mary (1978) 'The state and the oppression of women', in A. Kuhn and A. M. Wolpe (eds), *Feminism and Materialism*, London: Routledge and Kegan Paul.

Maguire, Patricia (1984) *Women in Development: An Alternative Analysis*, Amherst, MA: Center for International Education, University of Massachusetts Press.

— (1987) *Doing Participatory Research: A Feminist Approach*, Amherst, MA: University of Massachusetts Press.

Mandelbaum, D. G. (1982) 'The study of life history', in R. G. Burgess (ed.), *Field Research*, pp. 146–51.

Mansi, Ragaa Khalil (1995) 'Child labour from the insurance and social security perspective', paper presented to Ministry of Labour, ILO and UNICEF conference, March.

Mason, Jennifer (1996) *Quantitative Researching*, London: Sage.

Maynard, Mary and June Purvis (eds) (1994) *Researching Women's Lives from a Feminist Perspective*, London: Taylor and Francis.

Mayoux, Linda (1997) 'Impact assessment and women's empowerment in micro-finance programmes: issues for a participatory action and learning approach', background paper submitted to CGAP virtual meeting on Impact Assessment Methodologies in Micro-finance Programmes, 7–19 April.

Mernissi, Fatima (1977) 'Women, saints and sanctuaries', *Signs*, 3 (1): 101–12.

— (1985) *Beyond the Veil: Male–Female Dynamics in Modern Muslim Society*, London: Al-Saqi Books.

— (1991) *Women and Islam: An Historical and Theological Enquiry*, trans. Mary Jo Lakeland, Oxford: Blackwell.

Marrick, Thomas and Marianne Schmink (1983) 'Households headed by women and urban poverty in Brazil', in M. Buvinic, M. Lycette and W. P. McGreevy (eds), *Women and Poverty in the Third World*, Baltimore, MD: Johns Hopkins University Press, pp. 244–71.

Mill, J. S. (1970) [1869] *On the Subjection of Women*, Cambridge, MA: MIT Press.

Millar, Jane, Sandra Leepa and Celia Davies (1992) *Lone Parents: Poverty and Public Policy in Ireland*, Dublin: Combat Poverty Agency.

Ministry of Social Affairs (1992) 'Study for modifying and improving the social aid services', Cairo: MOSA.

— (1995) 'Achievements of the Ministry of Social Affairs in 10 years 1984–1994', Cairo: MOSA.

Ministry of Insurance (1997) 'Report on achievements: an annual report 1995–1996', Cairo: Ministry of Insurance.

Misra, Joya and Frances Akinis (1998) 'State welfare and women: structures, agency, and diversity', *Social Politics*, Fall.

Bibliography

Moghadam, Valentine (1992a) 'Women's employment in the M.E. and N.A.: the role of gender, class and state policies', working paper no. 229, East Lansing: Michigan State University.

— (1992b) 'Development and patriarchy: the Middle East and North Africa in economic and demographic transition', working paper no. 99, Tokyo: World Institute for Development Economics Research, UN University.

— (1995) *Economic Reform and Women's Unemployment in Egypt: Constraints and Opportunities*, Tokyo: World Institute for Development Economics Research, UN University.

Mohanty, Chandra Talpade (1991) 'Under Western eyes: feminist scholarship and colonial discourses', in C. T. Mohanty, Ann Russo and Lourdes Torres (eds), *Third World Women and the Politics of Feminism*.

Mohanty, C. T., Ann Russo and Lourdes Torres (eds) (1991) *Third World Women and the Politics of Feminism*, Bloomington: Indiana University Press.

Molyneux, Maxine (1981) 'Women's emancipation under socialism: a model for the Third World?', IDS Discussion Paper no. 157, Sussex: Institute of Development Studies.

Moore, Henrietta (1988) *Feminism and Anthropology*, Cambridge: Polity.

— (1994) 'Is there a crisis in the family?' Occasional Paper no. 3, Geneva: World Summit for Social Development.

Morris, Lydia (1994) *Dangerous Classes: The Underclass and Social Citizenship*, London: Routledge.

Moser, Caroline (1989) 'Gender planning in the Third World: meeting practical and strategic gender needs', 17 (11): 1799–826.

Moser, Caroline and Caren Levy (1986) 'A theory and methodology of gender planning: meeting women's practical and strategic needs', Gender and Planning Paper no. 11, London: Development Planning Unit, UCL.

Moser, Caroline O. N. and Linda Peake (eds) (1987) *Women, Human Settlements and Housing*, New York: Tavistock.

Mustafa, Hala (1992) 'Political Islam in Egypt: from the reform movement to violent groups', Cairo: Centre for Political and Strategic Studies.

Mustafa, Khalid and Arshad Hussain Hashmi (1990) 'Ushr, social welfare and development: a critical appraisal in Pakistan', *Journal of Rural Development and Administration*, XXVIII (3), Summer: 79–84.

Muthwa, Sibongile (1994) 'Female household headship and household survival in Soweto', *Journal of Gender Studies*, 3 (2): 165–75.

Myles, John (1995) 'When markets fail: social welfare in Canada and the United States', UNIRSD Discussion Paper no. 68, Geneva: United Nations Research Institute for Social Development.

Nagi, Saad Z. (1995) 'Economic liberalisation and problems of social policy in Egypt', paper prepared for conference 'Systems of Social Security: Egyptian and German Experiences', Cairo: Konrad Adenauer Foundation.

Nassar, Heba (1995) *Economic Aspects of Vulnerability of Children in Egypt*, Cairo: UNICEF.

— (1996) 'The employment status of women in Egypt', mimeo, Cairo: Social Research Centre, American University Cairo and Friedrich Ebert Stiftung.

— (1997) 'Vulnerability of women in poverty. Workshop on social security and income generation projects for vulnerable groups, with special focus on working children and female-headed households', Cairo: Social Research Centre, American University Cairo.

Nassar, Heba (1998) 'Social protection for the poor in Egypt', paper presented to the Inter-University Consortium for International Social Development in Affiliation with the Social Fund for Development Egypt for the 10th International Symposium 'Livelihoods, NGOs and Development: Global Dimensions and New Directions', Cairo.

National Centre for Sociological and Criminological Research (1981) 'Social assistance in Egypt: an experiment to address poverty', Cairo: NCSCR.

Nawar, Laila (1994) 'The status of women in non-traditional families: the size and characteristics', Population Council/UNICEF seminar.

Nelson, Barbara J. (1984) 'Women's poverty and women's citizenship: some political consequences of women's economic marginality', *Signs*, 10 (2).

— (1990) 'The origins of the two-channel welfare state: workmen's compensation and mothers' aid', in Linda Gordon (ed.), *Women, the State, and Welfare*.

Nelson, Cynthia (1968) 'Changing roles of men and women: illustrations from Egypt', *Anthropological Quarterly*, 41 (2): 57–78.

— (1974) 'Public and private politics: women in the Middle Eastern world', *American Ethnologist*, 1 (3): 551–63.

NGO Forum (1994) Research summary and recommendations drawn up by the Gender Equality and Empowerment Task Force of the Egyptian NGO Forum in preparation for ICPD, Cairo, September.

Norris, Christopher (1990) *What's Wrong with Postmodernism: Critical Theory and the Ends of Philosophy*, London: Harvester Wheatsheaf.

Oakely, Judith (1994) 'Thinking through fieldwork', in A. Bryman and R. G. Burgess (eds), *Analysing Quantitative Data*.

Oakley, Anne (1981) 'Interviewing women: a contradiction in terms', in Helen Roberts (ed.), *Doing Feminist Research*.

Orloff, A. S. (1993) 'Gender and the social rights of citizenship: the comparative analysis of gender relations and welfare states', *American Sociological Review*, 58, June: 303–28.

Ortner, Sherry and Harriet Whitehead (eds) (1981) *Sexual Meanings*, New York: Cambridge University Press.

Ostergaard, Lise (ed.) (1992) *Gender and Development: A Practical Guide*, London and New York: Routledge.

Ostner, Ilona 'Independence and dependency: options and constraints for women over the life course', *Women's Studies Int. Forum*, 17 (2/3).

Oteify, Amina (1994) 'The understanding of the contract in Islamic jurisprudence and the Islamic law, with an in-depth study of the historical development of the marriage contract', paper presented at NGO Forum, ICPD, Cairo.

Owen, David (ed.) (1997) *Sociology after Postmodernism*, London: Sage.

Parpart, Jane L. (ed.) (1989) *The Disorder of Women: Democracy, Feminism and Political Theory*, Cambridge: Polity.

— (1993) 'Who is the Other?', *Development and Change*, 24 (3), July: 439–59.

Pateman, Carole (1988) 'The patriarchal welfare state', in Amy Gutmann (ed.), *Democracy and the Welfare State*, Princeton, NJ: Princeton University Press, pp. 231–60.

Pateman, Carole and Elizabeth Gross (eds) (1986) *Feminist Challenges: Social and Political Theory*, Sydney: Allen and Unwin.

Bibliography

Patterson, Sybil (1994) 'Women's survival strategies in urban areas: CARICOM and Guyana', in Fatimer Meer (ed.), *Poverty in the 1990s: The Responses of Urban Women*, Paris: UNESCO/International Social Science Council, pp. 117–33.

Patton, Michael Quinn (1990) *Qualitative Evaluation and Research Methods*, London: Sage.

Pearce, Diana (1978) 'The feminisation of poverty: women, work and welfare', *Urban and Social Change Review*, 11: 28–36.

— (1985) 'Toil and trouble: women workers and unemployment compensation', *Signs*, 3, Spring: 439–59.

— (1990) 'Welfare is not for women: why the war on poverty cannot conquer the feminisation of poverty', in Linda Gordon (ed.), *Women, the State, and Welfare*.

Peristiany, J. G. (1966) *Honor and Shame: The Values of Mediterranean Society*, Chicago: University of Chicago Press.

Perlmutter, Amos (1967) 'Egypt and the myth of the new middle class: a comparative analysis', *Comparative Studies in Society and History*, 10 (2): 46–65.

Peteet, Jule and Barbara Harlow (1991) 'Gender and political change', *Middle East Report*, 173: 4–8.

Piven, Frances Fox (1976) 'The social structuring of political protest', *Politics and Society*, 6: 297–326.

— (1985) 'Women and the state: ideology, power, and the welfare state', in Alice Rossi (ed.), *Gender and the Life Course*, New York: Aldine, pp. 265–87.

— (1990) 'Ideology and the state: woman power and the welfare state', in Linda Gordon (ed.), *Women, the State, and Welfare*, pp. 250–61.

Poovey, Mary (1988) 'Feminism and deconstruction', *Feminist Studies*, 14 (1), Spring: 51–65.

Popkin, B. M. and M. Buvinic (1983) 'Rural women, work and child welfare in the Philippines', in M. Buvinic, M. Lycette and W. P. Mcgeevery (eds), *Women and Poverty in the Third World*, Baltimore, MD: Johns Hopkins University Press.

Quddus, Sayed Abdul (1989) *Pakistan: Towards a Welfare State*, Pakistan: Royal Book Company.

Rasam, Amal (1984) 'Towards a theoretical framework for the study of women in the Arab world', in UNESCO, *Social Science Research and Women in the Arab World*, London: Frances Pinter.

Roberts, Helen (ed.) (1981) *Doing Feminist Research*, London: Routledge and Kegan Paul.

Rosaldo, M. Z. (1980) 'The use and abuse of anthropology: reflections on feminism and cross-cultural understanding', *Signs: Journal of Women in Culture and Society*, 5 (3): 359–417.

Rose, Nancy E. (1993) 'Gender, race and the welfare state: government work programmes from the 1980s to the present', *Feminist Studies*, 19 (2).

Rosenhouse, Sandra (1989) 'Identifying the poor: is headship a useful concept?', LSMS Working Paper no. 58, Washington, DC: World Bank.

Ross, Heather and Isabel Sawhill (1976) *Families in Transition: The Growth of Households Headed by Women*, Washington, DC: Urban Institute.

Rugh, Andrea (1979) 'Coping with poverty in a Cairo community', *Cairo Papers in the Social Sciences*, 2 (1).

— (1984) *Family in Contemporary Egypt*, Syracuse, NY: Syracuse University Press.

Safa, Helen (1995) *The Myth of the Male Breadwinner: Women and Industrialisation in the Caribbean*, Boulder, CO: Westview Press.

el-Safty, Madiha with Friedrich Ebert Stiftung (1996) *The Sociological Profile of Women in Egypt*, Cairo: Social Research Center, American University in Cairo.

Said, E. (1985) *Orientalism*, New York: Pantheon.

el-Sakka, Ahmad (1995) 'Alternative social security systems: social security funds', in Thomas Scheben (ed.), *Systems of Social Security: Egyptian and German Experiences*, Egypt: Wahba Press, pp. 146–56.

Samuel, R. (1982) 'Local history and oral history', in R. G. Burgess (ed.), *Field Research: A Source Book and Field Manual*, London: Allen and Unwin, pp. 136–45.

Sassoon, Anne S. (1987) *Women and the State: The Shifting Boundaries of Public and Private*, London: Unwin and Hyman.

Saunders, L. W. and Mehana Soheir (1993) 'Women headed households from the perspective of an Egyptian village', in J. P. Mencer and Anne Okongwu (eds), *Where Did All the Men Go? Female-headed/Female-supported households in Cross-cultural Perspectives*, Boulder, CO, San Francisco and Oxford: Westview Press.

Scott, James C. (1985) *Weapons of the Weak: Everyday Forms of Peasant Resistance*, New Haven, CT: Yale University Press.

— (1990) *Domination and the Arts of Resistance: Hidden Transcripts*, New Haven, CT: Yale University Press.

Scott, Joan W. (1988) 'Deconstructing equality versus difference, or the use of poststructuralist theory for feminism', *Feminist Studies*, 14 (1), Spring: 33–50.

el-Sebaie, Mostafa (1960) *Socialism in Islam*, Egypt: el-Nashroon el-Arab.

Shanthi, K. (1996) 'Economic and social status of female heads of households – need for intervention under new economic policy', *Indian Journal of Social Work*, 57 (2), April: 309–26.

Shaver, Sheila (1990) 'Gender, social policy regimes and the welfare state', paper presented at annual meeting of the American Sociological Association, 15 August, Washington, DC.

Shukrallah, Hala (1991) 'The Islamic movement in Egypt', unpublished paper, Sussex: Institute of Development Studies.

Singerman, Diane (1989) *Avenues of Participation: Family, Politics and Network in Urban Networks on Urban Quarters in Cairo*, University Microfilms International.

Siyam, Eyad (1992) 'Activists of the Islamic movement and methods for building political power in an Egyptian village', *Al-Mijala Al-Igtmia'ia Al-Kawmiia*, Cairo: National Centre for Sociological and Criminological Research, pp. 1–41.

Skocpol, Theda (1992) *Protecting Soldiers and Mothers*, Cambridge, MA: Harvard University Press.

Skocpol, Theda and Amenta Edwin (1986) 'States and social policies', *Annual Review of Sociology*, 12: 131–57.

Smock, Audrey and Nadia Youssef (1977) 'Egypt', in Janet Giele and Audrey Smock (eds), *Women: Roles and Status in Eight Countries*, New York: John Wiley, pp. 35–79.

el-Solh, Camilia Fawzi (1994) 'The feminisation of poverty in selected Arab countries', paper presented to conference 'Women in the Middle East: New Frontiers', Centre for Middle Eastern and Islamic Studies, Collingwoods College, University of Durham.

Solomon, C. (1991) 'Transcending the qualitative, quantitative debate: the analytic and

systematic approaches to educational research', *The Educational Researcher*, 2 (6): 10–18.
Somers, Margaret R. (1993) 'Citizenship and the place of the public sphere: law, community and political culture', *American Sociological Review*, 58, October: 587–620.
Soper, Kate (1990) 'Feminism, humanism and postmodernism', *Radical Philosophy*, 55, Summer: 11–16.
Spencer, Gary (1982) 'Methodological issues in the study of bureaucratic elite: a case study of West Point', in E. G. Burgess (ed.), *Field Research: A Source Book and Field Manual*, London: Allen and Unwin.
Springborg, Robert (1989) *Mubarak's Egypt: Fragmentation of the Political Order*, Boulder, CO: Westview Press.
Stamp, Patricia (1990) *Technology, Gender and Power in Africa*, Canada: International Development Research Centre.
Stanley, Liz and Sue Wise (eds) (1983) *Breaking Out: Feminist Consciousness and Feminist Research*, London: Routledge and Kegan Paul.
Staudt, Kathleen A. (1985) *Women, Foreign Assistance and Advocacy Administration*, New York: Praeger.
— (1987) 'Women, politics, the state, and capitalist transformation in Africa', in Irving Leonard Marovitz (ed.), *Studies in Power and Class in Africa*, New York: Oxford University Press.
— (1990) 'Gender politics in bureaucracy: theoretical issues in comparative perspective', in K. Staudt, *Women, International Development, and Politics: The Bureaucratic Mire*, Philadelphia: Temple University Press.
Staudt, K. and Jane Jaquette (1988) 'Bureaucratic resistance to men's programmes: the case of women in development', in Ellen Boneparth (ed.), *Women, Power, and Policy*, New York: Pergamon.
Stephens, John D. (1995) 'The Scandinavian welfare state: achievements, crisis and prospects', DP 67, Geneva: UNRISD.
Stiehm, Judith Hicks (1982) 'The protected, the protector, the defender', *Women's Studies Int. Forum*, 5 (3): 367–76.
Skeggs, Beverley (1995) 'Situating the production of feminist ethnography', in Mary Maynard and June Purvis (eds), *Researching Women's Lives from a Feminist Perspective*.
Sullivan, Denis J. (1994) *Private Voluntary Organisations in Egypt: Islamic Development, Private Initiative and State Control*, Gainesville: University Press of Florida.
Sullivan, Earl (1986) *Women in Egyptian Public Life*, Syracuse, NY: Syracuse University Press.
Summers, Yvonne (1991) 'Women and citizenship: the insane, the involvement and the inanimate?', in Pamela Abbot and Claire Wallace (eds), *Gender, Power and Sexuality*, London: Macmillan.
Taher, Nadia Adel (1986) 'Social identity and class in a Cairo neighbourhood', *Cairo Papers in Social Science*, 9 (4).
Therborn, Göran (1980) *The Ideology of Power and the Power of Ideology*, London: Verso.
Titmuss, Richard A. (1958) 'War and social policy', in R. A. Titmuss, *Essays on the Welfare State*, London: Allen and Unwin.
— (1974) *Social Policy*, London: Allen and Unwin.
Tripp, Charles and Roger Owen (eds) (1989) *Egypt Under Mubarak*, New York: Routledge.

Tucker, Judith and Joe Stork (1982) 'In the footsteps of Sadat', *Middle East Report*, 107: 3–6.
UNICEF (1993) *Ein Helwan and Al-Nahda Progress Report*, New York: UNICEF.
Ursel, Jane (1986) 'The state and the maintenance of patriarchy: a case study of family labour and welfare legislation in Canada', in James Dickinson and Bo Russell (eds), *Family Economy and the State: The Social Reproduction Process under Capitalism*, Beckenham, UK: Croom Helm.
Varely, Ann (1996) 'Women-headed households: some more equal than others?', *World Development*, 24.
Walby, Sylvia (1986) *Patriarchy at Work*, Minneapolis: University of Minnesota Press.
— (1990) *Theorising Patriarchy*, Oxford: Blackwell.
Waterbury, John (1983) *The Egypt of Nasser and Sadat: The Political Economy of Two Regimes*, Princeton, NJ: Princeton University Press.
Watson, S. (ed.) (1990) *Playing the State: Australian Feminist Interventions*, London: Verso.
Weiss, Holger (1997) 'A tentative note on Islamic welfare: Zakat in theory and praxis in the Sokoto caliphate', Working Paper no. 11/97, IDS/University of Helsinki.
White, Sarah (1992) *Arguing with the Crocodile: Gender and Class in Bangladesh*, London: Zed.
Wilensky, H. L. (1975) *The Welfare State and Equality: Structural Ideological Roots of Public Expenditures*, Berkeley: California University Press.
Wilson, Elizabeth (1977) *Women and the Welfare State*, London: Tavistock.
Winchester, Hilary (1990) 'Women and children last: the poverty and marginalisation of one-parent families', Institute of British Geographers, *Transactions*, 15 (1): 70–86.
Wollstonecraft, M. (1967) [1792] *Vindication of the Rights of Women*, New York: W.W. Norton.
Wood, Geoffrey (ed.) (1985) *Labelling in Development Policy: Essays in Honour of Bernard Shaeffer*, London: Sage.
World Bank (1991) *Annual Report: Egypt*, Washington, DC: World Bank.
— (1993) *Implementing the World Bank's Strategy to Reduce Poverty: Progress and Challenges*, Washington, DC: World Bank.
Youssef, Nadia (1980) 'A woman-specific strategy statement: the case of Egypt', Cairo: AID Bureau of Programme and Policy Coordination.
Youssef, N. and C. Hetler (1983) 'Establishing the economic condition of women-headed households in the Third World: a new approach', in M. Buvinic, M. Lycette and W. P. Mcgreevery (eds), *Women and Poverty in the Third World*, Baltimore, MD: Johns Hopkins University Press.
Zaalouk, Malak (1985) 'The impact of male labour migration on the structure of the family and women left behind in the city of Cairo', *Al-Haq Revue de l'Union des Avocats*, Arabes Traveaux de la première conférence internationale de la femme Arabe et Africaine, Cairo, nos 2, 3.
Zaki, Eshrak Gamal (1993) 'Gender discrimination, social stratification: the case of female-headed households in the Greater Cairo region', unpublished MA thesis, Sociology and Anthropolgy Department, American University Cairo.
Zaretsky, E. (1982) 'The place of the family in the origin of the welfare state', in T. Barrie and M. Yalome (eds), *Rethinking the Family: Some Feminist Questions*, New York: Longman.

Ziller, A. (1980) *Affirmative Action Handbook: Review of New South Wales Government Administration*, New South Wales: Government Information Centre.

Zinn, Maxine Baca (1991) 'Family, feminism and race in America', in J. Lorber and S. A. Farrel (eds), *The Social Construction of Gender*, London: Sage.

Zubaida, Sami (1992) 'Islam, the state and democracy: contrasting conceptions of society in Egypt', *Middle East Report*, 179: 2–10.

Index

Abbas, 141–4
abduction of women, 19
U'm Adel, 63
adultery, as crime, 19, 20
Afaf, 61
Affaf, 172
A'l-A'hali newspaper, 108
ahl al kheir, 98
U'm Ali, 64
alimony, 52, 144
All Saints Church, Cairo, 107, 113
aloneness, coping with, 62–3
Amal, 64
Antaar, Mr, 60
assistance: conditions for eligibility, 116–17, 121; self-driven exclusion from, 117–18
Association for the Development and Enhancement of Women (ADEW), 18, 21, 31, 169
U'm Attiat, 96
authority, seen as taboo, 168
Azer, Adel, 77
Aziza, 2–3, 103

Bahie el-Din, Amira, 45
Bahro, Rudolf, 4
El Banat, Set, 62
bargaining power of women, 162
barren women, 172
beating of wives *see* wife-beating
Bedouins, 38–9, 57, 116, 118
bint al-balad, 128
Bothayna, 37
Brandon, Cynthia B., 68
breadwinner, women as *see* women: as breadwinners
breadwinning, as criterion for headship, 44
breastfeeding, time allowed for, 78

Brown, Carol, 11
bureaucracy, definition of, 13
bureaucrats: policy role of, 93; women's relationship with, 157 *see also* welfare bureaucracy
Burgess, R.G., 28
Burton, Clare, 164, 165, 177
Buvinic, Mayra, 65

census in Egypt, 55
Central Authority for Population Mobilisation and Statistics (CAPMAS), 55, 56, 68
de Certeau, Michel, 164, 165
Chant, Sylvia, 46, 53, 61, 135
chaperone, accompanies women, 141
Charlton, Sue Ellen, 17
chastity pension, 84, 86–7
childcare, 14, 20, 21, 63, 66, 126, 160; day centres, 78, 79, 85
circumcision of girls *see* female genital mutilation
citizenship: and soldiering, 17; of women, 9, 15, 16–20, 110, 154 (defined through sexuality, 156–7)
clothes washing ritual, 36
co-wives, 29, 39, 49, 51, 63, 64, 96, 98, 138–40; legally bound to husbands, 140
Communist Party (A'l-Tagm'u), 108, 109
conscription in Egypt, 18
consent, problematic notion for women, 17
coping mechanisms of women, 100–5, 160, 161, 162, 163, 165, 171
coping with aloneness, 62–3
Coptic Charity organisation (Jami'it al-Mas'aii A'l Khairiiya Al Keptia), 110
Coptic Church, 107; assistance

Index

programmes of, 108, 113–14, 120; attitude to women, 112
Coptic groups, 5; welfare programmes of, 7–8, 159
credit: women excluded from, 114; women's access to, 129, 131, 142
criminal activities pursued by women, 136–8
Crow, Graham, 61
cruel fathers, 125, 128, 147, 149
cultural relativism, 167–71, 175
custody, rights of women, 109, 110

Da'awa magazine, 108
Dahlerup, Drude, 12
Dallos, Rudi, 61
Il Daman il Ijtimaii, 94–100
data: of welfare offices, mistakes in, 95; problems of access to, 7, 27, 34, 54
daughters, exploited, 128
daya midwife, 147
decision-making: as criterion of headship, 44–5; women excluded from, 152
deflowering of women, 33, 36, 132, 154; faked by women, 160, 161, 166; manual, 133 *see also dukhla baladi*
deserted women, 29, 39, 46, 48, 51, 52, 57, 58, 64, 81, 96, 97, 105, 121, 140
destitution, proof of, 95, 101
Dews, Peter, 168
disguise and anonymity, politics of, 161
division of labour, sexual, 5
divorce, 3, 20, 51, 54, 62, 69, 89, 109, 110, 136, 143; initiated by women, 90, 91, 116, 121, 134, 140; rights of women, 19, 109
divorced women, 29, 39, 45, 46, 47, 48, 51, 52, 56, 57, 58, 59, 61, 62, 64, 70, 81, 83, 84, 88, 90, 91, 96, 97, 101, 103, 115, 121, 169; attitudes towards, 98; Islam's view of, 121; seen as threat, 60, 134, 156; status of, 144
Doreya, 92
dress codes, 35, 37, 38, 39, 147; Islamic, 35, 39, 116, 117, 173; traditional, 116, 118, 119
dukhla baladi, 120, 124, 132, 133, 166, 176, 177; subversion of, 140–1

earthquakes, resettlement of victims, 34, 37, 104

economic approach to raising income-earning, 79–80
education: free provision of, 77, 80; of girls, 144, 174, 175 (curtailed, 132, 151); of women, 3, 14, 78 (curtailed, 133–4)
Egypt: as welfare state, 77–81; Charter of, 79; Constitution of, 79
Ehrenreich, Barbara, 11
electricity, access to, 36 (illegal, 99)
Elham, 88–9
emergency assistance, 83
empowerment of women, 23, 29, 32, 149, 155–6; feminist research and, 30; of those researched, 31
English, Deirdre, 11
errands, running of, 104, 105
Esping-Andersen, Gosta, 73, 75
exclusion: Greeley's patterns of, 114; politics of, 88–106; programme-driven, 7, 90, 114–17; self-driven, 99–100, 117, 137
Ezba research site, 38, 57, 98, 103, 104

family: changes in, 155; nuclear, 43; structures, definition of, 114–16
fathers, dependency on, 102 *see also* cruel fathers
Fathia, 115
favours, exchanges of, 100, 104–5
Faysal Bank, 105
Fekri, 127
female genital mutilation (FGM), 45, 120, 124, 135, 154, 165, 168, 169, 170, 176; condemnation of, 168; degrees of, 149–51; maintained by women, 150
female headed households (FHHs), 1, 149, 166; as male-absent households, 21, 41; as target group, 169; as Western concept, 59; attitudes towards, 120; *de facto*, 45, 46, 53 (oppressed, 176); *de jure*, 45, 46, 53 (stigmatised, 176); definition of, 47; impact of welfare programmes on, 159; literature on, 7; marginalisation of, 114; obstacles facing, 1, 5; official attitudes towards, 96, 97; perceptions of, 108, 118; prevalence of, 54–6; punitive attitude towards, 67; resistance to status of, 140, 155–6;

social rights of, 16; status in society, 23, 160, stigmatisation of, 41
femininity, as product of state policies, 11
feminism, 6, 13, 23, 30, 76, 164, 167–71, 177–8; liberal, 9–10, 14; organisations banned in Egypt, 15; post-modern, 27; radical, 12, 14; socialist, 10–11; theory of, 9
feminist research, 26–40; concerns regarding, 29–33; definition of, 30
Fergany, Nader, 54
fertility of women, control of, 3
food subsidies, 80
Frankel, Boris, 4
Fraser, Nancy, 1, 4, 22, 72, 85
Frohman, Alicia, 11

Galal, 127
Gambia, women's resistance in, 166
gam'eyya credit group, 142
genital mutilation of girls *see* female genital multilation
Gihan, 104
girls, low valuation of, 89; monitoring of, 141
Goetz, Anne Marie, 4, 93
A'm Gomaa, 2
government employment, open to women, 174, 175
Greeley, Martin, 7, 90, 114

Habermas, Jurgen, 17, 168
hair, covering of, 35
Haj programme, 36, 107, 113, 119; budget of, 122
Halla, 99, 170
Hamida, 95–6
Hanan, 128, 144–6
Handoussa, Heba, 1, 6, 77, 86
Hanem, 62–3
Hardey, Michael, 61
U'm Haytham, 99, 119
headship: defining of, 43–7; female, 21, 23 (based on economic provision, 58; defining of, 41–71); male, 42; patriarchal definition of, 20; self-reporting of, 44
health insurance, 16
Health Insurance Organisation Programme (HIOP), 81

healthcare, 79, 134; free provision of, 77, 131
Hedeya, 125, 127, 132–6, 170
hegab, wearing of, 35
Hend, 61
heroines, women as, 125, 127, 128–38
Hetler, Carol, 46, 54
hidden transcripts of resistance, 161
Hind, 89
Hoda, 60
honour: of family, 125, 132, 133, 135, 173; of men, 159
household: definition of, 43; society's perception of, 41
housework, 126, 156; unpaid, 10
housing, 68; cost of, 63; problem for FHH, 69
Howayda, 173
humiliation of application procedures, 84, 86, 87, 89, 93, 105, 135, 136–7, 138, 139–40, 157

Ibtsam, 63
ID cards: not available to women, 18–19, 69, 70, problem for women, 90, 94, 97, 117, 156; requirement of, 16, 18
illiterate women, 16, 18, 34, 68, 95, 102, 103, 120, 130, 137, 161, 171, 177
Infitah, 14
informal sector, employment in, 38, 41, 66, 77, 79, 126
inheritance, women's rights, 110
Insurance and Pension Organisation (IPO), 81
interpretation of needs *see* needs of women, interpretation of
interviews, checklist for, 32
Intisar, 128, 140–4, 154, 161, 169
Iskander, 127
Islam, 15; attacks on, 164; fundamentalist, 38 *see also* dress codes, Islamic
Islamic Charity organisation (Al-Jami'iya A'l Khairiiya A'l Islamia), 110
Islamic groups, 5, 21, 27, 28, 36, 51, 52, 59, 130; conflict with Egyptian state, 15; welfare programmes of, 7–8, 100, 107–23, 159

Al-Jami'iyya al-Shari'iyya organisation,

Index

36, 51–2, 107, 112; budget of, 122; welfare programmes, 160
de Jasay, Anthony, 4
Jews, 110

Kabeer, Naila, 42, 43, 66, 68
Kafalet al-Yateem project of Shari'iyya organisation, 112, 113, 115, 116, 122, 159
Kahn, Alfred, 54
Kamerman, Sheila, 54
Kandiyoti, Deniz, 15, 165, 166, 167
katb el-ketab, 132, 142
Kenya, women's resistance in, 166
Kesma, 127–8
Khadiga, 90–1
khafed, 149
Om Khaled, 118
khemar, wearing of, 35, 116, 119
el-Kholy, Heba, 18–19
Knuttila, Murray, 9
Korpi, Walter, 73
Kosma, 138–40

labelling of Third World women, 163, 168, 177
Labour Force Sample Survey (LFSS), 68
Labour Party, 108
law, Islamic *see* Shari'a law
Levy, Caren, 54
liberalisation, economic, 111
Lloyd, Cynthia B., 68
loans, zero-interest, 36
'log-rolling', 104–5, 161
lunch, as socialising period, 35–6

Mackinnon, Catherine A., 11
Macleod, Arlene Elowe, 173–4
Maguire, Patricia, 31
male partner, presence of, 52–3
male-headed households, 31, 42, 53, 59
Mariam, 70, 102
marital status of women heads of households, 51–2
marriage, 3, 20, 33, 36, 109, 110, 139, 152, 155, 166; after rape, 19; at early age, 55, 124, 132; consummation of, 132, 145; in two stages, 92, 132; of girls to older men, 48, 50, 125, 147; pensions of daughters ended, 115;
renegotiation of power within, 167
see also remarriage *and* weddings
maternity leave, 14, 78
ma'zun, marriage official, 132
means-testing of assistance, 76, 82
men: abandonment by, 54; interviewed, 127; supremacy threatened, 127
Mernissi, Fatima, 159
Merrick, Thomas, 65
methodology: experimenting with, 27; non-probability sampling, 28
middle-class values, 32, 37, 126–7, 138; bias of research, 32, 170
middle classes, 162; Egyptian women, and veiling, 173–5
migration, 14, 15, 124; male, 45, 55, 57, 131 (impact on family, 6)
military, women's participation in, 17
Millar, Jane, 54
Ministry of Insurance and Social Affairs (MOISA), 81, 86, 91
Ministry of Social Affairs (MOSA), 2, 7, 28, 37, 46, 51, 81, 83, 84, 88, 93, 94, 98, 99, 100, 103, 105, 117, 122, 130, 131, 135, 136–7, 139–40, 156, 159; attitude of officials to women, 96; fear of approaching, 95; violence against officials of, 138
Mohammed Ali, 14
Mohanty, Chandra Talpade, 162
Mona, 99
monitoring of women, 60, 65, 87, 141
Moser, Caroline, 45, 54
mosque, 36, 39, 99, 105, 112, 117, 119, 136, 140; assistance from, 37, 118 (refused by women, 115); marriage in, 132
mother-in-law, 45
Mubarak, Hosni, 14, 15, 79; solidarity programme, 67, 84–5
Muslim Brotherhood, 108
mutual responsibility, 110

U'm Nagah, 119, 125, 127, 136–8, 157, 161
Naglaa, 115
Nassar, Heba, 79
Nasser, Gamal Abdel, 14, 77, 78, 80, 108, 111; revolution of, 174
Nasser Social Bank, 36, 105
nationality law, 20

natural leaders, women as, 103, 129
Nawar, Laila, 6
needs of women, interpretation of, 72, 85–7, 153, 159; politics of, 20–2, 120–2
networking of women, 102–4, 131, 154, 161
never-married women, 47, 50, 56, 58, 83, 97, 156, 169
non-governmental organisations (NGOs), 33, 81, 101, 107, 110, 130; access to data of, 7; as entry point for research, 29; Islamic, numbers of, 111; religious (importance of, 108–12; rising number of, 110)
Norris, Christopher, 168

opposition: by women, 8, 102, 153–4, 163, 171–3; definition of, 165, 167; versus resistance, 164–7
oppressed women *see* women, oppressed
oral history of women, 26
Organisation for Social Insurance, 4
Orientalism, 163, 164
orphan programmes, 28, 57, 107, 112, 113, 114, 116, 118, 119
orphans, definition of, 115

Pan-Arabism, 111
passivity of women, 162, 163, 166
passport applications by women, 16
Pateman, Carole, 17
patriarchy, 5, 10, 11, 13, 20, 26, 30, 32, 42, 114, 121, 170; classical, 155; in needs interpretation, 85–7; new forms of, 146, 149, 153 (emergence of, 154–5); women's bargaining with, 165, 169
Patterson, Sybil, 171
Pearce, Diana, 4
Penal Code, 20; discrimination against women, 20
Pension Programme of MOSA, 4
pensions, 52, 81, 82, 90; 'chastity' pension, 50, 83, 84, 86–7, 159; for spinsters, 50; for widows, 136; girls cut out of, 92; of deceased wife, 91–2; old-age, 16, 18, 78; Sadat pension, 83–4, 86
personal status law, 19, 20, 109
Piven, Frances Fox, 12

political outburst, as resistance, 161
Popkin, B.M., 6
post-modernism, 167–71
poverty, 1, 37, 38; feminisation of, 5, 41, 65; gender dimensions of, 67; in Arab world, 67; of women, 53, 63, 65–70; urban, 6
prayer mats, 36
pregnancy, unintended, 141, 144
Principal Bank for Development and Agricultural Credit, 79
prostitution, punishment for, 19

rape, 19; marital, 17, 169 (not recognised in law, 88); women punished for, 20
Rateb, Dr Ahsya, 92
religion, impact on state policies, 11
religious classes, attending of, 117
religious groups, 5; welfare programmes of, 7–8, 121 *see also* Islamic groups *and* Coptic groups
remarriage, 2, 48, 64, 96, 116, 156, 172
research methods, 26–40
research sites, described, 33–9
researcher, relationship with researched, 30, 163
The Resettlement, 37–8, 57, 118
resistance: as viewed by de Certeau, 165; definition of, 162, 166, 167; relation to opposition, 164–7; of women, 8, 10, 166, 171–3 (passive, 102; to being heads of household, 155–6)
Rosenhouse, Sandra, 54

Sabah, 62, 118
U'm Saber, 33, 101–2, 118, 125, 127, 128–31, 157
al-Sadat, Anwar, 14, 15, 78, 83–4, 108, 109, 111; Sadat pension, 83–4
Safaa, 61
U'm Salama, 99
U'm Samah, 35
Sanaa, 99
Sania, 102
savings schemes *see* gam'eyya
U'm Sayyeda, 93–4, 105
Schmink, Marianne, 65
Scott, James C., 160, 161, 164, 167, 176, 177
Sedika, 172

Index

sexism, 7, 11; of Egyptian welfare system, 72
sexual duties of wives, 126, 128, 145; avoidance of, 142, 148
sexual harassment of women, 152–3
sexuality: as defining element of citizenship, 156, 156; of women (control of, 1, 2, 7, 17, 116, 120, 121, 133, 140, 144, 150, 153, 159, 161, 169, 176; unsatisfied, 146)
shabka, 142, 145
Shadia, 32–3, 125, 128, 146–9, 161, 170
sharaf, 133 *see also* honour
Shari'a law, 19, 51, 109; reintroduction of, 108
Shari'iyya NGO *see* Al-Jami'iyya al-Shari'iyya
Shelters research site, 27, 29, 34–6, 57, 60, 95, 98, 116, 118
U'm Sherif, 64–5
single mothers, 12, 58; increasing numbers of, 55; vulnerability of, 69
Sithom, 2, 101
slavery, children trained into, 177
slums, 34, 37, 11
Social Aid Programme of MOSA, 4
social insurance, 72, 77, 80, 82; Contributory System, 81, 90–4; Non-Contributory System, 81; of women, 78, 82
Social Insurance Organisation (SIO), 81
Social Security Act no. 30 (1977), 82
Spasford, Roger, 61
spinsters *see* never-married women
squatter areas, 18, 33–4, 37, 39, 97, 113
Stanley, Liz, 31
state: analysis of, 11; Egyptian, relation to women, 14–16; fear of, 99–100; gendered nature of, 3–8, 12; hostility to, 12; nature of, 8–13; neutrality of, 13; non-neutrality of, 9; patriarchal, 11; policy impact on women, 12–13; role in subordinating women, 72; theory of, exclusion of gender analysis, 9; women's relationship with, 10, 22, 157
Staudt, Kathleen A., 4
stereotypes, women's conformity to, 154, 161
structural adjustment programmes, 6, 77, 79

subversion by women, 100–5, 118–20, 144, 162, 165, 169, 173, 176, 177; of *dukhla baladi*, 140–1

tabdid manqulat, 143
U'm Tafida, 60
tahara, 149
Tawfic Coptic organisation (Jami'it A'l-Tawfik A'l-Keptia), 110
telephones, access to, 36
Terez, Mme, 113, 115
Thatcher, Margaret, 74
Therborn, Göran, 74
Third World women, labelling of, 163, 168, 177
Titmuss, Richard, 74, 75
de Tocqueville, Alexis, 74
Tombs research site, 35–7, 57, 113, 119, 136
typologies, of women heads of household, 47–51

U'lfat, 128, 149–53, 170
U'm Nagah, 154
U'm Saber, 154
Ulfat, 125
unemployment, 37, 45, 46, 48–9; insurance, 81, 82
Unionist Party, 109
Universal Social Security scheme (1980), 82
universalism, 169
Ursel, Jane, 4
u'rzu'i, derivation of word, 49 *see also* wives, of *u'rzu'i men*
useless husbands, 125, 126, 128, 140–4, 146, 148, 156; common concept, 145

Varely, Ann, 54
veiling of women, 35, 37, 39, 107, 117, 119; as act of surrender, 175; as resistance to West, 174; as symbol of backwardness, 174; new, 173; political meaning of, 173–8
violence against women, 155 *see also* wife-beating
Virgin Mary's Church, Alexandria, 107, 113–14
virginity: examination of pensioners, 50 (*see also* pensions, 'chastity' pension); loss of, 142, 173; meaning of, 159;

monitoring of, 147, 156; proof of, 87; re-establishement of, 173; tied to honour, 132
voting rights of women, 14, 15

Wafd (Delegation Party), 108
wages of women, 172 *see also* work of women, waged
water, access to, 36, 38
Weber, Max, 13
weddings, 35
welfare: Egyptian system of, 81–5; war on, 1
welfare approach to poverty, 80–1
welfare bureaucracy, 72; as agents of patriarchal state, 13–14
welfare programmes: gendered nature of, 85; impact on autonomy of FHH, 107; regulations of, 27
welfare state: conservative, 75; correlated with expansion of democracy, 74; critique of, 11–12; definition of, 73–5; Egypt as, 7, 72, 77–81; liberal, 75; social democratic, 75–6; types of, 75–7; USSR model of, 80
welfare trap, 76
Western model, critique of, 168
White, Sarah, 163
WID programmes, discrimination against women, 5
widowhood, women's reaction to, 62
widows, 2, 21, 29, 45, 46, 47, 48, 51, 52, 56, 57, 58, 59, 62, 64, 81, 83, 96, 99, 101, 102, 103, 113, 114, 116, 118, 119, 121, 159; sympathy towards, 60
wife-beating, 62, 64, 88, 134, 136, 142, 145, 146, 147, 148, 155, 166, 170, 172, 176; lack of shelters for battered wives, 63
Wilensky, H.L., 73
winter assistance, 83
Wise, Sue, 31

wives: of disabled men, 50–1, 60; of drug addicts, 47, 49, 98, 115, 134; of drunkards, 49, 53, 96, 134, 172; of gamblers, 148; of imprisoned husbands, 29, 47, 58, 98; of old men, 58; of unemployed men, 29, 48–9, 51, 57, 58, 97; of *u'rzu'i* men, 3, 29, 47, 49, 51, 53, 56, 57, 63, 97, 99, 102, 118, 125, 130, 170
women: as breadwinners, 49–50, 132, 139, 142, 146, 148, 152 (sole, 114); as reproducers of oppression of women, 176; as survivors, 124–58; as victims, 124–58; below-survival incomes of, 2, 3; characterised as *naqisat 'aql wa din*, 143; equal rights of, 108; marginalisation of, 88; multiple roles of, 5; non-universality of experience, 27; oppressed, 146–53
women heads of household, 103, 120, 125, 128; as priority target, 65–7; classification of, 56; experience of, 61–5; factors affecting status of, 51–4; marital status of, 51–2; self-perception of, 60–1; status of, 52, 58–61; typologies of, 47–51
women's work: as source of stigma, 155–6; domestic, 151; double workload of, 3, 152; men's view of, 126, 127; progressive legislation, 4; waged, 78, 85, 144, 148, 172 (disparaged, 139) *see also* housework
women-maintained households, use of term, 46
work of women *see* women's work
workers' movement, 38
working hours of women, 66, 79
World Bank, study by, 86

Youssef, Nadia, 46, 54

Zakat Committee, 36
Zarifa, 102

Printed in the USA
CPSIA information can be obtained
at www.ICGtesting.com
LVHW091817130624
783112LV00003B/367